PEACE WITHIN
THROUGH
GOD'S WAY

Inspirational Words of God and Commentary

JOHN H. (JAN) DOLCATER, JR.

Copyright © 2021 by John H. (Jan) Dolcater, Jr.

All rights reserved. No part of this publication may be reproduced, distributed, or transmitted in any form or by any means, including photocopying, recording, or other electronic or mechanical methods, without the prior written permission of the author, except in the case of brief quotations embodied in critical reviews and certain other noncommercial uses permitted by copyright law.

Scripture quotations ts taaken from the New American Standard Bible® (NASB), Copyright © 1960, 1962, 1963, 1968, 1971, 1972, 1973, 1975, 1977, 1995 by Th e Lockman Foundation used by permission. www.Lockman.org/

Printed in the United States of America.

Library of Congress Control Number: 2019903678

ISBN	Paperback	978-1-68536-027-6
	eBook	978-1-68536-028-3

Westwood Books Publishing LLC
Atlanta Financial Center
3343 Peachtree Rd NE Ste 145-725
Atlanta, GA 30326

www.westwoodbookspublishing.com

I dedicate my spiritual legacy to:
My loving and thoughtful wife, June Unger Dolcater
My daughter, Catharine Clarke
My son, John H. Dolcater, III
My granddaughters, Sarah Paulson and Elizabeth Paulson Huser
My grandsons, Daniel, Justin, and Jake Dolcater
My great-grandchildren, Ethan, Hannah, and Eleanor
My godson, David Jernigan
And all members of my family.

FOREWORD

I was moved often as I read Jan Dolcater's book, *Peace Within Through God's Way*. It brought to mind the many times we prayed and worked together for God's mission and the good of the church. His faith and the steps he's taken to keep his own faith vibrant and true can be truly meaningful to others.

Jan is a man of integrity whose upright character has been formed by God's grace and tested in life's fires. He shares his story through key selections of Scripture and his reflections upon them. Practical and down-to-earth, Jan shows how God's Word applies to everyday teaching. This challenges and strengthens us – if we will allow it.

Coming from his own experience of both hardship and blessing, Jan encourages and inspires us to put God at the center of our lives and be guided by His Word.

I especially appreciate his encouragement to read Scripture frequently and to ponder it carefully and be consistently guided by it.

The Rev. Dr. Michael Rowe
Rector, St Mary's Church
Bonita Spring, Florida

MESSAGE OF GUIDANCE FROM THE AUTHOR

I want to encourage committed Christians, Sunday church attendees, and non- believers alike to search for a deeper sense of understanding of how and where to find true peace within themselves.

Remember that each of us has both a gift and a purpose that we should fulfill and utilize as we proceed on our life's journey. Always do your best to exhibit to others in your countenance and your actions that you are a follower of Jesus. Let patience, faithfulness, love, mercy, and self-control be exercised on a consistent basis. If we follow this pathway in a conscientious manner, others will be interested in our realm of happiness and peace of mind.

It's equally important for us to read the Bible on a regular basis. This both deepens our faith and aids us in explaining to others the promises of God that broaden our understanding and commitment. By following this initiative, we will bring others to Christ while deepening our own faith and commitment.

Most importantly, have a purposeful prayer connection with our Lord. Open your heart in praise and thanksgiving for the blessings that have been extended to you and your family. Ask humbly for forgiveness for the transgressions that you have committed throughout the week.

Only then, ask for the needs or desires that you feel will lead you to a more committed life for God and the Lord Jesus Christ.

Ask the Lord for guidance as you proceed forward in your quest to learn more and ask for the understanding and experience that will increase your own personal closeness with God. Now, as you feel purpose for yourself, do not be selfish but enthusiastically share your peace of mind with others.

May the unfolding of my words ignite your search for the true riches of peace of mind through your faith and reliance in Jesus Christ.

Sincerely,
Jan Dolcater
March 2019

INTRODUCTION

I wrote this book to provide guidance to individuals of all ages in recognizing and considering the options that we encounter in our lives. Far too many people are caught up in our fast-moving world and lose themselves in a self-important, me-first, self-absorbed attitude. Have you ever considered that you might have made self-gratification the most important priority in your life? If so, I encourage you to consider another option.

Let me explain, as I want to share my own shortcomings and errors to help you avoid the pitfalls I fell into. I proceeded down the path of doing things my own way and it proved to be very costly. When you proceed to live without God, as I did, you fall into a sinful life and with a skewed view of the truth. It is so easy to get caught in this unproductive and debilitating way of being, instead of feeling full of life.

This is particularly true in the atmosphere that permeates our world today. As a result, many are prone to follow their way and not God's Way. All too often, people drift into habits and relationships that are not productive. This leads to feelings of emptiness and despair (or something close to it) and as a result we venture into various, unanticipated entanglements.

I am keenly aware of how these circumstances can come to be, as I have experienced it personally. It began, for me, in the dark ages of the late 1940's. I floundered about without purpose; an immature kid who was influenced by the good brothers of the fraternity just back from World War II. I was quickly swept up into an aura of fun and pleasure and paid little attention to my studies or things of genuine importance.

My mother sensed my plight and encouraged me to read the Bible as a means of establishing a solid and sound footing. Her initial recommendation to me was to discern the guiding principles in the Book of Proverbs. Unfortunately, I did not take her sound advice, as my priorities were elsewhere,

I often wonder how my life would have been different, and probably far more productive, had I paid attention to this advice. Even more importantly, how much more would I have interacted to better advantage with my family.

Without question, I would have set a more favorable example for my children. Obviously, there is no way to change or correct the errors of the past. But I cannot stress too strongly the need to provide the best example for our children to emulate. I ask that you consider the need to emphasize prayer and dependence on God. How I wish I had done this myself. It is so important to recognize the need for making necessary changes in our lives as life is really very short

Throughout the centuries, mankind has sought, by various means, the elusive quality of life defined as "peace of mind." As with many aspects of daily living, we tend to complicate this search in distinctly different ways, but with the same results – a failure of the spirit within to gain the freedom so necessary for true happiness

How many times have you seen friends or family try to gain peace of mind by attempting to buy it? Sometimes, it may be with the acquisition of a fancy car or an upscale home or some other material possession. With others, it may be the attainment of status within a business or profession. Yet another may mistakenly believe this can be gained by the acceptance of a social organization or an established group of one's peers. I personally recognize each of these situations having, in some manner, indulged myself in each.

Strangely, it was by loss, and not by gain, that I began my successful search. As with many mortals, I was in a position of having to overcome a fearsome level of personal pride. Pride was initially drilled into me by my parents and resulted in my becoming too self-important. It was later inflated by my own thrusting myself forward in various levels of business and social achievement.

Success at whatever cost seemed to matter the most – purpose was the loser. As you pursue your own personal quest for peace of mind, know that it will never be attainable without acknowledging your dependence and commitment to our Almighty God. No matter how hard you work or how highly innovative you may be, all will be in vain without this commitment. You cannot win on your own, utilizing just sheer willpower.

Do not allow yourself to follow misguided philosophies such as the one recently proposed by Facebook founder Mark Zuckerberg who encouraged people to find a sense of purpose and support somewhere other than church, and, instead, focus on Facebook.

Our forefathers who established this nation were predominately Christian. The Declaration of Independence and the Constitution were written with freedom of religious expression in mind and it is critically important for our country's future that this religious foundation be maintained. Participation in the Christian religious faiths in our country is in serious decline, as noted by a recent Pew Research Center survey. This survey further revealed that the millennial generation is the least churched generation in the history of our country. I am deeply concerned that we are becoming far too secular and if this trend continues the future of our great and beloved nation will be at risk. It is up to each of us to take this very seriously and not just coast along.

Hopefully, you will find that the pathway I am proposing, which is God's Way and not your own way, will lead you to your goal of finding true peace of mind. I cannot express too strongly the need to make God's Way the focus of your life. As we proceed, it will be helpful to you to carefully consider the Words of God and to utilize them in your daily life wherever you feel they are appropriate.

CONTENTS

Foreword...v
Message of Guidance from the Author vii
Introduction... ix
Words of God... 1

A...1
Acceptance..1
Advice..2
Assurance..12

B..15
Baptism...15
Believe...16
Bible...18
Blessed...21
Blessings...23

C..25
Commandments..25
Commitment..27
Communion...29
Compassion..30
Confession..31
Confidence..33

Courage. 34
Cross 35
Crucifixion. 36

D. **39**
Deliverance. 39
Diligence. 41
Discipline 42
Do's & Don'ts. 44

E. **47**
Eternal Life. 47
Everlasting 48

F. **51**
Faith 51
Faithfulness 58
Forgiveness. 59

G. **63**
Gentleness 63
God 64
Goodness 86
Grace. 87
Guidance 90

H. **95**
Holy. 95
Holy Spirit 96
Honor 102
Humility. 103

I **109**
Integrity 109

J 111
Jesus Christ 111
Joy 198
Judgment 201

K 205
Kindness 205
Knowledge 207

L 211
Love 211
Lovingkindness 218

M 221
Mercy 221
Morality 223

N 227
Nurturing 227

O 229
Obedience 229
Opportunity 231

P 237
Patience 237
Peace 238
Perseverence 241
Planning 243
Praise 245
Prayer 246
Purpose 251

Q 257
Quietness 257
Questioning 258

R 261
Reconciliation 261
Redemption 262
Repentance 263
Resurrection 265
Reverence 267
Righteous 268
Righteousness 271

S 275
Salvation 275
Sanctification 277
Self-Control 279
Sin 280
Sorrow 290
Spirit 291

T 295
Teaching 295
Thankful 296
Thanksgiving 298
Trust 299
Truth 302

U 305
Understanding 305

V 311
Vanity 311
Vision 313

W ... 315
Wisdom ... 315
Witness ... 321
Worship ... 324

Y ... 327
Yearning ... 327

Z ... 329
Zeal ... 329
Zealous ... 330

My Closing Thoughts ... 333
About the Author ... 335
Bibliography ... 337

NOTE TO THE READER:

Before we review my alphabetical listing and begin examining these Biblical verses, let me explain how they came to be. During my daily Bible readings over the past forty years, these words, and the verses connected with them, jumped out at me as I read them. When this occurred, I would either underline the verse or verses with a magic marker or make a note in the margin with a personal thought on the meaning or importance of the verse. Please give each of these verses and my accompanying words consideration as to how they might apply to your life today. Also, consider whether your own life might experience a significant change if you adopted a combination of them into your own lifestyle. Now, let's explore.

ACCEPTANCE

I believe that most all of us want to be accepted by our acquaintances, friends, family, and others. However, I ask you, "Who is it most important for you to be accepted by: those individuals or God?"

As we proceed on our pathways through life, it is essential for each of us to open our hearts and minds and agree to accept God as our central focus. Without this acceptance, our lives may appear to be full, but in fact they will be very empty. I encourage you to make the acceptance of God a cornerstone for your life.

And do not be conformed to this world, but be transformed by the renewing of your mind, that you may prove what the will of God is, that which is good and acceptable and perfect. (Romans 12:2)

It is far more important to be accepted by God than by any contemporary.

Wherefore, accept one another, just as Christ also accepted us to the glory of God. (Romans 15:7)

Be of the same mind as the Lord Jesus in accepting others.

Greet all the brethren with a holy kiss. (1 Thessalonians 5:26)

This was a symbol of Christian fellowship and acceptance.

...The grace of our Lord was more than abundant, with the faith and love which are found in Christ Jesus. It is a trustworthy statement deserving full acceptance that Christ Jesus came into the world to save sinners; among them I am the foremost of all. (1 Timothy 1:14–15)

Here, the apostle Paul expresses his acceptance by Jesus Christ despite the prior evils that he had committed. Have you ever felt that you could not be forgiven of a sin that you had committed? Understand the breadth of the forgiveness that Jesus provides us by His sacrifice of dying on the cross. If we will confess with our mouths, and commit to believing and following Him, our sin or sins will be forgiven whatever they are. It should be remembered that our Lord and Savior, Jesus Christ, was accepting of all individuals without showing partiality to anyone regardless of position, status, or race.

ADVICE

Are you open to advice, or do you ignore it when it is offered to you? Please maintain an open mind as you review the various statements of advice that God has put forward in His Holy Word. There is no better source of advice to consider now or at any time in your future. Each of our lives needs to be both guided and affected by His words. Far too often in today's society, there are individuals who scoff at the words and meanings in the Bible as being outdated or irrelevant. Do not let that deter you from following His Word.

I believe it is meaningful for you to consider two verses of scripture that stress the importance of asking God humbly for His advice. They are as follows:

I will instruct you and teach you in the way which you should go; I will counsel you with My eye upon you. (Psalm 32:8)

Trust in the Lord with all your heart. And do not lean on your own understanding. In all your ways acknowledge Him, and He will make your paths straight. (Proverbs 3:5-6)

I encourage you to listen for His guidance and to meditate on these two verses prior to making any important decision. Keep in mind that the guidance God gives you may be completely contrary to what you were considering. Please keep these verses in mind as you make your decision whether to follow your way or God's way.

And we know that God causes all things to work together for good to those who love God, to those who are called according to His purpose. (Romans 8:28)

Remember, His Word is infallible and will *never* be out of date. Keep this in mind as you examine the remaining verses in this section.

And you shall not swear falsely by my name, so as to profane the name of your God; I am the Lord. (Leviticus 19:12)

Avoid doing this at all times, as this is one of the Ten Commandments.

For six days may work be done; but on the seventh day there is a Sabbath of complete rest, a holy convocation. You shall not do any work; it is a Sabbath to the Lord in all your dwellings. (Leviticus 23:3)

Do you observe this? If not, I encourage you to make a sincere effort to do so.

You shall not put the Lord your God to the test, as you tested Him at Massah. (Deuteronomy 6:16)

Why would you or any thinking individual try and put God to the test? Stop a moment and review your situation, and, then, put yourself to the test.

Cast your burdens upon the Lord and He will sustain you; He will never allow the righteous to be shaken. (Psalms 55:22)

This is sound advice in any age or time. This will be reality forever. Do not make the mistake of not doing this. Remember that the Lord is always available to those who surrender and commit themselves to Him.

I will set no worthless thing before my eyes. (Psalms 101:3)

What can you gain by being involved in worthless pursuits? Perhaps you may experience a short-term pleasure or gain, but you will probably also find long-term consequences in return.

Because He has inclined His ear to me. Therefore, I shall call upon Him as long as I live. (Psalms 116:2)

I do this each and every day, and by doing this, I have found peace that I would not have experienced in any other manner.

How can a young man keep his way pure? (Psalms 119:9)

By keeping it according to His Word. Far too often, many young people put their way first and not God's way, but I encourage you to start by putting your faith and trust in Him while humbly asking for His guidance.

It was good that I was afflicted. That I may learn Thy statutes. (Psalms 119:71)

I believe that the seven years of my business bankruptcy, although very costly financially, was the best thing that ever happened to me. By working my way through these difficulties, as demanding as they were (both mentally and physically), I learned the most important lesson of my life: to know where my values and trust must always be.

Thy word is a lamp to my feet. And a light to my path. (Psalms 119:105)

Memorize this verse and keep it as a lesson for your life. I read the preceding verse each morning. It provides sound guidance for me. Try it for yourself.

Deliver my soul, O Lord from lying lips, from a deceitful tongue. (Psalms 120:2)

If you do not follow this advice, you will deceive yourself, and this will very likely lead you into an unpleasant situation.

As you proceed through these various words of advice, I encourage you to pay particular attention to the thoughtful and caring things that are expressed in the Book of Proverbs. I sure wish that I had at a much earlier time in my life. I hope that they will be meaningful to you.

A little sleep, a little slumber, a little folding of the hands to rest and your poverty will come to you like a vagabond. (Proverbs 6:10–11)

Procrastination is guaranteed to bring unexpected disasters to you.

Ill-gotten gains do not profit. But righteousness delivers from death. (Proverbs 10:2)

If you proceed on this path, it will lead to you into a dead end street.

Through presumption comes nothing but strife. But with those who receive counsel is wisdom. (Proverbs13:10)

Avoid making decisions without adequate forethought.

Better is a little with the fear of the Lord, than great treasure and turmoil with it. (Proverbs 15:16)

What would you rather have? Great treasure, or the Lord's hand guiding you? Think this over carefully. Do you have any doubt as to which you'd choose?

The refining pot is for silver and the furnace for gold. But the Lord tests hearts. (Proverbs17:3)

Are you up to it? Have faith and trust regardless of your circumstances. He is *always* faithful to those who trust in Him.

He who gives an answer before he hears, it is folly and shame to him. (Proverbs 18:13)

Strive to be a good listener and not a blusterer.

He who guards his mouth and his tongue, guards his soul from trouble. (Proverbs 21:23)

Trouble awaits those who do not act cautiously.

A good name is to be more desired that great riches. Favor is better than silver and gold. (Proverbs 22:1)

As one gets older, this takes on greater importance and significance.

Train up a child in the way he should go, even when he is old, he will not depart from it. (Proverbs 22:6)

The child's inclinations and interests should be taken into consideration. However, you should stress the importance of faith, honor, trust and belief in God to your children at every opportunity.

The rich rules over the poor, and the borrower becomes the lenders slave. (Proverbs 22:7)

Avoid burdening yourself with debt. It is a backbreaking load that I understand through painful experience. I found that it was far easier to borrow a million dollars than to pay it back with high interest as I struggled for seven long years to repay creditors after a business Chapter 11.

Do not associate with a man given to anger; Or with a hot-tempered man. Lest you learn his ways and find a snare for yourself. (Proverbs 22:24–25)

Choose your friends and associates wisely, lest you become like those of poor repute.

Who has woe? Who has sorrow? Who has contentions? Who has complaining? Who has wounds without cause? Who has redness of eyes? Those who linger long over wine. Those who go to taste mixed wine. Do not look on the wine when it is red. When it sparkles in the cup. When it goes down smoothly; At the last it bites like a serpent and stings like a viper. (Proverbs 23:29–32)

Profound advice regarding the consumption of alcohol and the consequences when consumed in excess. Do you know anyone who overindulges? Is this a pattern in your life? If so, change. Disaster is waiting for anyone who does this.

If your enemy is hungry, give him food to eat; And if he is thirsty, give him water to drink; for you will heap burning coals on his head. (Proverbs 25:21–22)

This is an application of the "Golden Rule." There may be some that do not know what this is. For those who are not sure, this is it: do unto others as you would have them do unto you.

He who hates disguises it with his lips, but he lays up deceit in his heart. (Proverbs 26:24)

A smooth smile often hides sharp teeth.

As in water face reflects face. So, the heart of man reflects man. (Proverbs 27:19)

Be always aware of another's countenance. Be cautious. Read the other person's eyes as they are a pathway to their soul. I have successfully used this many times in my sales career. I guarantee that it will be fruitful for you to do so as well.

The Book of Ecclesiastes, like most of the Book of Proverbs, was authored by King Solomon who was considered the wisest individual that the world had ever known. His perspective of things, as they relate to vanity, is exceptional.

I said to myself, "Come now, I will test you with pleasure, so enjoy yourself." And behold it too was futility. (Ecclesiastes 2:1)

The pursuit of pleasure, achievements, or great wealth all fail to bring genuine satisfaction and peace of mind.

Enjoy life with the woman, whom you love all the days of your fleeting life which He has given you under the sun; for this is your reward in life, and in your toil in which you have labored under the sun. (Ecclesiastes 9:9)

How true and powerful this passage is. Be grateful for this reward.

So, remove vexation from your heart and put away pain from your body, because childhood and the prime of life are fleeting. (Ecclesiastes 11:10)

This is very sound and practical advice for young people to keep in mind. Be thankful for the years given to you by our Almighty God.

Woe to one, who quarrels with His Maker – An earthenware vessel among the vessels of the earth! Will the clay say to the potter, "What are you doing?" (Isaiah 45:9)

It is folly to question God's way. The self-reliant person who tries to illumine the darkness by their own light will only come to sorrow. This is a very hard lesson that I learned in business. I mistakenly thought that if I worked hard enough that would solve all my problems. I did it my way rather than God's way. I hope that you will profit from my errors in judgment and follow God's way.

Can man make gods for himself? Yet they are not gods! (Jeremiah 16:20)

Some may make gods of money, possessions, prestige and imagined power, but they will always fail. There is only one who can accomplish all things, and that is with Almighty God, now and forever.

But everyone will die of his own iniquity; each man, who eats sour grapes, his teeth will be set on edge. (Jeremiah 31:30)

People excuse themselves by saying they were punished for the sins of their fathers. In reality, each person is punished for his own sins.

Woe to you who make your neighbors drink. Who mix in your venom even to make them drunk so as to look on their nakedness! You will be filled with disgrace, rather than honor. Now you yourself drink and expose your own nakedness. The cup in the Lord's right hand will come around to you, and utter disgrace will come upon your glory. (Habakkuk 2:15–16)

Never be tempted to involve yourself in such a situation. Flee from it with haste.

I hope that you have read these statements of advice carefully. Despite coming from ancient times, they are very relevant today. Try and apply these guidelines, as best you can, on your pathway through life. Now, let's continue.

And after that He called the multitude to Him, and He said to them, "Hear and understand. Not what enters into the mouth defiles the man, but what proceeds out of the mouth, this defiles the man." (Matthew 15:10–11)

This parable from Jesus makes us think of how we should conduct our speech. Do not bluster. Pause first and do not rush your thoughts.

Therefore be careful how you walk not as unwise men but as wise, making the most of your time, because the days are evil. So then do not be foolish, but understand what the will of the Lord is. (Ephesians 5:15–17)

Make every effort to follow God's way and not your own.

Finally, brethren, whatever is true, whatever is honorable, whatever is right, whatever is pure, whatever is lovely, whatever is of good repute, if there is any excellence and if anything worthy of praise, let your mind dwell on these things. (Philippians 4:8)

Here, the apostle Paul expresses very sound advice for all to consider as they pass through life. This advice from long ago will never be out of date.

See to it that no one takes you captive through philosophy and empty deception, according to the tradition of men; according to the elementary principles of the world, rather than according to Christ. (Colossians 2:8)

This was sound advice centuries ago and it still is today.

For the time will come when they will not endure sound doctrine; but wanting to have their ears tickled, they will accumulate for themselves teachers in accordance with their own desires; and will turn away their ears from the truth, and will turn aside to myths. But you, be sober in all things, endure hardship, do the work of an evangelist, fulfill your ministry. (2 Timothy 4:3–5)

Consider everything you hear talked about in today's secular world. They sound very similar to these verses. Does this make you question if the end times are near?

Let your character be free from the love of money, being content with what you have; for He Himself has said, "I will never desert you, nor will I forsake you," so that we confidently say "The Lord is my helper, I will not be afraid. What shall man do to me?" (Hebrews 13:5–6)

Stop and think seriously on these words. As long as the Lord is your helper, your safety is secure.

But if any of you lacks wisdom let him ask of God, who gives to all men generously and without reproach, and it will be given to him. (James 1:5)

How often do you take the time to ask God for guidance and listen for His response? Or, do you just move ahead trusting to luck that everything will be all right? Which choice will provide you with the most positive results? Choose wisely!!

Be of sober spirit, be on the alert, Your adversary, the devil, prowls about like a roaring lion, seeking someone to devour. (1 Peter 5:8)

Do not be misled, the devil is real and is always on the lookout to tempt us and lead us astray.

Does your walk with the Lord match your talk and your actions? If not, the convictions you espouse will be confusing to your fellow man.

Be cautious always in making decisions as all of them have consequences, some good and many bad. Ask the Lord for guidance to help you avoid problems.

ASSURANCE

As we proceed on our journey through life, we need to feel confident that we are on the right path. When you are faced with a problem or concern, who do you rely on for guidance? Only by placing your trust and faith in Almighty God and making a commitment to follow Him can you truly have assurance that the guidance you receive is on the mark.

And we know that God causes all things to work together for good to those who love God, so those who are called according to His purpose. (Romans 8:28)

Be assured that He is always listening to you even when your words are difficult to express.

That their hearts may be encouraged, having knit together in love, and attaining to all the wealth that comes from the full assurance of understanding, resulting in a true knowledge of God's mystery, that is Christ Himself. (Colossians 2:2)

Here, the apostle Paul is offering encouragement to those who accept Jesus Christ.

And we desire that each of you show the same diligence so as to realize the full assurance of hope until the end, that you may not be sluggish, but imitators of those who through faith and patience inherit the promises. (Hebrews 6:11–12)

Do you exert diligence in both your planning and your work? Don't let either slip away from you. Maintain your faith and assurance at all times regardless of the pressure you face.

I have a question for you. Do you believe that God wants you to have absolute assurance of your salvation? For those who believe in Jesus Christ, I refer you to:

These things I have written to you who believe in the name of the Son of God, in order that you may know that you have eternal life. (1 John 5:13)

Let us draw near with a sincere heart in full assurance of faith, having our hearts sprinkled clean from an evil conscience and our bodies washed with pure water. Let us hold fast the confession of our hope without wavering, for He who promised it is faithful; and let us consider how to stimulate one another to love and good deeds. (Hebrews 10:22–24)

Always remember that Jesus is faithful in *all* things forever and ever.

In addition to reading the Bible on a daily basis, over the past forty years I have also read a book called *Streams in the Desert*. I will be including references to it as we proceed on this spiritual journey. Here's an example: "Be assured, if you walk with God and expect help from Him, He will never fail you."

Now faith is the assurance of things hoped for, the conviction of things not seen. (Hebrews 11:1)

A vivid description of assurance in faith. I suggest that you read and reread this passage several times. Let it soak in.

BAPTISM

The sacramental rite of admission to the Christian Church either by immersion or sprinkling with water. Water baptism is the outward sign of both repentance and the forgiveness of sins. It is the acknowledgment of an individual's need of repentance for the forgiveness of sins.

"Go therefore and make disciples of all the nations, baptizing them in the name of the Father and the Son and the Holy Spirit; teaching them to observe all that I commanded you and lo I am with you always even to the end of the age." (Matthew 28:19–20)

Jesus gives instructions to His disciples to spread the Word of God to all mankind and to baptize each of the new converts. He did this prior to His ascension.

And it came about in those days that Jesus came from Nazareth in Galilee, and was baptized by John in the Jordan. And immediately coming up out of the water, He saw the heavens opening, and the Spirit like a dove descending upon Him; and a voice came out of the heavens "Thou art My beloved Son; in Thee I am well pleased." (Mark 1:9–11)

John did not feel worthy to baptize Jesus but agreed to do so and when John baptized Him with water God expressed his love and approval.

And Jesus said to them "I will ask you one question, and you answer Me, and then I will tell you by what authority I do these things. "Was the baptism of John from heaven or from men? Answer Me." And they began reasoning among themselves saying "if we say, 'From heaven,' then He will say, "Then why did you not believe him?" "But shall we say, 'from men?' – they were afraid of the multitude, for all considered John to be a prophet indeed. And answering Jesus they said, "We do not know." And Jesus said to them, "Neither will I tell you by what authority I do these things." (Mark 11:29–33)

Jesus displays His wisdom in responding to the inquiring scribes and Pharisees.

And Paul said, "John baptized with the baptism of repentance, telling the people to believe in Him who was coming after him, that is, in Jesus." And when they heard this, they were baptized in the name of the Lord Jesus. (Acts 19:4–5)

Being baptized in the name of Christ emphasizes their faith in Him.

And corresponding to that, baptism now saves you – the removal of dirt from the flesh, but an appeal to God for a good conscience – through the resurrection of Jesus Christ... (1 Peter 3:21)

Baptism with water is the vivid symbol of the changed life of one who has a conscience at peace with God through faith in Christ.

BELIEVE

It is essential to accept as true the existence of your faith in God and His Son, the Lord Jesus Christ. Keep this in mind as you proceed through life. I was reading a booklet recently called *In Touch* and it put forward the proposition of how to discern whether we were following

God's will or our own. To help you in determining the right approach, I suggest that you ask yourself the following questions when you're faced with making an important decision in your life.

Is it consistent with the Word of God? If you feel called to do something contrary to Scripture, you can be certain that it is not what God is guiding you to do.

Can you confidently ask God to enable you to do this? If you feel uneasy about requesting God's help and empowerment, that may well be a sign that the direction did not originate from Him. Confidence for God-given challenges never comes from within ourselves. But when we believe the Lord and rely on His Word instead of our feelings, He'll give us the ability and courage we need to accomplish His will.

Is it wise? If there is not a discernable purpose to the action, you need to ask yourself if the purpose is from Him.

Does it fit with your identity with Christ? If you feel led to do something that goes against the image of Jesus in your life, then you can be sure God has not called you to do it.

I recommend that you thoughtfully review these questions (which I gleaned from an *In Touch* daily lesson) prior to committing to any plan or action of consequence, as it may very likely have a significant impact in your future.

The naïve believes everything, but the prudent man considers his steps. (Proverbs 14:15)

Be thoughtful and careful in what you believe. As you struggle with difficulties, utilize God's Word as it is the only true and sound foundation for your belief.

"All things asked in prayer believing, you shall receive." (Matthew 21:22)

True faith and prayer have no bounds. Believers have faith based on the eternal truth of Almighty God.

Jesus said to him, "Because you have seen Me, have you believed? Blessed are they who did not see, and yet believe." (John 20:29)

This was said to the disciple Thomas who had not believed until he saw and touched Jesus after His resurrection.

Allow nothing to deter you from belief in God, not friend or acquaintance, nor empty chatter or philosophy of any type. Remember that each individual is held accountable for unbelief.

Years ago, in my business career, I attended a three-day seminar and, on the last morning, the leader posed several questions. The first was how many of our group knew what "being in the groove" was? All raised their hands. He then asked how many knew what "being in a rut" was. Again, all raised their hands.

He then explained that the only difference in the two examples was a matter of depth and asked us which we were in – the groove or the rut? I ask you to think thoughtfully where you stand in your life with God. Where do you fit? Hopefully, you will commit to believe and have the proper depth of faith in our Lord and Savior, Jesus Christ.

BIBLE

The purpose of the Bible is to reveal the one and only true God. This book has the answers for everything in your life. Develop the habit of reading it on a regular basis. Do not delay or procrastinate, just make

PEACE WITHIN THROUGH GOD'S WAY

the time. It is important for you to understand and accept that this is the Word of God spoken through individuals and not fables or half-truths. Pay particular attention to the verses in 2 Peter found later in this title. Allow the Bible to become the directional compass in your life and your anchor for stability. The Word of God will never be out of date. Lastly, remember that the Bible is relevant for every situation you will encounter in life. The Bible is more than a book; it is truly the heart of God and it was written for each of *us*.

I recently listened to a sermon by Dr. Charles Stanley and he described a method that I believe will be very useful for you to follow. Let's begin with the following verse.

This book of law shall not depart from your mouth, but you shall meditate on it day and night, so that you may be careful to do according to all that is written in it; for then you will make your way prosperous, and then you will have success. (Joshua 1:8)

Think on these powerful words. Now, with this firmly implanted in your mind, shut the world out from your thoughts. It is important for you to focus on the scripture that is meaningful to you and listen. What you are doing is establishing a platform to have a conversation with God. These sound suggestions will help you, if you will do the following:

Make this a priority in your day

1. Find a quiet place
2. Make this time have a purpose
3. Have a plan.

Ask for directions and, by all means, listen carefully as He will guide you on the proper pathway to successfully meet your needs or the trial you face. Finally, please take the time and ask the Lord to teach you and to guide you. He is *always* accessible for those who believe in Him.

Thy word is a lamp to my feet and a light to my path. (Psalms 119:105)

Never forget the word of God is infallible. Please try and memorize this verse as it is very meaningful.

The grass withers and the flower fades; But the Word of God stands forever. (Isaiah 40:8)

Another example of the permanence and power of God.

But the Scripture has shut up all men under sin, that the promise by faith in Jesus Christ might be given to those who believe. (Galatians 3:22)

A thought to keep in mind is that the Bible is the Word of God in print. Don't ever forget this and make every effort to live your life in a manner that is focused and consistent with the Holy Scriptures. The Bible is the only Book whose Author is always present when it is read.

All Scripture is inspired by God and profitable for teaching, for reproof, for correction, for training in righteousness. (2 Timothy 3:16)

Pay particular attention to this passage. Not part, but *all* Scripture is inspired by God.

For the word of God is living and active and sharper than any two-edged sword, and piercing as the division of the soul and the spirit, of both joints and marrow, and able to judge the thoughts and intentions of the heart. (Hebrews 4:12)

His word has the power to reach the innermost parts of a person's personality and judge his innermost thoughts.

But know this first of all that no prophecy of Scripture is a matter of one's own interpretation, for no prophecy was ever made by an act of human will, but by men moved by the Holy Spirit spoke from God. (2 Peter 1:20–21)

I mentioned this verse at the beginning of this topic. Read this verse thoroughly and utilize the Bible on a consistent basis. Remember the fear of the Lord is the beginning of wisdom and that *all* scripture is inspired by God. There is no better tool for you than to both study, and meditate on, His Word. It truly has all the answers and guidelines you will need to lead a happy and productive life.

Remember, the only true and sound foundation for you to utilize in your life is God's Word.

BLESSED

Each of us has been blessed with a great number of opportunities. Be sure to take the time to thank our Almighty God on a regular basis for being blessed by Him.

And he said, "Naked I came from my mother's womb, and naked I shall return there. The Lord gave and the Lord has taken away. Blessed be the name of the Lord." (Job 1:21)

Humility is shown here by Job, not selfishness or self-importance.

How blessed is man that does not walk in the counsel of the wicked, nor stand in the path of sinners, nor sit in the seat of scoffers. (Psalms 1:1)

Wisdom and understanding are illustrated in this verse.

How blessed is he, whose transgression is forgiven, Whose sin is covered! (Psalms 32:1)

There is nothing better than this.

Blessed is the nation, whose God is the Lord. The people whom He has chosen for His own inheritance. (Psalms 33:12)

Today, I am afraid for our country as it is leaning away from God. Please make the effort to prevent this from becoming reality.

How blessed is the man, who considers the helpless; The Lord will deliver him in a day of trouble. (Psalms 41:1)

Make every effort to be kind and helpful to those who are less fortunate.

Blessed be the Lord, who daily bears our burden. The God who is our salvation. God is to us a God of deliverances... (Psalms 68:19-20)

Consider the burden of sin that the average person carries and be thankful for His compassion.

Blessed is the man whom Thou dost chasten, O Lord, and dost teach out of Thy law. That Thou mayst grant him relief from the days of adversity. (Psalms 94:12-13)

I am very blessed to have faced seven hard and demanding years of adversity and that through faith and trust in God I not only survived them but am a better person because of them.

How blessed is the man who finds wisdom. And the man who gains understanding. (Proverbs 3:13)

Do not allow these benefits to escape your grasp.

A righteous man who walks in his integrity – How blessed are his sons after him. (Proverbs 20:7)

It is very important to set a proper example for your children.

Blessed be the God and Father of our Lord Jesus Christ, the Father of mercies and God of all comfort; who comforts us in all our affliction so that we may be able to comfort those who any affliction with the comfort with which we ourselves are comforted by God. (2 Corinthians 1:3–4)

It is very important to comfort those in need and to nurture with compassion those that need comfort.

Blessed is a man who perseveres under trial, for once he has been approved, he will receive the crown of life; which the Lord has promised to those who love Him. (James 1:12)

Keep this in mind and persevere in all things.

Blessed is the one who reads and those who hear the words of this prophecy, and heed the things which are written in it; for the time is near. (Revelation 1:3)

This is the first beatitude in the Book of Revelation for the seven churches.

BLESSINGS

I believe that each of us receives, in so many ways, far more blessings than we realize. I feel certain that most people can acknowledge this if they'd think about it for a moment. Therefore, I recommend that you make it a habit, as you begin each day, to thank Almighty God for all of the blessings that have been extended to you. Be ever thankful and humble whether blessings are small or great.

It is the blessing of the Lord that makes rich, And He adds no sorrow to it. (Proverbs 10:22)

True prosperity is a blessing accompanied by neither anxiety nor trouble.

I want to tell you about a blessing that I experienced as I faced a major crisis. I discovered, the day after our corporate bankruptcy was announced, that the bank would take 100 % of any account receivable that we generated. Without any cash flow, I was really in a dark corner.

Not knowing what else to do, I decided to contact twenty accounts that were dependable customers. I asked if they would allow all of our sales to them be on a COD basis. This would allow us to keep 40% of the sale with the remainder going to reduce our debt to the bank. I was asked for how long, and I said, "for one year."

Obviously, this would be a nuisance for them, but all agreed to do it except for one person who was as financially strapped as myself. Instead of working with me for a year, this group did so for eighteen months. Without this help, we would not have survived. Remarkably, several had been thirty to sixty-day accounts. What a blessing I received from these understanding and generous individuals. I am thoroughly convinced that this would never have happened without the presence of God.

"There is no burden that, if we lift it cheerfully and bear it with love in our hearts, will not become a blessing." This is another message from *Streams in the Desert*.

A faithful man will abound with blessings, but he who makes haste to be rich will not go unpunished. (Proverbs 28:20)

Far too often, the desire to get rich quick results in dishonest dealings.

Now, take a minute and open your heart and thank the caring and compassionate God who has brought you many blessings.

COMMANDMENTS

The commandments of our God are to be adhered to in a consistent and conscientious manner. If we ignore them, or observe them inconsistently, we should understand that there will be consequences for our neglect or avoidance of them.

"You shall have no other gods before Me. (Exodus 20:3)

You shall not make for yourself an idol or any likeness of what is in heaven above or on the earth beneath or in the water under the earth. (Exodus 20:4)

You shall not take the name of the Lord your God in vain, for the Lord will not leave unpunished who takes His name in vain. (Exodus 20:7)

Remember the Sabbath day to keep it holy. (Exodus 20:8)

Honor your father and mother, that your days may be prolonged in the land, which the Lord your God gives you. (Exodus 20:12)

You shall not murder. (Exodus 20:13)

You shall not commit adultery. (Exodus 20:14)

You shall not steal. (Exodus 20:15)

You shall not bear false witness against your neighbor. (Exodus 20:16)

You shall not covet your neighbor's house, you shall not covet your neighbor's wife, or his male servant or his female servant or his ox or his donkey or anything that belongs to your neighbor." (Exodus 20:17)

It is important for you to know and understand the significance of the Ten Commandments and that they are not just His ten suggestions.

For six days a work may be done, but on the seventh day, there is a sabbath of complete rest, a holy convocation. You shall not do any work; it is a sabbath to the Lord in all your dwellings. (Leviticus 23:3)

Today's secular world ignores this. Please consider this carefully and pay heed to it.

Beware lest you forget the Lord your God by not keeping His commandments and His ordinances and His statutes which I am commanding you today. (Deuteronomy 8:11)

Moses said this centuries ago but it is still relevant for us today.

The fear of the Lord is the beginning of wisdom; A good understanding have all those who do His commandments. His praise endures forever. (Psalms 111:10)

The fear of the Lord is the starting point and the essence of wisdom. It also exhibits a reverence for God and submission to His will.

Teach me good discernment and knowledge, for I believe in Thy commandments. (Psalms 119:66)

...And all Thy commandments are truth. (Psalms 119:151)

I refer to these verses daily in my quiet time. Why not give them a try?

The conclusion, when all has been heard, is fear God and keep His commandments, because this applies to every person. For God will bring every act to judgment, everything which is hidden, whether it is good or evil. (Ecclesiastes 12:13–14)

It certainly makes sense to pay attention to this statement.

"If you love Me you will keep My commandments." (John 14:15)

Jesus explains this to His disciples, but it applies to all of us now and in the future.

…God is greater than our heart and knows all things. Beloved, if our heart does not condemn us, we have confidence before God; and whatever we ask we receive from Him, because we keep His commandments and do the things that are pleasing in His sight. And this is His commandment, that we believe in the name of His Son Jesus Christ and love one another, just as He commanded us. (1 John 3:20–23)

It is a comfort to know that God is both all-knowing and all-loving.

COMMITMENT

If you have no true commitment in your life, any road will get you there. However, when you arrive, you might find it a very difficult and unpleasant place; where you do not wish to be under any circumstances. Without commitment, your life will be a futile search for happiness. Commit yourself to God and follow His way in your life.

Commit yourself to the Lord; let Him deliver him. Let Him rescue him, because He delights in him. (Psalms 22:8)

To *commit* means for you to have a firm an unwavering commitment to God.

"Commit your troubles to the Lord and leave it all in His good hands"—another thought from *Streams in the Desert*.

...For Thou art my strength. Into Thy hand I commit my spirit; Thou hast ransomed me, O Lord, God of truth. (Psalms 31:4–5)

Committing one's life to God is the epitome of faith. Die to self and live by the Holy Word of God.

Commit your way to the Lord, trust also in Him and He will do it. (Psalms 37:5)

You can always trust the Lord when you make your commitment to Him.

Commit your works to the Lord and your plans will be established. (Proverbs 16:3)

Roll your burdens upon the Lord when they overwhelm you with anxiety. Never forget His presence.

Jesus answered and said to him, "Truly, truly, I say to you unless one is born again, he cannot see the kingdom of God." (John 3:3)

Obviously, an individual cannot enter again into his mother's womb. We must commit to Christ and have a spiritual rebirth.

And Jesus crying out with a loud voice, said, "Father, into Thy hands I commit My spirit." And having said this He breathed His last. (Luke 23:46)

There is no more powerful and meaningful commitment than this.

COMMUNION

A holy service where each person is offered the body and blood of our Lord and Savior, Jesus Christ, so that we recipients may be forgiven our sins and renew our faith and commitment to Him. All persons who receive this must be aware that this is done with reverence and with a contrite heart. Never participate in this without asking for genuine forgiveness, or with a half-hearted or wishy-washy approach.

And while they were eating, Jesus took some bread and after a blessing, He broke it and gave it to the disciples and said, "Take eat; this is My body." And when he had taken a cup and given thanks, He gave it to them saying, "Drink from it all of you; for this is My blood of the covenant, which is poured out for many for forgiveness of sins." (Matthew 26:26–28)

Never forget that the Lord's Supper is a significant reminder of the sacrifice that Jesus made for all mankind. It must be plainly understood that if communion is taken in an unworthy manner (that is, with unconfessed sin) this may result in unpleasant consequences. It is exceedingly important for each of us to carefully examine our hearts and souls prior to receiving communion.

Is not the cup of blessing which we bless a sharing in the blood of Christ? Is not the bread we break a sharing in the body of Christ? (1 Corinthians 10:16–17)

By sharing in the bread and cup of blessing, these individuals, being one in spirit, become one in the body of Christ.

You cannot drink the cup of the Lord and the cup of demons; you cannot partake of the table of the Lord and the table of demons. Or do we provoke the Lord to jealousy? We are not stronger than He, are we? (1 Corinthians 10:21–22)

Some may mistakenly believe that it is no problem to participate in the communion service while also pursuing a life that is inconsistent with the Word of the Lord. However, anyone who follows that logic is, without a doubt, deluding themselves. A statement that I particularly like is this: you cannot walk with the Lord and run with the devil. Think about it? Where do you fit?

COMPASSION

This is the understanding and willingness to care for others regardless of the circumstances surrounding them. What does this word mean to you? How does it make you feel? Does it have a sense of caring for you? It should always be remembered that life does not necessarily extend the same good fortune or opportunity to all of us. I encourage you to offer yourself in whatever manner is appropriate to help others who are in need whether it's because they are sick, sorrowful, or destitute. Allow yourself to be an instrument of God's peace.

Thou O Lord will not withhold Thy compassion from me; Thy lovingkindness and Thy truth will continually preserve me. (Psalms 40:11)

We must give of ourselves in humility. "God does not comfort us to be comfortable, but to be comforters." This statement from *Streams in the Desert* reminds us to show compassion to those who need to be comforted.

…According to the greatness of Thy compassion blot out my transgressions. Wash me thoroughly from my iniquity and cleanse me from my sin. (Psalms 51:1–2)

Every one of us needs to use this prayer from their heart.

Will the Lord reject forever? And will He never be favorable again? Has His lovingkindness ceased forever? Has His promise come to an end forever Has God forgotten to be gracious? Or has He in His anger withdrawn His compassion? (Psalms 77:7-9)

Sometimes, when we are in fear or peril, we cry out to God for help and beg for mercy yet hear and feel nothing from God. Is it because we have cut ourselves off from God rather than God abandoning us? We must repent, fear (respect) and praise Him not only each day but forever.

......He said, "It is not those who are healthy who need a physician, but those who are sick. But go and learn what this means, I desire compassion, and not sacrifice, for I did not come to call the righteous, but sinners." (Matthew 9:12-13)

Jesus calls all sinners to His compassion.

And so, as those have been chosen by God, holy and beloved, put on a heart of compassion, kindness, humility, gentleness and patience; bearing with one another and forgiving each other whoever has a complaint against anyone. Just as the Lord forgave you, so you should also. (Colossians 3:12-13)

Ask the Lord to lead you in this pattern of living. Reread this several times as the advice provided is priceless.

CONFESSION

No human, regardless of their level of intelligence, is perfect and as a result all are guilty of sin. Confession simply means we agree with God that our thoughts, words or actions are out of sync with His way and His commandments. It is up to each of us to confess our sins and when we do this, we should be specific and not vague. Ask Jesus Christ for forgiveness and ask for His guidance as you proceed through life. If you will follow through and do this, you will develop a pure spirit.

He, who conceals his transgressions will not prosper, but he that confesses and forsakes them will find compassion. (Proverbs 28:13)

Open your heart, confess your transgressions and ask Jesus for forgiveness.

If you confess with your mouth Jesus as Lord, and believe in your heart that God raised Him from the dead, you shall be saved. (Romans 10:9)

If you wish to have Salvation from the Lord, this statement is of utmost importance.

Fight the good fight of faith take hold of the eternal life to which you were called, and you made the good confession in the presence of many witnesses. (1 Timothy 6:12)

This is Timothy's public confession at the time of his baptism. Never be shy or hesitant to acknowledge your confession and belief in the Lord Jesus Christ.

Let us hold fast the confession of our hope without wavering, for He who promised is faithful, and let us consider how to stimulate one another to love and good deeds. (Hebrews 10:23–24)

The only way you can be forgiven of your sins is through Jesus Christ and His sacrificial, substitutionary death at Calvary.

If we confess our sins, He is faithful and righteous to forgive us our sins and to cleanse us from all unrighteousness. (1 John 1:9)

Open your heart and your soul to our Lord and Savior Jesus Christ and be ever thankful.

CONFIDENCE

Do you feel confident in all that you do? Each of us has varying degrees of confidence in our abilities and the exercise of them. However, regardless of your degree of self-confidence, it is still our responsibility to rely on guidance and direction from the Lord. Please do not make the mistake of relying strictly on your own devices. If you do, the probability is that your results will lack clarity and, most likely, will be poor. Trust me, as I erred big time in this regard and I hope this reminder will help you.

For Thou art my hope; O Lord God, Thou are my confidence from my youth. (Psalms 71:5)

Allow the Lord to guide your confidence.

That they should put their confidence in God; and not forget the works of God. (Psalms 78:7)

When you are in a tight spot in whom do you put your confidence? Is it God? If not, why not? Can you think of anyone more dependable than He is?

Like a bad tooth and an unsteady foot is confidence in a faithless man in time of trouble. (Proverbs 25:19)

Truer words were never spoken even though they are centuries old. Confidence may demolish a man's business, but if his faith in Christ is strong, it will build his character. Consider this thoughtfully.

Let us therefore draw near with confidence to the throne of grace, that we may receive mercy and find grace to help in time of need. (Hebrews 4:16)

Draw near to Jesus Christ and experience the attributes of this verse.

Now faith is the assurance of things hoped for; the conviction of things not seen. (Hebrews 11:1)

This verse expresses having full confidence in our Lord and Savior, Jesus Christ, regardless of whatever daunting fear you may be experiencing.

COURAGE

When you feel threatened or in danger, stand firm and exhibit a position of strength and understanding. When you respond in this manner, you are displaying courageous behavior. Be sure when you face a tenuous situation to place yourself into the hands of our Lord and Savior, Jesus Christ.

"Have I not commanded you? Be strong and courageous. Do not tremble or dismayed for the Lord your God is with you wherever you go." (Joshua 1:9)

Be patient and wait for the Lord to guide you.

Wait for the Lord: Be strong, and let your heart take courage; Yes, wait for the Lord. (Psalms 27:14)

Courage is fear that has said its prayers. Consider this thought from *Streams in the Desert*: "Look at the soil of your heart – do you have the courage, honest purpose and the earnest desire to fulfill your obligations?"

Wait for the Lord; Be strong and let your heart take courage all you, who hope in the Lord. (Psalms 31:24)

Use all your courage to help those who are discouraged.

A quotation from Nelson Mandela is appropriate here: "I learned that courage was not the absence of fear, but the triumph over it. The brave man is not he who does not feel afraid, but he who conquers that fear."

For God has not given us a spirit of timidity, but of power, and love and discipline. (2 Timothy 1:7)

The apostle Paul says to the believers they should display courage in spite of what they face. Mark Twain once said that "courage is resistance to fear, mastery of fear, and not the absence of fear." Keep this in mind as you move forward in your life.

CROSS

The cross is the world's most important symbol as it is the emblem of the sacrifice that Jesus Christ made for all mankind. He was crucified on a cross to forgive the sins of all those who believe and commit to Him.

And He was saying to them all, "If anyone wishes to come after Me, let him deny himself, and take up his cross and follow Me. For whoever wishes to save his life shall lose it, but whoever loses his life for My sake, he is the one who will save it. For what is a man profited, if he gains the whole world and loses or forfeits himself? For whoever is ashamed of Me and My words, of him will the Son of Man be ashamed when He comes into His glory and the glory of the Father and of the holy angels. (Luke 9:23–26)

Separation from the "old life" is the measure for His believers.

...this Man delivered up by the predestined plan and foreknowledge of God, you nailed to a cross by the hands of godless men and put Him to death. And God raised Him up again, putting an end to the agony of death, since it was impossible for Him to be held in its power. (Acts 2:23–24)

Understand that God's plan was exercised in everything that transpired in the life of Jesus while He was on earth.

For the word of the cross is to those who are perishing foolishness, but to us that are being saved It is the power of God. Because the foolishness of God is wiser than men, and the weakness of God is stronger than men. (1 Corinthians 1:18 & 25)

Strive to gain the wisdom of God through Jesus Christ. This is simplicity yet perfection. The worldly wisdom prized by the Corinthians was the very antithesis of the wisdom of God. The cross of Christ revealed our sin at its worst and God's love at its best. However, I ask you to consider that everything that would condemn us before our Almighty God was placed upon Jesus, our Savior, on the cross for the forgiveness of our sins.

This note from *Our Daily Bread* is quite expressive: "God's love for us is as expansive as the open arms of Christ on the cross."

CRUCIFIXION

Putting an individual to death by the excruciating method of nailing him to a cross was initiated by the Romans during the first century. Our Lord and Savior Jesus Christ experienced this for all mankind so that we may all be forgiven of our sins. It should be understood that

Jesus' crucifixion was a public demonstration of God's hatred of sin and His immense love of mankind.

I am poured out like water, and all my bones are out of joint; My heart is like wax; it is melted within me. My strength is dried up like a potsherd, and my tongue cleaves to my jaws; and Thou doest lay me in the dust of death. For dogs have surrounded me; a band of evildoers has encompassed me; they pierced my hands and my feet. I can count all my bones, they look, they stare at me; they divide my garments among them, and for my clothing they cast lots. (Psalms 22:14–18)

David gives a prophetic description of the crucifixion of Jesus even though crucifixion was not known until Roman times many centuries later.

When Pilate therefore heard these words, he brought Jesus out, and sat down on the judgment seat at a place called The Pavement, but in Hebrew Gabbatha. Now it was the day of preparation for the Passover; it was about the sixth hour. And he said to the Jews "Behold your King"! They therefore cried out, "Away with Him, away with Him, crucify Him!" Pilate said to them, "Shall I crucify your King?" The chief priests answered, "We have no king but Caesar." So he then delivered Him to be crucified. (John 19:13–16)

Pilate's sarcasm was directed at the chief priests who he had no use for. They responded blasphemously by denying the kingship of God over their nation.

For the death that He died, He died to sin, once for all; but the life He lives, He lives to God. (Romans 6:10)

Jesus was crucified on the cross so that the sins of all mankind would be forgiven if only we confess Him as Lord and Savior and fully commit to Him.

But may it never be that I should boast, except in the cross of our Lord Jesus Christ, through which the world has been crucified to me and I to the world. (Galatians 6:14)

Paul expresses his commitment to Jesus.

DELIVERANCE

When we commit our souls and bodies to Jesus Christ we are delivered into salvation. Decisions that you make on this subject should never be made without thorough efforts of thoughtful prayer.

Thou art my hiding place; Thou dost preserve me from trouble; Thou dost surround me with songs of deliverance. (Psalms 32:7)

This becomes true when you confess your sins and acknowledge Christ as your Savior.

O give us help against the adversary. For deliverance by man is vain. (Psalms 60:11)

Deliverance can come only through Jesus and not man.

Blessed be the Lord who daily bears our burdens. The God who is our salvation. God is to us a God of deliverances; and to God the Lord belong escapes from death. (Psalms 68:19–20)

The Lord relieves the daily burden of sin that we all carry for those who follow Him.

JOHN H. (JAN) DOLCATER, JR.

Before beginning the next topic, I want to offer for your consideration other types of deliverance that I have experienced.

Looking back on my life, I know that the Lord has delivered me from death on a number of occasions. When I was a young boy, I accompanied my parents to Atlanta because my Mom wanted to see the première of *Gone with the Wind*. We stayed at the Winecoff Hotel which was near the theater and we left the next day after seeing the film. The following night, a devastating fire broke out in that hotel killing 120 people. The location of our hotel room was in one of the most severely-burned areas. My parents and I were barely delivered from death. Have you ever had a close encounter like that?

The next time I escaped death came while I was attending high school. There was a large water tank next to the school. One day after class, and on a dare, a friend and I climbed the ladder to the walkway at the top of the tank and then proceeded up the curved ladder to the very top. Very exciting, but quite foolish, as on the way down on the curved portion I lost my footing and slipped. If I had not grabbed the ladder, I would have fallen about 60 feet. In spite of these occurrences, I did not think much of them at the time.

Some years later, as I was winding up college, I was called up to attend summer camp as part of my commitment to ROTC. I went to Webb AF base in Big Spring, Texas. Our group was really hustled to sign up for flight school. One enticement was a flight in a jet trainer similar to our top fighter jet. I climbed into the jump seat and the pilot did several interesting and exciting maneuvers as we climbed to 15,000 feet. We leveled off and to my surprise he asked if I would like to take the stick and see how it felt to fly it myself. I said, "Yes!" and took hold of it, trying at first to be steady. I was thinking about banking the plane, as I held the stick firm in my hand but before doing it, I told the pilot my plan. He told me to look over my right shoulder. I did as I was told and shivered as there was another plane flying very close on our wing. If I had not spoken up, there is no question we would have had a mid-air collision. During our month at Webb, there were six fatal training flight accidents and I was very thankful not to have been the seventh one. I dodged another one. It did not make a big impression on me at the time. Of course, when you are twenty-two, you think that you're bulletproof, and I did at that time. I will describe more experiences later on.

Always remember this from *Streams in the Desert*: "God orders the time for our deliverance from whatever we face."

DILIGENCE

This trait is highly desirable as it demonstrates a committed determination to excel in spite of obstacles and difficulties. Very often, we find ourselves facing an obstacle that appears to be almost impossible to overcome. Regardless, stay strong and strive to develop the habit of diligence.

"Only give heed to yourself and keep your soul diligently; lest you forget the things which your eyes have seen, and lest they depart from your heart all the days of your life; but make them known to your sons and grandsons…" (Deuteronomy 4:9)

It is our duty and obligation to pass on the love of God and the teaching of Jesus Christ to our children and beyond.

Watch over your heart with all diligence. For from it flows the springs of life. (Proverbs 4:23)

Maintain an open and caring heart in spite of any difficulty you face.

Poor is he who works with a negligent hand. But the hand of the diligent makes rich. (Proverbs 10:4)

Work always in a consistent and thorough manner and you will be well rewarded for your efforts.

The plans of the diligent lead surely to advantage. But everyone who is hasty comes surely to poverty. (Proverbs 21:5)

A very accurate description of diligence as compared to carelessness.

And we desire that each one of you show the same diligence so as to realize the full assurance of hope until the end, that you may not be sluggish, but imitators of those through faith and patience inherit the promises. (Hebrews 6:11–12)

Strive to be fully committed in your faith.

DISCIPLINE

By maintaining a sense of order despite the changing circumstances that face you, you create a successful way of life. We all have choices but being consistent is not a sometime thing. By being consistent, the results of your actions now and in the future will be dramatically enhanced.

"Behold, how happy is the man whom God reproves; So do not despise the discipline of the Almighty…" (Job 5:17)

Remember that God loves those He disciplines.

The Lord has disciplined me severely, but He has not given me over to death. (Psalms 118:18)

I was strongly disciplined during the seven years of resolving my Chapter 11 bankruptcy which cost my family and myself a half-million dollars, but I survived with the guidance of God and am a better person for it.

Whoever loves discipline loves knowledge, but he who hates reproof is stupid. (Proverbs 12:1)

Makes sense to me. How about you?

Poverty and shame will come to him, who neglects discipline. But he who regards reproof will be honored. (Proverbs 13:18)

Life lived recklessly is a guarantee that it will come to no good.

He, who neglects discipline despises himself. But he who listens to reproof acquires understanding. The fear of the Lord is the instruction for wisdom and before honor comes humility. (Proverbs 15:32–33)

This should be the basic foundation of anyone's life if they wish to be successful and acquire peace of mind.

Do not hold back discipline from a child. Although you beat him with the rod he will not die. (Proverbs 23:13)

Be a good parent and not just a good buddy.

This verse takes me back to when our priest asked me to teach the ninth grade Sunday School class. It is an understatement to say this age group is challenging. My initial goal was to make a firm impression on them by providing a disciplined approach. I started by telling them that this year would be different for them.

When I was asked what I meant, I said that, to begin with, there would be tests every six weeks and I did not want anyone to have to tell their parents that they were flunking Sunday School. It took a little time, but the class size, which originally was 6 swelled to 19 by the end of the year. Looks like discipline had a positive result here.

For we hear that some among you are leading an undisciplined life, doing no work at all, but acting like busybodies. Now such persons we command and exhort in the Lord Jesus Christ to work in quiet fashion and eat their own bread. (2 Thessalonians 3:11–12)

Some of this group was under the mistaken belief that the end of the world was soon to occur and, therefore, did not work. Paul expressed his recommendation to prevent this from continuing.

…"My son, do not regard lightly the discipline of the Lord, Nor faint when you are reproved by Him; For whom the Lord loves He disciplines and He scourges every son whom He receives." (Hebrews 12:5)

I am curious; do you feel you have the bodily or godly discipline that you need in your own life? If it were to be increased, do you believe your life would be more vibrant and produce a dramatic improvement?

One of life's most difficult challenges is waiting for the Lord's guidance as we deal with problems. As a rule, most of us struggle when faced with decisions that require discipline. Be patient and do not shrink from it. When it is available to you, utilize it.

DO's & DON'TS

We are faced with choices every day of our lives. What we choose will determine our commitment to God and bad choices may have exceptionally serious consequences. Always avoid impulsive decisions. In past years, I have made a few of those and none were productive.

"Only be strong and very courageous; be careful to do all according to the law, which Moses, my servant, commanded you; do not turn from it to the right or to the left, so that you may have success, wherever you should go…" (Joshua 1:7)

Never be hesitant to follow God's word.

Cease from anger and forsake wrath. Do not fret it only leads to evildoing. (Psalms 37:8)

Fretting over problems never produces anything of value.

Do not let kindness and truth leave you; Bind them around your neck. Write them on the tablet of your heart. (Proverbs 3:3)

These are priceless gifts to share.

Another *don't* is don't take foolish chances.

I had been making some sales calls on customers in the Bradenton/Sarasota area and wanted to get back for a Rotary Fellowship party. I was running late, so I decided to speed up my driving as I approached the community of Ruskin. It was raining but not too hard. I should have used better judgment. As I entered the town, I came to an overpass. I touched the brakes and, all of a sudden, my car did a 360° spin.

I was very fortunate as the car came to a stop at the traffic light at the bottom of the overpass in exactly the correct position. I couldn't believe what had happened. It was scary. There is no question that I had had another close call. So, I encourage you to slow down and better utilize your time to much better advantage than I did.

Do not weary yourself to gain wealth. Cease from your consideration of it. (Proverbs 23:4)

Do not covet another's wealth or way of life. Place your faith in God's hands, let Him lead you, and be content with the results.

Do not speak in the hearing of a fool. For he will despise the wisdom of your mouth. (Proverbs 23:9)

Choose your friends and associates with care. For the heavy drinker and the glutton will come to poverty and drowsiness will clothe a man with rags.

Too often this is unobserved; the foolish only look for a "good time."

Do not say, "Thus shall I do to him as he has done to me; I will render to the man according to his work." (Proverbs 24:29)

Apply the Golden Rule and do unto others as you would have them do unto you.

Do not answer a fool according to his folly; Lest you be also like him. (Proverbs 26:4)

Never forget this lesson that is so well-stated.

Do not let your speech cause you to sin, and do not say in the presence of a messenger of God that it was a mistake. Why should God be angry on account of your voice and destroy the work of your hands? (Ecclesiastes 5:6)

Instead of replying hastily, pause. Patience pays dividends.

This compilation of things *not* to do makes a great deal of sense to me. What is your opinion? Have you learned anything of value?

ETERNAL LIFE

This topic is so boundless, it is very difficult for most all of us to consider. However, bear in mind that God has given to mankind the ability to look beyond the routine of life and into the limitless posterity of the future. When you ponder the enormity of this, it is overwhelming. However, do not make the error of ignoring this reality.

"For he whom God has sent speaks the words of God, for He gave the Spirit without measure. The Father loves the Son, and has given all things into His hand. He who believes in the Son has eternal life; but he who does not obey the Son shall not see life, but the wrath of God abides on him." (John 3:34–36)

What course or direction do you have in your life? Consider this carefully.

"You search the Scriptures because you think that in them you have eternal life; and it is these that bear witness of Me." (John 5:39)

This statement occurred during a discourse that Jesus had with the scribes and Pharisees at a feast in Jerusalem.

"For this the will of My Father that everyone who beholds the Son and believes in Him, may have eternal life and I, Myself will raise him up on the last day." (John 6:40)

The promise of Jesus plainly stated.

"My sheep hear My voice and I know them, and they follow Me; and I give eternal life to them, and they shall never perish; and no one shall snatch them out of My hand." (John 10: 27–28)

The promise to those that believe and trust in Jesus as their Lord and Savior.

But now having been freed from sin and enslaved to God, you derive your benefit resulting in sanctification and the outcome, eternal life. For the wages of sin is death, but the free gift of God is eternal life in Christ Jesus our Lord. (Romans 6:22–23)

Every person has free will to discern such matters. Does this make sense to you?

And the witness is this, that God has given us eternal life and this life is in His Son. He that has the Son has the life; he who does not have the Son of God does not have the life. (1 John 5:11–12)

Plainly said. Easy to comprehend.

EVERLASTING

The condition that has no end and can only be supplied by our Almighty God. Nothing from humankind can ever provide anything of this nature.

…Even from everlasting to everlasting Thou art God. (Psalms 90:2)

Think on this profound statement.

For the Lord is good. His lovingkindness is everlasting, and His faithfulness to all generations. (Psalms 100:5)

How can anyone ask for more than this?

But the lovingkindness of the Lord is from everlasting to everlasting on those who fear Him. And His righteousness to children's children. (Psalms 103:17)

A comforting thought for those that respect the Lord.

The sum of Thy word is truth, and every one of Thy righteous ordinances is everlasting. (Psalms 119:160)

Here lies a foundation for our lives.

And see if there is any hurtful way in me, and lead me in Thy everlasting way. (Psalms 139:24)

Put aside any unforgiveness that exists in you.

Trust in the Lord forever, for in God the Lord, we have an everlasting Rock. Isaiah 26:4)

A Rock for all the ages.

...The Everlasting God the Lord, the Creator of the ends of the earth does not become weary or tired. His understanding is inscrutable. He gives strength to the weary. (Isaiah 40:28–29)

What a comfort to be aware of.

It is very important for all to remember that He is a Living God now and forever. When you consider the magnitude of this, it makes humankind so very small in comparison.

FAITH

I ask that you consider these elements of faith that I have learned. These are drawn from years of reading from *Streams in the Desert*.

1) "Faith is taking God at His word. God gives promises in a quiet hour.
2) The beginning of anxiety is the end of faith and the beginning of faith is the end of anxiety." (This is a quotation from George Mueller.)
3) You will never learn faith in comfortable surroundings. As you face adversity, place your complete faith and trust in God. Do not allow whatever problem you encounter to be an overwhelming burden, but instead make it a bridge for you to cross to become closer to God as you surrender your heart and soul to Him.
4) Tis better to walk with faith than with sight.
5) Faith leads you forward to triumphs.
6) Faith is the substance of things hoped for, the evidence of things not seen.
7) Faith takes away self-works and also all want.
8) Little faith will bring souls to heaven, but great faith will bring heaven to your soul. Perfect faith focuses on God completely

and not on yourself. Never forget there are no limitations on God.
9) There is no shortcut to the life of faith.
10) Faith has nothing to do with feelings, improbabilities, or outward appearance. Faith rests on the naked word of God. When we take Him at His word, the heart is at peace."

I hope the lessons of faith listed above will help you as you examine the verses of faith listed below. I particularly like these:

Now faith is the assurance of things hoped for, the conviction of things not seen. (Hebrews 11:1)

In God, whose word I praise; In God I have put my trust; I shall not be afraid. (Psalms 56:4)

Fear nothing, if your faith in God is sincere

A notation from *Our Daily Bread*: "Fear can paralyze, but faith propels us to follow God."

Quite a few years after my experience with the 360° spin, I was on a business trip to the West Coast. I had been seeing a customer in Atlanta and was on a non-stop flight from Atlanta to Los Angeles to see some west coast suppliers. The plane was a Boeing 727, a favorite plane of mine at the time. We started on time and were cruising at 35,000 feet over Texas when the pilot came on and in a fairly matter-of-fact voice told us we were going to make an unscheduled stop in Waco as we had a problem with an engine on fire. He said, "I do not know for sure, but I believe I can put it on the ground OK." While his intent was to calm us, this was not exactly reassuring to say the least. Down we came and as I looked out the window our port engine was blazing.

As the note prior to this story says, "fear nothing, if your faith in God is sincere." I applied this as we finally touched down without incident. Crash trucks extinguished the fire, but we were not able to pull up close to the terminal and before we deplaned, we were told to be very cautious as the runways to the terminal usually had a fair number of rattlesnakes on them. Ho hum, just another quiet day. Believe this was number five on my close calls. All of these occurrences have made me wonder, "why me?"

"Faith arises amidst storms, so remember fair-weather faith is no faith at all." Another excellent thought from *Streams in the Desert*.

And immediately He made the disciples get into the boat, and go ahead of Him to the other side, while He sent the multitudes away. And after He went up to the mountain by Himself to pray; and when it was evening, He was there alone. But the boat was already many stadia away from the land, battered by the waves; for the wind was contrary. And in the fourth watch of the night He came to them walking on the sea. And when the disciples saw Him walking on the sea, they were frightened saying "it is a ghost" and cried out for fear. But immediately Jesus spoke to them saying, "Take courage it is I; do not be afraid." And Peter answered Him and said, "If it is You command me to come to You on the water." And He said, "Come!" And Peter got out of the boat and walked on the water and came toward Jesus. But seeing the wind, he became afraid, and beginning to sink, he cried out saying, "Lord save me!" And immediately Jesus stretched out His hand and took hold of him, and said to him, "O you of little faith, why did you doubt?" (Matthew 14:22–31)

Instead of Peter, assume it was you who asked Jesus if He would allow YOU to walk on the water. Would you have sunk in the water like Peter, or would your faith have been maintained fully? How strong is your faith? Are you sure?

For in it the righteousness of God is revealed from faith to faith; as it is written "But the righteous man shall live by faith." (Romans 1:17)

No one can be righteous in the sight of God without faith.

For we maintain that a man is justified by faith apart from the works of the law. (Romans 3:28)

Faith is the radar that sees through the fog of life.

Therefore having been justified by faith, we have peace with God through our Lord Jesus Christ. (Romans 5:1)

What a comforting and satisfying feeling to have.

For through the grace given to me I say to every man among you not to think more highly of himself than he ought to think; but to think so as to have sound judgment as God has allotted to each a measure of faith. (Romans 12:3)

Be humble as you exercise your faith.

…for we walk by faith, not by sight. (2 Corinthians 5:7)

Let your path be one of confidence and assurance in the Lord.

Test yourselves to see if you are in the faith; examine yourselves! Or do you not recognize this about yourselves, that Jesus Christ is in you – unless indeed you fail the test? (2 Corinthians 13:5)

Have you ever tested your faith? Do you believe you would pass the test? I encourage you to always maintain your faith regardless of any trial or difficulty you face; when you do so you will lead a joyful life.

...nevertheless knowing that a man is not justified by the works of the Law but through faith in Jesus Christ, even we have believed in Christ Jesus, that we may be justified by faith in Christ, and not by works of the Law; since by the works of the Law shall no flesh be justified. (Galatians 2:16)

If a man is to be vindicated of any charge of sin in connection with failure to keep God's law, he must show his faith and commitment to Christ Jesus.

Now that no one is justified by the Law before God is evident; for, "The righteous man shall live by faith." (Galatians 3:11)

One can be justified in God's sight only by faith.

For by grace you have been saved through faith; and that not of yourselves; it is the gift of God; not as a result of works that no one should boast. (Ephesians 2:8–9)

Faith in Jesus Christ is the answer and not works alone.

...so that Christ may dwell in your hearts through faith; and that you being rooted and grounded in love, may be able to comprehend with all the saints what is the breadth and length and height and depth, and to know the love of Christ which surpasses knowledge, that you may be filled up to the fullness of God. (Ephesians 3:17–19)

Please read and reread this several times as these verses have significant meaning.

As you therefore have received Christ Jesus the Lord, so walk in Him, having been firmly rooted and now being built up in Him and established in your faith, just as you were instructed and overflowing with gratitude. See to it that no one takes you captive through philosophy and empty deception, according to the tradition of men, according to the elementary principles of the world, rather than according to Christ. (Colossians 2:6–8)

Do not allow the misguided philosophies of today's secular society lead your footsteps astray.

But the Spirit explicitly says that in later times some will fall away from the faith paying attention to deceitful spirits and doctrines of demons. (1 Timothy 4:1)

With so many strange philosophies discussed in the world today, I cannot help but wonder whether we are in the later times. Your thoughts?

But those who want to get rich fall into temptation and a snare and many foolish and harmful desires which plunge men into ruin and destruction. For the love of money is a root of all sorts of evil, and some by longing for it have wandered away from the faith and pierced themselves with many a pang. But flee from these things, you man of God, and pursue righteousness, godliness, faith, love, perseverance and gentleness. (1 Timothy 6:9–11)

Do not allow any success you may achieve cloud your dependence on, and your faith in, God.

I have fought the good fight, I have finished the course, I have kept the faith. (2 Timothy 4:7)

Here, the apostle Paul expresses his faith as he knows his death is imminent. Soon after, he was beheaded by the Emperor Nero.

But My righteous one shall live by faith; And if he shrinks back, My soul has no pleasure in him. But we are not of those that shrink back to destruction, but of those who have faith to the preserving of the soul. (Hebrews 10:38–39)

I want to ask you this question. Are you a believer or are you a doubter? I encourage you to not allow human reasoning to cloud or interfere with your faith.

Now faith is the assurance of things hoped for, the conviction of things not seen. (Hebrews11:1)

This was stated previously but is very pertinent. Never forget that faith is a cherished virtue.

By faith we understand that the words were prepared by the word of God, so what that is seen was not made of things which are visible. (Hebrews 11:3)

The above verse has words of guidance for all to follow.

My brethren, do not hold your faith in our glorious Lord Jesus Christ with an attitude of personal favoritism. (James 2:1)

Jesus shows no partiality to one with wealth or position.

For just as the body without the spirit is dead, so also faith without works is dead. (James 2:26)

Remember this and put this into practice in your life.

In this you greatly rejoice, even though for a little while, if necessary you have been distressed by various trials, that the proof of your faith, being more precious than gold which is perishable, even though tested by fire, may be found to result in praise and glory and honor at the revelation of Jesus Christ; and though you have not seen Him, you love Him, and although you do not see him now, but believe in Him, you greatly rejoice with joy inexpressible and full of glory obtaining as the outcome of your faith the salvation of your souls. (1 Peter 1:6–9)

No happiness exists that is greater than what is expressed in these words.

For whatever is born of God overcomes the world and this is the victory that has overcome the world – our faith. (1 John 5:4)

Our faith grows stronger when we trust Him in times of affliction. One who trusts in faith is one who can be trusted.

I want you to consider some thoughts from an *In Touch* booklet in regard to faith.

"The pathway of faith has a divine purpose and we are to obey the Lord no matter what. Are you journeying on the pathway of faith? Or is something holding you back from all God intended for your Life?" He never fails.

FAITHFULNESS

An element of good character shown in loyalty, trustworthiness and constancy in all that we do. Endeavor to establish this in your persona and maintain it without exception, no matter what difficulty or problem you may face.

The Rock! His work is perfect. For all His ways are just; A God of faithfulness and without injustice, righteous and upright is He. (Deuteronomy 32:4)

What a privilege is available to humankind to have a Creator like this.

God is dependable in all His words and works which are characterized in righteousness, justice and grace. His faithfulness endures forever. Keep in mind that God is far more dependable than any of your employers or your 401K. Who could possibly ask for a more trustworthy and reliable source to depend on for their security?

For the Lord is good; And His lovingkindness is everlasting and His faithfulness to all generations. (Psalms 100:5)

We are truly blessed to have our Almighty God. "Unfaltering faith will always prove the faithfulness of God." – from *Streams in the Desert*

Thy faithfulness continues throughout all generations. (Psalms 119:90)

This is reality for believers in the Lord; now, and for all time.

But the fruit of the Spirit is love, joy, peace, patience, kindness, goodness, faithfulness, gentleness, and self-control; against such things there is no law. Now those who belong to Christ Jesus have crucified the flesh with its passions and desires. If we live by the Spirit, let us also walk by the Spirit. (Galatians 5:22-25)

These verses are a genuine treasure. I encourage you to commit these to memory. I recite them every day as part of my quiet time.

FORGIVENESS

The state of being forgiven for misdeeds in word or action. If you are to have a happy and meaningful life, it is essential to be able to forgive. Keep in mind that it is extremely important to forgive promptly, for, if you do not, oftentimes anger held within will fester. When a person does not forgive another for a wrong, it is very much like developing a cancer that will not heal. If God can forgive us of our sins should we really not be able to do likewise for others? Make this an essential element in your life.

How blessed is he whose transgression is forgiven; whose sin is covered. Psalms 32:1)

Thank you, Lord. Forgiveness sparks spiritual freedom.

And Peter said to them, "Repent, and let each one of you be baptized in the name of Jesus Christ for the forgiveness of your sins; and you shall receive the gift of the Holy Spirit." (Acts 2:38)

All have this opportunity, today, just as it was in Peter's time, but only if this advice is followed.

"Therefore let it be known to you, brethren, that through Him forgiveness of sins is proclaimed to you, and through Him everyone who believes is freed from all things, from which you could not be freed through the Law of Moses..." (Acts 13:38-39)

Grace and forgiveness are unearned gifts from Jesus Christ.

Let all bitterness and wrath and anger and clamor and slander be put away from you; along with all malice. And be kind to one another tender-hearted, forgiving each other, just as God in Christ also has forgiven you. (Ephesians 4:31–32)

I encourage you to adopt this policy in order to have peace of mind.

> "People are often unreasonable, illogical and self-centered; forgive them anyway."
> –Mother Teresa in Calcutta, India

And so, as those who have been chosen of God, holy and beloved, put on a heart of compassion, kindness, humility, gentleness, and patience;

bearing with one another and forgiving each other, whoever has a complaint against anyone; just as the Lord forgave you so also should you. And beyond all these things put on love, which is the perfect bond of unity. (Colossians 3:12–14)

What a beautiful expression of love, forgiveness, and understanding. Does this have meaning for you? I sure hope so.

Consider these words from a booklet entitled *Our Daily Bread*; "Lord, I know I am not even close to being perfect and that is why I need You."

GENTLENESS

The ability to apply softness and compassion in your behavior regardless of the circumstances. This is truly one of the most important fruits of the Spirit.

A gentle answer turns away wrath, but a harsh word stirs up anger. (Proverbs 15:1)

Very true, now and forever. Utilize this virtue in your daily life.

The fruit of the spirit is love, joy, peace, patience, kindness, goodness, faithfulness, gentleness and self-control; against such things there is no law. Now those who belong to Christ Jesus have crucified the flesh with its passions and desires. If we live by Spirit, let us also walk by the Spirit. (Galatians 5:22–25)

These particularly meaningful verses will appear several more times in this book and are certainly appropriate here.

Brethren, even if a man is caught in any trespass, you who are spiritual, restore such a one in a spirit of gentleness; each one looking to yourself, lest you too be tempted. (Galatians 6:1)

This is difficult to do. Try and do it anyway.

I, therefore, the prisoner of the Lord, entreat you to walk in a manner worthy of the calling with which you have been called with all humility and gentleness, with patience, showing forbearance to one another with love, being diligent to preserve the unity of the Spirit in the bond of peace. (Ephesians 4:1–3)

What an outstanding template for a person's life.

...but sanctify Christ as Lord in your hearts, always being ready to make a defense to everyone who asks you to give an account for the hope that is in you, yet with gentleness and reverence. (1 Peter 3:15)

Show reverence to Christ, in this manner, now and at all times.

As we close this topic, I ask that you consider this suggestion from *Streams in the Desert:* "Mind the checks, when you are about to do or to say something. Pay attention to God's gentleness in His touch of caution."

I recognize that we have covered many meaningful topics that open hearts to thoughtful consideration. Before you proceed into the topic of God, take a few moments to relax and pray that the Lord will guide your thoughts as we go forward. Amen.

GOD

I am sure that many who read this book have only vague or uncertain feelings about the existence of God. Others will question the reality of God or what His purposes or actions relate to. However, I want you to understand that God is paramount. He controls everything. I ask that in reading these verses in reference to God, you keep these words in mind. There is absolutely nothing beyond Him in anything. He is the Almighty and Everlasting One in lovingkindness and is ever available to each and every one of us as we deal with the complexities of life. God has allowed each of us free will; we can either accept or reject Him, but I encourage you to choose carefully. Always take God at His Word.

Is anything too difficult for the Lord? (Genesis 18:14)

The answer to this question is a resounding, "No!"

And God said to Moses, "I AM WHO I AM; and He said, "Thus you shall say to the sons of Israel, I AM has sent me to you." (Exodus 3:14)

This verse emphasizes His dynamic self-existence.

Know therefore today, and take it in your heart, that the Lord, He is God in heaven above and on the earth below; there is no other. (Deuteronomy 4:39)

Scatter away any unbelief that you have ever felt before as He is a living God, now and forever. As you look around you, remember that all you see in earth, sky, and sea was created by God.

"You should not put the Lord your God to the test, as you tested Him at Massah…" (Deuteronomy 6:16)

Don't be foolish and undisciplined. Make every effort to obey the laws of God that have been revealed to you.

You shall follow the Lord your God and fear Him; and you shall keep His commandments, listen to His voice, serve Him, and cling to Him. (Deuteronomy 13:4)

For those who are living in sin with no regard for Him, it is a fact that they should fear the Almighty God as each is accountable in judgment. Believers should follow Him with complete trust.

The Rock! His work is perfect; For all His ways are just; A God of faithfulness and without injustice. Righteous and upright is He. (Deuteronomy 32:4)

An ideal description of our Almighty God.

...for God sees not as a man sees, for a man looks at the outward appearance, but the Lord looks at the heart. (1 Samuel 16:7)

Keep this thought embedded in your mind. Be humble.

For the Lord knows the way of the righteous, but the way of the wicked will perish. (Psalms 1:6)

The wicked are spiritually dead and already guilty before God.

O Lord, our Lord, How majestic is Thy name in all the earth. Who has displayed the splendor above the heavens? (Psalms 8:1)

Men of all eras and times should consider the wonder of what God has entrusted us with and treasure it.

I will bless the Lord who has counseled me: Indeed, my mind instructs me in the night. (Psalms 16:7)

Sleepless nights provide opportunity for instruction such as facing hard facts and difficult issues. When you are troubled, under stress, and faced with trials, pray, listen, and learn.

I have set the Lord continually before me; Because He is at my right hand, I will not be shaken. (Psalms 16:8)

Both of the apostles Peter and Paul used this verse, at one time, while making a point to others.

Lord is my rock and my fortress and my deliverer, My God, my rock in whom I take refuge; My shield and the horn of my salvation, my stronghold. (Psalms 18:2)

This is true for me and I hope it is for you as well.

God is at cross-purpose with those who art at cross-purposes with Him. (Psalms 18:26)

Simple and straight to the point.

Let the words of my mouth and the meditation of my heart be acceptable in Thy sight, O Lord my rock and my Redeemer. (Psalms 19:14)

I strongly urge you to read this verse several times and, perhaps, commit it to memory. In my opinion, this verse is exceptional and should never be forgotten.

The Lord is my light and my salvation; Whom shall I fear? The Lord is the defense of my life; Whom shall I dread? (Psalms 27:1)

No one, if you have faith.

The Lord is my strength and my shield; my heart trusts in Him and I am helped; Therefore my heart exults, and with my song I will thank Him. (Psalms 28: 7)

Don't lock your thoughts solely on the sunshine of your life, but also perceive your sorrows. Our Lord, who is always with us, never gives us more than we can comprehend or understand. Thanks be to God!

Into Thy hand I commit my spirit; Thou has ransomed me, O Lord, God of truth. (Psalms 31:5)

Committing one's life to God is the epitome of faith.

But as for me, I trust in Thee O Lord, I say "Thou art my God. My times are in Thy hand. Deliver me from the hand of my enemies, and those who persecute me." (Psalms 31:14–15)

Follow God's guiding hand only. For some, this may seem difficult to even try or get used to doing. Let me give some advice that I came across recently in a booklet called *In Touch* for those interested in becoming stronger in their spiritual life.

1) "Become less attracted to the multitude of ungodly practices of our world today; instead, strive to learn more about Jesus and how to become more like Him
2) Start replacing ungodly habits with activities that please the Lord
3) Make a concerted effort to comprehend biblical truths and begin to apply them in your life.
4) As you follow the course of action noted previously you will find it far easier to recognize unrighteous ideas and behaviors and instead place yourself in the hands of God and allow His guidance to lead your footsteps."

There are no shortcuts in following God but the reward is a full and joyful life, now and forever. Place your loyalty with Him and be ever thankful of His love for each of us.

Blessed is the nation whose God is the Lord; the people whom He has chosen for His own inheritance. (Psalms 33:12)

Any nation whose God is the Lord is truly blessed.

I sought the Lord and He answered me, and delivered me from all my fears. (Psalms 34:4)

Never be reluctant to pray to God. He always hears us. He is willing to help and minister to those who freely admit their weakness and sin and humbly ask for His forgiveness.

Why are you in despair O my soul? And why have you become disturbed within me? Hope in God for I shall yet praise Him, the help of my countenance and my God. (Psalms 42:11)

When you feel that you are at your wit's end, facing overwhelming obstacles, quietly open your heart for His help. Allow His will to be done in guiding you in overcoming your difficulty. I know this is reality from past experiences. God's caring for me puts my heart at ease.

Would not God find this out? For He knows the secrets of the heart… (Psalms 44:21)

Nothing is hidden from God. Never forget this.

"Cease striving and know that I am God. I will be exalted among the nations; I will be exalted in the earth." (Psalms 46:10)

In other words, acknowledge God's supremacy.

For such is God. Our God forever and ever; He will guide us until death. (Psalms 48:14)

May God be with us as stated here.

Create in me a clean heart O God, and renew a steadfast spirit within me. Do not cast me off from Thy presence, and do not take Thy Holy Spirit from me. Restore me to the joy of Thy salvation, and sustain me with a willing spirit. (Psalms 51:10–12)

I urge you to read and reread these meaningful, powerful verses. They truly offer comfort and peace to all of us. They are worth memorizing.

The sacrifices of God are a broken spirit; A broken and a contrite heart O God, Thou will not despise. (Psalms 51:17)

We must acknowledge our sins and express our dependence on Him.

The fool has said in his heart, there is no God. They are corrupt and have committed abominable injustice; there is no one who does good. (Psalms 53:1)

I feel pity for anyone who believes this. Their future is desolate.

As for me, I shall call upon God and the Lord will save me. (Psalms 55:16)

I know from personal experience that this is absolutely true. Earlier, I described several near-death experiences I've had. Here is one more. As I mentioned earlier, I was winding down my commitment to Air Force ROTC just prior to graduation. I was sent, along with others from college, to Big Spring, Texas for summer camp. Those of us who qualified for flight school were strongly pushed to make that commitment.

In order to encourage us, they flew a number of us to Eglin Field in Florida to witness a demonstration of the firepower of our combat planes. On the flight back to Texas, I was asked to come to the pilot's cabin. When I got there, the pilot asked me if I would like to take the stick of this Flying Boxcar. I said, "yes," but as we were approaching Barksdale AFB in Louisiana, he told me to get back behind him into a jump-seat because we "had a little trouble."

I got back and then looked out of the window and realized that the port engine on this twin-engine aircraft was on fire. We did not make a procedure turn as is typical when landing, but instead headed directly for the main runway. I can assure you, I did not have a positive feeling as I spotted five crash trucks waiting for us. I definitely called on the Lord as the pilot put landing gears down and we headed in. Fortunately, we were able to land safely. However, a week later, on a plane just like ours with ROTC cadets on board, they were not as fortunate as they crashed in Oklahoma killing all 46 on board.

"Faith in God grows significantly by overcoming impossible obstacles." This is another pearl from *Streams in the Desert.*

Cast your burden on the Lord and He will sustain you; He will never allow the righteous to be shaken. (Psalms 55:22)

Follow the Lord God on a consistent basis and you will find the path for a better life.

Keep these words of thoughtful advice from *Streams in the Desert* close to your thinking. "Never steal tomorrow out of God's hands."

Thou, even Thou art to be feared; And who may stand in His presence when once Thou art angry? (Psalms 76:7)

No one, nor anything.

My voice rises to God and I will cry aloud; My voice arises to God and He will hear me. In the day of trouble I sought the Lord. (Psalms 77:1–2)

God thinks past our words but goes instead to our hearts.

Will the Lord reject me forever? And will He never be favorable to me again? Has His loving-kindness ceased forever? Has His promise come to an end forever? Has God forgotten to be gracious? Or has He in anger withdrawn His compassion? (Psalms 77:7–9)

Sometimes when in fear or peril, we cry out to God for help. We beg for mercy yet hear nothing or feel nothing from God. Is it that we have cut ourselves off from God rather than God abandoning us? We must repent, fear (respect), and praise Him *only*.

For He is our God and we are His people of His pasture and the sheep of His hand. Today, if you hear His voice. (Psalms 95:7)

I encourage you not only to listen, but to obey His words.

Know that the Lord Himself is God. It is He, who had made us and not we ourselves. We are His people and the sheep of His pasture. (Psalms 100:3)

Never forget this reality.

He is the Lord our God; His judgments are in all the earth. (Psalms 105:7)

Be slow to judge others but quick to judge yourself as God judges all of us.

...The word of the Lord tested him. (Psalms 105:19)

We are tested in different ways. It is important to stay true to His statutes. Stay on His path and not on your own or the path of others.

Because He has inclined to hear me, therefore I shall call upon Him as long as I live. (Psalms 116:2)

Do this yourself and I am positive you will not be disappointed.

The Lord preserves the simple. I was brought low and He saved me. (Psalms 116:6)

This verse has a significant meaning to me as I was brought to my knees and definitely humbled. After flying high and being exceptionally successful, the recession of 1975-76 devastated my business and I sloughed my way through a Chapter 11 bankruptcy for seven long and exhausting years as I struggled to repay creditors.

As that period wound down, I had repaid $1,643,000 while using only very meager funds for operation. At that point, I started my life over again. When the collapse came in 1976 at 4 AM on a September morning, I poured out my heart to God and asked for forgiveness and guidance. I told Him that it was not my will to lose everything I had but if that was His will, I would accept it.

At that point, I had a most unusual feeling; it was like an enormous load was lifted from my shoulders. From that point forward, and for the next several years, I had no idea on every Monday morning how I was going to be able to pay the wages of my five loyal employees (who had stuck it out with me) on the coming Friday. However, by the grace of God, during those first two very trying years, I somehow never missed making payroll except for myself on several occasions.

There is no question in my mind I could have never accomplished this without the help, understanding, and guidance of Almighty God. I must also add that I was blessed by having a faithful and supporting wife, which was an immense help and comfort throughout this exhausting and demanding experience.

The Lord is for me, I will not fear. What can man do to me? (Psalms 118:6)

We should never forget this. For if the Lord is with you, nothing else matters.

This is the day which the Lord has made. Let us rejoice and be glad in it. (Psalms 118:24)

Show Him your appreciation each and every day.

The Lord will guard your going out and your coming in from this time forth and forever. (Psalms 121:8)

Consider the comfort this statement provides.

Unless the Lord builds the house, they labor in vain who build it; Unless the Lord guards the city, the watchman stays awake in vain. (Psalms 127:1)

It is necessary to establish a solid foundation for your life. Please do not forget to ask for His approval and guidance as you move forward to unknown surroundings and possibilities. There is no doubt in my mind that if you follow this course your future will be bright.

Out of the depths I have cried to Thee, O Lord, Lord hear my voice... (Psalms 130:1–2)

Do not permit hardship to dampen or halt your resolve. Hardship met firmly in faith in our Lord builds character. The more difficult the trial that is overcome, the more character is developed. When you face temptation, double down in your strength with the Lord.

O Lord Thou has searched me and known me. Thou dost when I sit down and when I rise up; Thou dost understand my thoughts from afar; Thou dost scrutinize my path and my lying down, and art intimately acquainted with all my thoughts. (Psalms 139:1–3)

There is absolutely nothing hidden from God.

Set a guard over my mouth, keep watch over the door of my lips. Do not incline my heart to any evil thing. To practice deeds of wickedness with men who do iniquity and do not let me eat of their delicacies. (Psalms 141:3-4)

I read this passage for guidance on a daily basis. Why not give it a try?

The fear of the Lord is the beginning of knowledge. Fools despise wisdom and instruction. (Proverbs 1:7)

There are six things that the Lord hates: yes, seven are an abomination to Him; Haughty eyes, a lying tongue, and hands that shed innocent blood, a heart that devise wicked plans, feet that run rapidly to evil, a false witness who utters lies, and one who spreads strife among brothers. (Proverbs 6:16-19)

Test yourself regarding your spiritual growth and determine how well you measure up in regard to these verses. If you fall short, work diligently to make the needed changes to get back on the right path.

The reward of humility and the fear of the Lord are riches, honor and life. (Proverbs 22:4)

Sounds like a jackpot winner to me.

I know everything God does will remain forever; there is nothing to add to it and there is nothing to take from it, for God has so worked, that man should fear Him. (Ecclesiastes 3:14)

Enjoy the gifts of God but also recognize His presence with reverence.

I said to myself, "God will judge, both the righteous man and the wicked man" for a time for every matter and for every deed is there. (Ecclesiastes 3:17)

Though both man and beast face a common fate and return to dust, only man will face God in judgment. Therefore, we should serve God faithfully in this life.

I encourage you to give particular attention to these words of wisdom that are expressed in such a vivid and meaningful way.

Do not be hasty in word or impulsive in thought to bring up a matter in the presence of God. For God is in heaven and you are on the earth, therefore, let your words be few. (Ecclesiastes 5:2)

Do not be careless in your discussion of Him or with Him.

When you make a vow to God, do not be late in paying it, for He takes no delight in fools. Pay what you owe! (Ecclesiastes 5:4)

Be diligent when you respond to our Lord, especially when you have made a commitment to Him.

For in many dreams and in many words there is emptiness. Rather fear God. (Ecclesiastes 5:7)

There is vanity in preoccupation in one's work and also in careless worship.

In the days of prosperity be happy, but in the days of adversity consider -- God has made the one as well as the other. So that man may not discover anything that will be after him. (Ecclesiastes 7:14)

Utilize adversity to your advantage. Learn from it and grow.

...I, the Lord, am the first, and the last. I am He. (Isaiah 41:4)

Take a moment to comprehend the significance of these words.

"For My thoughts are not your thoughts. Neither are My ways your ways," declares the Lord. "For as the heavens are higher than the earth, so are My ways higher than your ways and My thoughts than your thoughts." (Isaiah 55:8–9)

God's ways are always best.

But now, O Lord, Thou art our Father, we are the clay, and Thou our potter; And all of us are the work of Thy hand. (Isaiah 64:8)

Please mold us and guide our footsteps.

Can man make gods for himself? Yet they are not gods! (Jeremiah 16:20)

He may try with money, possessions, prestige, and imagined power; however, he will always fail. There is only one Almighty God, now and forever.

God will decide about man and not man decide about God. Without God as your compass, you are very likely on a troubled course.

In the beginning was the Word, and the Word was with God and Word was God. (John 1:1)

A definitive statement of the divinity of Jesus Christ, our Lord and Savior.

"For God so loved the world, that He gave His only begotten Son, that whoever believes in Him should not perish, but have eternal life…" (John 3:16)

Please consider this powerful commitment and the everlasting purpose of it. There will never be anything as meaningful as this. Please take a moment and try and memorize this verse.

"For He whom God has sent speaks the words of God, for He gives the Spirit without measure. The Father loves the Son, and has given all things into His hand. He who believes in the Son has eternal life, but he who does not obey the Son shall not see life, but the wrath of God abides on him." (John 3:34–36)

A passage that all need to understand without doubt or question.

Jesus said to them, "If God were your Father, you would love Me, for I proceeded forth and have come from God, for I have not even come on my own initiative, but He sent Me." (John 8:42)

Jesus acknowledges that He was sent on a mission by God and that only through His sacrifice may mankind have forgiveness for the sins of the world.

We know that God does not hear sinners; but if anyone is God-fearing, and does His will, He hears him. (John 9:31)

Never forget this and do not overlook the opportunity afforded to you. Think on this for a moment – life without God is like an unsharpened pencil – there is no point to it.

"For this reason the Father loves Me, because I lay down My life that I may take it up again. No one has taken it away from Me, but I lay it down on My own initiative, I have the authority to lay it down, and I have the authority to take it up again. This commandment I received from My Father." (John 10:17–18)

Thoughtfully consider the power of this verse.

"If I do not do the works of My Father, do not believe Me; but if I do them, though you do not believe Me, believe the works, that you may know and understand that the Father is in Me, and I am in the Father." (John 10:37–38)

Here, Jesus addresses the leaders who have witnessed the miracles He has performed yet do not believe that He is the Son of God.

"The God who made the world and all things in it, since He is Lord of heaven and earth, does not dwell in temples made with hands; neither is He served by man hands, as though He needed anything, since He Himself gives to all life and breath and all things; and He made from one every nation of mankind to live on the face of the earth, having determined their appointed times, and the boundaries of their habitation; that they should seek God, if perhaps they might grope for Him and find Him, though He is not far from each of us; for in Him we live and move and exist as even some of your own poets have said, "For we are His own offspring." (Acts 17:24–28)

The apostle Paul said this while speaking in the Areopagus in Athens in his attempt to explain to the Epicureans and Stoics the meaning of belief in God. Some years ago, on a visit to Greece, my wife and I had the privilege of standing in this very place. It was an inspiring experience.

...for all have sinned and fall short of the glory of God, being justified as a gift by His grace through the redemption which is in Christ Jesus. (Romans 3:23–24)

Are you willing to accept His gift of grace?

But God demonstrates His own love toward us, in that while we were yet sinners, Christ died for us. (Romans 5:8)

What a blessing for all those who believe.

But now having been freed from sin and enslaved to God, you derive your benefit resulting in sanctification and the outcome, eternal life. For the wages of sin is death and the free gift of God is eternal life in Jesus Christ our Lord. (Romans 6:22–23)

I urge you to consider these words and carefully weigh the benefits of embracing this passage against the consequences of ignoring it.

And we know that God causes all things to work together for good to those who love God, to those who are called according to His purpose. (Romans 8:28)

Do not ever forget the content of this verse. Comfort lies within.

What shall we say to these things? If God is for us, who is against us? He who did not spare His own Son, but delivered Him up for us all, how will He not also with Him freely give us all things? (Romans 8:31–32)

Never fear, always trust God.

Never take your own revenge, beloved, but leave room for the wrath of God, for it is written "Vengeance is Mine, I will repay" says the Lord. (Romans 12:19)

Although this action may be contrary to most opinion, remember that this is the Word of God. Never forget His advice.

…that no man should boast before God.…that just as it is written, "Let him who boasts, boast in the Lord." …that your faith should not rest on the wisdom of men, but on the power of God. (1 Corinthians 1:29, 31 and 2:5)

The apostle Paul did not want faith to be based on clever arguments or discussions, but on God's power.

Or do you not know that your body is a temple of the Holy Spirit who is in you, whom you have from God, and that you are not your own? (1 Corinthians 6:19)

Do not defile your body in any unworthy or evil manner.

Let each one do as he has purposed in his heart; not grudgingly or under compulsion for God loves a cheerful giver, and God is able to make all grace abound to you, that always having all sufficiency in everything, you may have an abundance for every good deed;... (2 Corinthians 9:7–8)

God will supply the generous giver with not only enough to meet his own needs but enough to give.

For am I now seeking the favor of men, or of God? Or am I striving to please men? If I were still trying to please men, I would not be a bond-servant of Christ. (Galatians 1:10)

Paul gives us a choice; to please either those around us ...or God. Choose with care as the wrong choice here has serious consequences.

But when the fullness of time came, God sent forth His Son, born of a woman, born under the Law, in order that He might redeem those who were under the Law, that we might receive adoption as sons. And because you are sons, God has sent forth the spirit of His Son into our hearts crying "Abba Father." Therefore you are no longer a slave, but a son, and if a son, then an heir through God. (Galatians 4:4–7)

Think in gratitude of the grace of God offered to us here.

Do not be deceived, God is not mocked; for whatever a man sows, this he shall also reap. (Galatians 6:7)

I recommend that you always keep this in mind. If you don't, prepare to reap the consequences.

But God being rich in mercy, because of His great love with which He loved us, even when we were dead in our transgressions, made us alive together with Christ (by grace you have been saved), and raised us up with Him and seated us with Him in the heavenly places, in Christ Jesus, in order that in the ages to come He might show the surpassing riches of His grace in kindness toward us in Christ Jesus. (Ephesians 2:4–7)

Through the grace of God, and our commitment to Jesus Christ, we have the opportunity of eternal life.

...that at the name of Jesus every knee should bow, of those who are in heaven and on earth and under the earth, and that every tongue should confess that Jesus Christ is Lord to the glory of God the Father. (Philippians 2:10–11)

Please keep this in mind always, now, and forever.

Be anxious for nothing, but in everything by prayer and supplication with thanksgiving let your requests be made known to God. And the peace of God, which surpasses all comprehension, shall guard your hearts and your minds in Christ Jesus. (Philippians 4:6–7)

Seek this peace with all your heart and all your strength as it is priceless.

And whatever you do in word or deed, do all in the name of the Lord Jesus giving thanks through Him to God the Father. (Colossians 3:17)

The apostle Paul encourages the Colossians to be thankful to Jesus Christ for all things achieved by either word or action.

For there is one God, and one mediator also between God and men, the man Christ Jesus, who gave Himself as a ransom for all, the testimony borne at the proper time. (1 Timothy 2:5–6)

Jesus mediates for mankind through His death on the cross.

For everything created by God is good and nothing is to be rejected, if it is received with gratitude; for it is sanctified by means of the word of God and prayer. (1 Timothy 4:4–5)

Never fail to open your heart and soul in gratitude for the blessings that you receive.

All Scripture is inspired by God and profitable for teaching, for reproof, for correction, for training in righteousness. (2 Timothy 3:16)

The Bible came about through men that God had superintended and directed.

But if any of you lacks wisdom let him ask of God, who gives to all men generously and without reproach, and it will be given to him. (James 1:5)

Do not be shy. Ask Him and believe.

Let no one say when he is tempted, I am being tempted by God; for God cannot be tempted by evil, and He Himself does not tempt anyone. (James 1:13)

When someone experiences temptation it is always from the evil one, the devil. Pray to God for strength and direction to turn away from whatever temptation you face. Any attempt to excuse yourself is based on ignorance of both God and of the nature of temptation. Place your loyalty to God above all personal welfare.

God tests our lives to make us stronger and not to break us.

Submit therefore to God. Resist the devil and he will flee from you. Draw near to God and He will draw near to you. Cleanse your hands, you sinners, and purify your hearts, you double minded. Humble yourselves in the presence of the Lord, and He will exalt you. (James 4:7, 8 &10)

You can never be only partially, or half-way, committed to God. It is all or nothing.

Blessed be the God and Father of our Lord Jesus Christ, who according to His great mercy has caused us to be born again to a living hope through the resurrection of Jesus Christ from the dead. (1 Peter 1:3)

What a blessing that has been provided for us by our loving God.

But know first of all that no prophecy of Scripture is a matter of one's own interpretation, for no prophecy was ever made by an act of human will, but men moved by the Holy Spirit spoke from God. (2 Peter 1:20–21)

Make no mistake, *all* Scripture is from God and not from man.

Beloved, let us love one another, for love is from God; and every one who loves is born of God and knows God. The one, who does not love, does not know God, for God is love. By this the love of God was manifested in us, that God has sent His only begotten Son into the world so that we might live through Him. In this is love, not that we loved God, but that He loved us and sent His Son to be the propitiation for our sins. (1 John 4:7–10)

Consider how strongly God expresses His love for us in this passage.

No one has beheld God at any time; if we love one another God abides in us, and His love is perfected in us. (1 John 4:12)

Be ever thankful that God loves each of us unconditionally.

For this is the love of God, that we keep His commandments, and His commandments are not burdensome. (1 John 5:3)

Let the love of God guide you in your life and your footsteps will be sure. And never parse the Word of God.

Grace, mercy and peace will be with us, from God the Father and from Jesus Christ, the Son of the Father, in truth and love. (2 John 1:3)

Embrace all the elements expressed here and hold them close to you.

Beloved, do not imitate what is evil, but what is good. The one who does good is of God; the one who does evil has not seen God. (3 John 1:11)

Pay attention to this principle; it is penetrating.

Keep yourselves in the love of God, waiting anxiously for the mercy of Lord Jesus Christ to eternal life. (Jude 1:21)

Never allow anything to draw you away from the love of God and never ever be too busy for God.

Now to Him who is able to keep you from stumbling, and to make you stand in the presence of His glory blameless with great joy, to the only God our Savior, through Jesus Christ our Lord, be glory, majesty, dominion, and authority, before all time and now and forever. Amen. (Jude 1:24–25)

One of the greatest benedictions of the New Testament.

I feel certain that many of the people who have taken the time to read this book have been searching for true peace of mind. No matter what worldly possessions you may accumulate, there is nothing that suffices until you make the decision to confess your sins to Jesus Christ, ask for forgiveness, and commit your life and soul to Him. When this is done, it is a certainty you will truly find the peace of mind that only He can extend. It is my prayer that those who have taken seriously the words and meanings of these verses, and studied the explanations of them, will fully understand the unconditional love that God has for each of us.

Make your commitment to the Lord Jesus so that the sins you have committed will be forgiven. No one else has this power that He, our Almighty and Merciful God, has and His kingdom is alive and active in all generations and in all parts of the world. Remember happiness and peace are doing things God's way.

I want to close this topic with a quotation from the booklet *Our Daily Bread*: "Do what you can with what you have and leave the results to God."

GOODNESS

A virtue of gentleness and faithfulness that is exhibited by reaching out to others in a helpful and caring manner. When the cause that you are putting forward is good – keep calm – do not fret and worry, just ask God for His help and let Him guide you in your efforts. This is a trait I hope you wish to have and to follow.

Surely goodness and loving-kindness will follow me all the days of my life, and I will dwell in the house of the Lord forever. (Psalms 23:6)

David sees himself as a recipient of God's covenant.

How great is Thy goodness; Which Thou has stored up for those who fear Thee; Which Thou has wrought for those who take refuge in Thee, before the sons of men! (Psalms 31:19)

Be thankful for God's extension of goodness to us.

But the fruit of the Spirit is love, joy, peace, patience, kindness, goodness, faithfulness, gentleness, and self control; against such things there is no law. Now those who belong to Christ Jesus have crucified the flesh with its passion and desires. If we live by the Spirit, let us also walk by the Spirit. (Galatians 5:22–25)

Once again, this passage appears for us to understand, appreciate, and be ever thankful for.

Beloved, do not imitate what is evil, but what is good. The one who does good is of God; the one who does evil has not seen God. (3 John 1:11)

Make this a rule to follow at all times.

I would like you to consider the fact that whoever we are, whatever our background, and whatever our failings (and we all have them) if we would but reach our hand to God, He will take it, will walk beside us, and will never let us go.

GRACE

This is God's unmerited favor. It is never achieved by an individual doing good works for others. It is God's kindness and His mercy for us. Grace can never be earned in any way; it is a gift from God.

I want to offer several thoughts in regard to grace for you from the book, *Streams in the Desert:*

- "Real growth in grace is the result of sanctified trials.
- Extraordinary afflictions are not always the punishment of extraordinary sins, but sometimes the trial of extraordinary grace.
- Never turn God's facts into hopes or prayers but turn them into realities. 'My grace is sufficient unto thee.'
- Grace is an unearned gift from God.
- God's love energizes us in service and to obey His holy word which, in turn, maximizes His grace."

And the Word became flesh, and dwelt among us, and we beheld His glory, glory as of the only begotten from the Father, full of grace and truth. (John 1:14)

He will exist forever as the God-man in His resurrection body.

For the Law was given through Moses; grace and truth were realized through Jesus Christ. (John 1:17)

Although grace was manifested in the Old Testament, it was dim when compared with the brightness that appeared in the incarnation.

for all have sinned and fall short of the glory of God, being justified as a gift by His grace through the redemption which is in Jesus Christ. (Romans 3:23–24)

The sinner who believes in Christ Jesus receives God's gift of salvation through grace.

I want to offer some words regarding grace from the booklet *Day by Day:* "Grace is as broad and open as the sky and as deep and beautiful as the ocean. If I have and give grace, the loving gift of the Father and Lord Jesus, I have and give peace. Grace and peace encourage me to follow Jesus come what may."

For sin shall no longer be a master over you, for you are not under the law, but under grace. (Romans 6:14)

By the grace of God and belief in Jesus Christ salvation is ours.

For through the grace given to me I say to every man among you not to think more highly of himself than he ought to think; but to think so as to have sound judgment, as God has allotted to each a measure of faith. (Romans 12:3)

Keep vanity far from you at all times.

For by grace you have been saved through faith, and that not of yourselves, it is the gift of God; not as a result of works that no one should boast. (Ephesians 2:8-9)

Rejoice in faith when you are receiving God's grace. Be humble and reach out to others in your faith and share your blessings.

Grace does something quite remarkable as it frees us from guilt. Furthermore, it should encourage us to serve the Lord and also to obey Him. Never forget all that He has done for each of us in so many and various ways and be thankful.

Let us therefore draw near with confidence to the throne of grace, that we may receive mercy and may find grace to help in time of need. (Hebrews 4:16)

Our Lord God knows all we go through and He can provide mercy and grace for those in need.

Grace, mercy and peace will be with us, from God the Father and from Jesus Christ, the Son of the Father, in truth and love. (2 John 1:3)

Embrace all the elements referred to here and hold them close to you.

These words from *Our Daily Bread* are a meaningful way to close this topic: "God's Grace is immeasurable, His mercy is inexhaustible, and His peace is inexpressible. We are indeed fortunate to have such a caring and loving Heavenly Father and Son, our Lord and Savior, Jesus Christ. Amen."

"Grace provides us with everything we need to live in perfect freedom, pardon for sins, healing for our heart and companionship with God." Words of wisdom from the booklet *In Touch*.

GUIDANCE

Do you ever feel the need for guidance as you struggle with decisions that seem overwhelming? Remember, guidance is really advice for dealing with problems. Free as we are and would wish to be, we cannot sustain ourselves without the guiding hand of God. Regardless of the obstacle or difficulty, never hesitate to place them in the hands of our Almighty God. No man lives by himself. As we live our lives, there are many days we struggle with difficulties. Use the hardships you encounter to strengthen you. Never lose sight of the light of our everlasting God. Do not be misled by others but maintain your faith and trust in God always. Remember He does not make mistakes and His love for you is infinite. Keep this in mind as you proceed through this section as I'm sure this will be helpful to you as you proceed through life. I know this approach has been beneficial in my life. I only ask, if you truly intend to be guided by God, that you consider three very important things. The thoughts listed below are from one of Dr. Charles Stanley's sermons. You must listen to God to hear Him. To do this, you must take the time to open your heart and your mind. Be still, and know that you need to listen to:

- What He says
- How to do what He says
- When to do what He says.

Remember, God does not function on the timetable of instant gratification. After this first step is taken, you then need to trust and, again, I reiterate:

- Trust in what He says
- Embed your trust in how He says to do it
- And trust when He says to do it.

He says, "go forward without fail" even if you do not feel that secure in doing it. Remember, God does not make mistakes. I truly believe if you will establish these principles in your life you will find success. Perhaps not at the speed you desire, but it will come.

Teach me Thy way O Lord, and lead me in a level path, because of my foes. (Psalms 27:11)

I encourage you to make this verse a part of your life.

It was good for me, that I was afflicted. That I may learn Thy statutes. (Psalms 119:71)

There is no question in my mind that the Lord sometimes brings afflictions or problems on those He loves. He does this for a reason. It may seem difficult to accept being thankful that He does this. I assure you that thought was not on my mind when I got up early one morning in January 1976.

JOHN H. (JAN) DOLCATER, JR.

I had an appointment with a new, important customer in Ft. Lauderdale. In order to be punctual, I was on my way from Tampa at 5 a.m. In spite of the early getaway, I had a serious problem; very heavy, dense fog. After making the first leg of the trip without incident, I had the misfortune of getting stuck behind an old pickup truck going just 15 miles an hour. After putting up with that for ten or twelve miles, I reached a long straightaway that I was familiar with. So, I decided to pass him. My thought as I began to pass was that if I spotted something coming ahead in the passing lane, I would go for the shoulder to avoid a collision. As I began to pass the pickup truck, I could see the outline of a tractor-trailer ahead. Apparently, he had seen me before I had seen him and had already applied his brakes but by doing so his trailer jackknifed across onto the shoulder.

Moments later, I took him head on. Fortunately for me, I was driving an Olds 98. On impact the engine was in the passenger side of the front seat. I had a firm grip on the steering wheel, but it had broken off in my hands. If I had not had my seatbelt on, I would have been impaled on the steering column. It was a terrible impact, and I suffered severe pain in my abdomen. Someone stopped and helped me across the highway to a pickup truck where I could lay down until an ambulance arrived to take me to the local small-town hospital.

It was determined that I was bleeding internally at a dangerously serious rate. My blood pressure was so low that I had to have an incision in my abdomen (done without anesthesia) to get the blood out. During surgery, two quarts of blood and my spleen were removed. They stitched up my intestines as well as other areas and I then spent the next two weeks fighting for my life in intensive care.

Finally, I rallied and began to recover. (I'll explain more about this unforgettable experience later on.) It finally dawned on me that God was trying to get my attention. You see, prior to that time I was doing things my way and not God's way.

After arriving home to recuperate, I began daily Bible readings from the booklet *Day by Day* and also in a book called *Streams in the Desert*. This has been a daily habit for me for the past forty years. Without a doubt, this was a genuine turnaround point for me. I am not suggesting that you need to experience a wake-up call like mine, but ask yourself honestly, do you really need to make a change in your lifestyle and begin a genuine spiritual journey? Please give this prayerful consideration.

Behold, as the eyes of servants look to the hand of their master, as eyes of the maid looks to the hand of her mistress; So our eyes look to the Lord our God until He shall be gracious to us. (Psalms 123:2)

It is important to receive guidance and comfort with thanksgiving and respect and to do as this verse plainly states.

And this is the confidence which we have before Him, that if we ask anything according to His will, He hears us. And if we know that He hears us in whatever we ask, we know that we have the requests we have asked from Him. (1 John 5:14 –15)

I encourage you to make it a habit to ask God in your prayers for guidance in your life. Do this not only at the beginning of each day but all throughout the day as well.

I offer a prayer for your consideration when you feel the need for dependable guidance. This prayer is from the booklet *Our Daily Bread*.

"Dear God, I thank you that I can always turn to You when I am faced with the difficulties of life. I can put my trust in You. Thank You that You are my 'refuge and strength, a very present help in trouble'..." (Psalms 46:1)

HOLY

Be morally and spiritually clean in all ways. Make every effort to be as blameless as possible and to set yourself apart for our maker, Almighty God. By following this course, you will be holy for Him.

Who may ascend into the hill of the Lord? And may stand in His holy place? He who has clean hands and a pure heart. Who has not lifted up his soul to falsehood, and has not sworn deceitfully. (Psalms 24:3–4)

This effort should be extended to all that you think and do.

There is no one holy like the Lord. Indeed, there is no one besides Thee, nor is there any rock like our God. (1 Samuel 2:2)

Very true. He who has not lifted up his soul to falsehood.

Where do you stand in regard to this passage? If you have not followed God's will, what do you plan to do about it? Decide to place yourself in His hands and not just your own.

Thy way, O God is holy; What god is great like our God? (Psalms 77:13)

There is nothing to compare our God to, nor will there ever be.

"But it will come about, if you listen attentively to Me," declares the Lord, "to bring no load through the gate of this city on the sabbath day, but to keep the sabbath day holy by doing no work on it." (Jeremiah 17:24)

Please pay heed to this.

And so, as those who have been chosen of God, holy and beloved, put on a heart of compassion, kindness, humility, gentleness and patience. (Colossians 3:12)

Pertinent advice to follow.

As obedient children, do not be conformed to the former lusts which were yours in ignorance, but like the Holy One who called you, be holy yourselves also in your behavior; because it is written "You shall be holy for I am holy." (1 Peter 1:14–16)

Follow God's will and authority if you are to live a holy life.

HOLY SPIRIT

The third person of the Trinity of God. This spirit of God is our Helper in time of need as we proceed on our spiritual journey. Never be shy. Open your heart and ask the Holy Spirit to guide you each and every day. The Holy Spirit is a gift to all who believe and not a reward for some. Please do not forget to ask.

Here are some thoughts on the various aspects of the works of the Holy Spirit as explained from a booklet called *In Touch*.

1. The Spirit illumines the mind, enabling believers to understand the things of God.

2. The Spirit energizes the physical body to serve the Lord.
3. The Spirit enables the will to follow through on doing what is right.
4. The Spirit quickens emotions to feel and express the fruit of the Spirit. (Galatians 5:22–25)

Only the Holy Spirit living inside us has the strength and wisdom to live out the Christian life victoriously.

And the earth was formless and void and darkness was over the surface of the deep, and the Spirit of God was moving over the surface of the waters. (Genesis 1:2)

The Spirit of God has been present since the beginning of time.

Create in me a clean heart O God, and renew a steadfast spirit within me. Do not cast me away from Thy presence, and do not take Thy Holy Spirit from me. Restore me to the joy of Thy salvation, and sustain me with a willing spirit. (Psalms 51:10–12)

When you feel in need, take the time to refresh yourself with this passage.

Where can I go from Thy Spirit? Or where can I flee from Thy presence? (Psalms 139:7)

Nowhere, if man has conscience.

And after being baptized Jesus went up immediately from the water; and behold, the heavens were opened, and he saw the Spirit of God descending as a dove, and coming upon Him, and behold a voice out of heaven saying, "This is My beloved Son, in whom I am well pleased." (Matthew 3:16–17)

This is the very first clear expression of the Trinity; God, Jesus and the Holy Spirit.

And Jesus, full of the Holy Spirit, returned from the Jordan and was led about by the Spirit in the wilderness. (Luke 4:1)

Jesus was led into the traditional site of temptation.

"It is the Spirit who gives life; the flesh profits nothing, the words that I have spoken to you are spirit and are life." (John 6:63)

Jesus explains that the Holy Spirit provides influence and guidance and the flesh is of little account.

Have you ever experienced being truly touched by the Holy Spirit? I have, and I want to explain. This happened to me in Tampa many years ago during a healing service.

I and several others were kneeling at the altar in the chapel and Father Francis McNutt was saying prayers and laying hands on each of us as he came to us in turn. I was slain in the spirit as were several others. This is best described as the power of the Holy Spirit so filling a person through the laying on of hands that a heightened inner awareness takes away the body's energy and the person collapses on the floor. You are completely relaxed, and will come to shortly, but you are also keenly aware of what is happening.

I assure you it is a meaningful event and is very special. This is something no one plans or prepares for, as it is simply an act of the hand of God. I hope that one day you may also have this experience in your life.

Every day strive to receive the renewing of the Holy Spirit in your life. This is excellent advice from the book, *Streams in the Desert*.

But the Helper, the Holy Spirit, whom the Father will send in My name, He will teach you all things, and will bring to your remembrance all I have said to you. (John 14:26)

The Holy Spirit will come to those who believe in the Father and the Son.

"I have many more things to say to you, but you cannot bear them now. But when, He, the Spirit of truth comes, He will guide you into all the truth for He will not speak on His own initiative, but whatever He hears, He will speak and He will disclose to you what is to come." (John 16:12–13)

He seals us with Christ.

And Peter said to them, "Repent, and let each of you be baptized in the name of Jesus Christ for the forgiveness of your sins; and you shall receive the gift of the Holy Spirit." (Acts 2:38)

If you are troubled or frustrated, open your heart to Jesus and allow the Holy Spirit to guide and comfort you. Do not allow adversity to tempt you to ignore the guidance of the Holy Spirit. Do not pass up this opportunity. Please don't miss it.

Advice from *Our Daily Bread* should be considered here: "Yielding to the Holy Spirit leads to right living."

And when they had prayed, the place where they had gathered together was shaken, and they were all filled with the Holy Spirit, and began to speak the word of God with boldness. (Acts 4:31)

Just imagine the experience and feelings of the disciples.

For the mind set on the flesh is death, but the mind set on the Spirit is life and peace. (Romans 8:6)

All of us have our minds set on various things. I only ask where and on what is your mind set on? *Uh, oh. Straighten up.*

However, you are not in the flesh but in the Spirit, if indeed the Spirit of God dwells in you. But if anyone does not have the Spirit of Christ, he does not belong to Him. (Romans 8:9)

Never overlook this fact.

But, if the Spirit of Him who raised Jesus from the dead dwells in you, He who raised Christ Jesus from the dead will also give life to your mortal bodies through His Spirit who indwells you. (Romans 8:11)

Never resist the indwelling of the Holy Spirit in your being.

For all who are being led by the Spirit of God, these are the sons of God. (Romans 8:14)

Those committed to God are now the sons of God.

Or do you not know that your body is a temple of the Holy Spirit who is in you, whom you have from God, and that you are not your own. (1 Corinthians 6:19)

Watch over the manner in which you maintain your body so that it is free from evil.

But the fruit of the Spirit is love, joy, peace, patience, kindness, goodness, faithfulness, gentleness, and self control; against such things there is no law. Now those who belong to Christ Jesus have crucified the flesh with its passions and desires. If we live by the Spirit, let us also walk by the Spirit. (Galatians 5:22–25)

Here is this passage again. When we keep our mind on God, His Spirit keeps our mind in peace.

For one who sows to his own flesh, shall from the flesh reap corruption, but the one who sows to the Spirit shall from the Spirit reap eternal life. (Galatians 6:8)

Allow the Spirit of God, and not the world, to shape your mind.

"Seek your stimulus not through the body but through the Spirit." This sound advice is from the book, *Streams in the Desert*. Check it out.

And do not grieve the Holy Spirit of God, by whom you were sealed for the day of redemption. (Ephesians 4:30)

It is very important for all of us to remember this.

And do not get drunk with wine, for that is dissipation, but be filled with the Holy Spirit. (Ephesians 5:18)

Bear in mind that when one is filled with the Holy Spirit this is not a half-full situation. You are truly filled.

But the Spirit explicitly says that in later times some will fall away from the faith, paying attention to deceitful spirits and doctrines of demons. (1 Timothy 4:1)

I wonder if we are in the later times now as there are many strange and unusual philosophies discussed in the world today.

He saved us not on the basis of deeds, which we have done in righteousness, but according to His mercy, by the washing of regeneration and renewing by the Holy Spirit. (Titus 3:5)

Personal good deeds are not the means of salvation.

As we move forward, please keep in mind this quotation from *Our Daily Bread*: "The Christian's heart is the Holy Spirit's home."

HONOR

This represents respect, love and understanding of all that is honest and dependable in us. May this always be important to each of us as we go through life. Think on this: God promises to provide everything we need if we will honor Him with our lives.

Honor the Lord from your wealth, and from the first of all your produce. (Proverbs 3:9)

Remember that all the benefits you receive are allowed by Almighty God.

The wise will inherit honor but fools display dishonor. (Proverbs 3:35)

While the wise inherit honor, fools promote the shame that is consistent with their character.

Keeping away from strife is an honor for a man, but any fool will quarrel. (Proverbs 20:3)

Make every effort to avoid quarrelsome individuals.

The reward of humility and the fear of the Lord are riches, honor and life. (Proverbs 22:4)

Please implant this thought into your mind.

Be devoted to one another in brotherly love; give preference to one another in honor not lagging behind in diligence, fervent is spirit, serving the Lord. (Romans 12:10–12)

Make every effort to maintain a good attitude. A bad attitude is like a flat tire as you are stuck and cannot go anywhere.

In this you greatly rejoice, even now for a little while, if necessary, you have been distressed by various trials, that the proof of your faith, being more precious than gold which is perishable, even though tested by fire, may be found to result in praise and glory and honor at the revelation of Jesus Christ; and though you have not seen Him, you love Him, and do not see Him now, but believe in Him you greatly rejoice with joy inexpressible and full of glory obtaining as the outcome of your faith the salvation of your souls. (1 Peter 1:6-9)

O faith, blessed faith! Caring for others honors Jesus' love for us.

HUMILITY

Try not to take yourself too seriously. Respect the feelings of others and treat them as you wish to be treated. And, by all means, exercise sound judgment in all matters. Humility is the path of promotion in the kingdom of God and it is the strength of character God wants to see in us. Make effort to establish this as a cornerstone of your life as you proceed down the pathway of commitment to God.

Boast no more so very proudly. Do not let arrogance come out of your mouth; For the Lord is a God of knowledge. (1 Samuel 2:3)

Although this was spoken over 2000 years ago, it is 100% relevant today and will be so well into the future.

The wicked strut about on every side. When vileness is exalted among the sons of men. (Psalms 12:8)

A display of arrogance rather than humility.

He leads the humble in justice, and He teaches the humble His way. (Psalms 25:9)

When we ask God for His help it should be done in a humble manner.

Blessed be the man, whom Thou dost chasten, O Lord, and dost teach out of Thy law; That Thou mayest grant him relief from the days of adversity, until a pit is dug for the wicked. (Psalms 94:12–13)

Problems are not all bad. They may lead us to concentrate on real values. It is really up to us to lay our troubles before the Lord and let Him guide us. I say this as I have experienced this myself.

I shall always remember a night when I was not able to sleep, but instead tossed and turned; my pajamas soaking wet with sweat. My business was falling apart, my fifty-plus employees were depending on me and I feared the perils that my family faced.

At about four in the morning, I collapsed into my Lazy-Boy chair. After another half-hour of despair, I humbly prayed to God that if I lost everything, I would follow His guidance and be committed to Him as long as I lived. Shortly after that, I suddenly felt as if a very heavy burden was lifted off my shoulders.

Although the next seven years of working through a Chapter 11 bankruptcy were exceptionally difficult, I never doubted that God would guide me through this nightmare. He was always with me regardless of the multitude of obstacles I faced. Allow your self-will to be crushed as mine was and permit this experience of mine to be a spiritual lesson of humility for you.

Whoever secretly slanders his neighbor, him I will destroy; No one who has a haughty look and an arrogant heart will I endure. (Psalms 101:5)

Put any form of vanity and lack of humility far away from you. It is poison.

The Lord preserves the simple; I was brought low and He saved me. (Psalms 116:6)

This was certainly true for me from 1976 through 1983 as I battled my way through my Chapter 11 bankruptcy and repaid $1,643,000 with a very limited amount of working capital. I am confident that if I had not had God's guidance and help, I could have never accomplished this.

Pride goes before destruction and a haughty spirit before stumbling. (Proverbs 16:18)

Pride precedes a fall with certainty. It is only a matter of time when the fall occurs.

The reward of humility and the fear of the Lord are riches, honor and life. (Proverbs 22:4)

The Lord God provides many things for those who exercise humility.

Do not boast about tomorrow, for you do not know what a day may bring forth. Let another praise you and not your own mouth. A stranger, and not your own lips. (Proverbs 27:1–2)

Make every effort to be humble at all times, particularly when you achieve some measure of success and others extend their praise based on your accomplishments. Yours truly was, unfortunately, too caught up in my own success and the recognition of my accomplishments and became very self-absorbed. As a result, I paid a very high price in financial loss. The consequences of not being responsible and not placing myself humbly in the hands of God for direction was a hard fact to face, but I am a better man for the experience. Please learn from the errors of my ways.

The crucible is for silver and the furnace is for gold, and a man is tested by the praise accorded him. (Proverbs 27:21)

Handle favorable recognition with humility.

A man's pride will bring him low, but a humble spirit will obtain honor. (Proverbs 29:23)

Avoid being full of yourself and of the things that you have achieved.

Do nothing from selfishness or empty conceit, but with humility of mind let each of you regard one another as more important than himself; do not merely look out only for your own personal interests, but also for the interests of others. (Philippians 2:3–4)

This is the attitude that Christ wants each of us to have.

Have this attitude in yourselves which was also in Christ Jesus, who, although He existed in the form of God, did not regard equality with God a thing to be grasped, but emptied Himself, taking the form of a bond-servant, and being made in the likeness of men. And being found in appearance as a man, He humbled Himself by becoming obedient to the point of death, even death on a cross. (Philippians 2: 5–8)

There is no greater love or humility expressed for mankind than His decision to take onto Himself the sins of the world.

This you know, my beloved brethren. But let everyone be quick to hear, slow to speak, and slow to anger; ...Therefore putting aside all filthiness and all that remains of wickedness, in humility receive the word implanted, which is able to save your souls. But prove yourselves doers of the word, and not merely hearers who delude themselves. (James 1:19 & 21–22)

Receive this humbly as the word of truth.

Submit therefore to God. Resist the devil and he will flee from you. Draw near to God and He will draw near to you. Cleanse your hands, you sinners, and purify your hearts, you double minded. Humble yourselves in the presence of the Lord, and He will exalt you. (James 4:7, 8 & 10)

Your allegiance to God must be full and complete; never just half way.

You younger men, likewise, be subject to your elders and all of you, clothe yourselves with humility toward one another, for God is opposed to the proud, but gives grace to the humble. Humble ...yourselves, therefore, under the mighty hand of God, that He may exalt you at the proper time, casting all your anxiety upon Him, because He cares for you. (1 Peter 5:5–7)

All people, whether they are Christian or not, should always make humility a major virtue.

I want to leave this topic with the following thought for you: Christianity made humility a major virtue. Humility is an attitude of mind whereby one realizes that one is without distinction in God's sight.

INTEGRITY

This word brings together many characteristics that any genuine individual should have. Integrity includes honesty, unblemished moral principles, trustfulness, a sincere attitude, and fairness in dealing with our fellowman.

"Lo, God will not reject a man of integrity, Nor will He support the evil doers…" (Job 8:20)

A real positive thing for you to remember. Now, don't forget it!

Let integrity and uprightness preserve me, for I wait for Thee. (Psalms 25:21)

Ask this of the Lord as you proceed on your pathway of life.

He who walks in integrity walks securely. But who perverts his way will be found out. (Proverbs 10:9)

Very accurate statement. It's not whether he'll be found out but when.

Better is a poor man who walks in his integrity than he who is perverse in speech and is a fool. (Proverbs 19:1)

This is a very valid statement.

Have you ever had your integrity tested? Let me tell you about an experience that I had as my business was caving in. I told you earlier about my night of decision. However, I did not say anything about what had happened several days before that.

I had been to see our company attorney for advice as I was trying to decide whether or not to file for bankruptcy. In the course of our conversation, the lawyer asked me a very unusual question and I asked what he meant, and he said, "I know a person that will do almost anything for money." I was taken off guard, to say the least, but what he was suggesting was to have this man torch our building material warehouse and thereby solve my problem with an illegitimate insurance claim. I was stunned, but, in a moment, I turned and told the lawyer I did not ever want to see him again. My integrity was tested, and I am grateful I did not come close to losing it.

God will not reject a man of integrity. (Job 8:20)

Never forget this fact.

JESUS CHRIST

He is the Son of God. This is expressed in the first chapter of the Book of John, verse one. In the beginning was the Word and the Word was with God, and the Word was God. He was in the beginning with God. Jesus is the only person that has ever lived who was completely unblemished and without sin. He died for all that they may be forgiven of their sins and have eternal life. He is the Way, the Truth, and the Life this day and forever more!

Any life separated from the only true anchor, Jesus, is in danger. Do not let that person be you.

"Therefore the Lord Himself will give you a sign; Behold a virgin will be with child and bear a son, and she will call His name Immanuel." (Isaiah 7:14)

A profound prophecy of the birth of Jesus Christ.

I am going to depart now from my previous pattern by not referring to the individual topics listed. This portion is about the life and ministry of Jesus in the four books of the Gospels; Matthew, Mark, Luke, and John. They thoroughly describe the life and ministry of Jesus Christ. Although, each of the authors describes the events of His life a bit differently, each is authentic. Although they were written later than other books of the New Testament, they take priority position in describing His earthly life and ministry.

Let us now begin with our understanding of Jesus Christ. The meaning of His life, His purpose for all humankind, is of more importance than anything else you will ever encounter. I encourage you to open your mind and learn.

The Book of Matthew is the first book of the four gospels. Matthew was originally a tax collector and agent for the despised Roman government but when he was asked by Jesus Christ to follow Him he became one of His original twelve disciples. The Book of Matthew was the first of the gospels to be written, either in the 50's AD or in the early 60's AD (*Ryrie Study Bible*).

"And she will bear a Son and you shall call His name Jesus, for it is He who will save His people from their sins." (Matthew 1:21)

An angel of the Lord appeared, in a dream, to Mary's husband, Joseph, to relate this to him.

And the tempter came and said to Him, "if You are the Son of God, command that these stones become bread." But He answered and said, "it is written, Man shall not live on bread alone, but on every word that proceeds out of the mouth of God." (Matthew 4:3–4)

Here Satan tries to tempt Jesus and fails.

Then Jesus said to him, "Begone, Satan! For it is written, You shall worship the Lord your God, and serve Him only." (Matthew 4:10)

This is the conclusion of Jesus' experience with Satan. Satan had tried, in many ways, to tempt Jesus to worship him.

And when He saw the multitudes, He went up on the mountain; and after He sat down, His disciples came to Him and opening His mouth He began to teach them, saying,

> "Blessed are the poor in spirit for theirs is the kingdom of heaven.
>
> Blessed are those who mourn for they shall be comforted.
>
> Blessed are the gentle for they shall inherit the earth.
>
> Blessed are those who hunger and thirst for righteousness for they shall be satisfied.
>
> Blessed are the merciful for they shall receive mercy.
>
> Blessed are the pure in heart for they shall see God.
>
> Blessed are the peacemakers for they shall be called sons of God.
>
> Blessed are those who have been persecuted for the sake of righteousness, for theirs is the kingdom of heaven.
>
> Blessed are you when men cast insults at you, and persecute you and say all kinds of evil against you falsely, on account of Me.
>
> Rejoice, and be glad for reward in heaven is great, for so they persecuted the prophets who were before you." (Matthew 5:1–12)

For those in God's family, the Sermon on the Mount does not present the way of salvation but the way of righteous living. It contrasts the new Way with the old one of the scribes and the Pharisees. Without question, this listing of blessings is both inspiring and beautiful to behold.

"Everyone therefore who shall confess Me before men, I will also confess him before My Father who is in heaven. But whoever shall deny Me before men, I will also deny him before My Father who is in heaven." (Matthew 10:32–33)

True freedom is most accurately found in both knowing and serving Jesus Christ. Our free will allows us to choose. Choose with care.

"Come to Me, all who are weary and heavy laden, and I will give you rest" (Matthew 11:28)

Some thoughtful words from an *In Touch* booklet: "Life's pressures may not lessen, but if you are intimately linked with Jesus, your soul is free from churning anxiety and His peace is ruling in your heart." Keep this advice close to you as you travail through any tough times.

And when He went ashore, He saw a great multitude, and felt compassion for them, and healed their sick. And when it was evening the disciples came to Him saying, "the place is desolate and the time is already past; so send the multitudes away; that they may go into the villages and buy food for themselves." But Jesus said to them, "They do not need to go away; you give them something to eat!" And they said to Him, "We have only five loaves and two fish." And He said "Bring them here to Me." And ordering the multitudes to recline on the grass, He took the five loaves and two fish and looking up toward heaven, He blessed the food and breaking the loaves He gave them to the disciples, and the disciples gave to the multitudes, and they all ate and were satisfied. And they picked up what was left over of the broken pieces, twelve full baskets. And there were about five thousand men who ate, aside from women and children. (Matthew 14:14–21)

I ask you to consider this miraculous act. Who was capable of doing this unless they possessed unlimited power? There are no limits on the power of Jesus Christ.

Then Jesus said to His disciples, "If anyone wishes to come after Me, let him deny himself and take up his cross, and follow Me. For whoever wishes to save his life shall lose it; but whoever loses his life for My sake, shall find it. For what will a man be profited, if he gains the whole world and forfeits his soul? Or what will a man give in exchange for his soul. For the Son of Man is going to come in the glory of His Father with His angels; and will then recompense every man according to his deeds." (Matthew 16:24-27)

This sound instruction was given by Jesus to His disciples, but it also applies to all of us today. Have you ever thought about forfeiting your soul?

"Whoever then humbles himself as this child, he is the greatest in the kingdom of heaven. And whoever receives one such child in My name receives Me." (Matthew 18:4-5)

Here Jesus explains the need for all to come to Him with openness and trust, as would a child.

And Jesus came up and spoke to them saying," All authority has been given to Me in heaven and on the earth. Go therefore and make disciples of the nations, baptizing them in the name of the Father and of the Son and the Holy Spirit, teaching them to observe all that I commanded you, and lo I am with you always, even to the end of the age." (Matthew 28:18-20)

Prior to His ascension into heaven, Jesus instructs His disciples as to their mission and responsibilities.

Mark was not one of the original twelve disciples of Jesus but was believed to be a convert of the apostle Peter. Peter looked on Mark as a son. He became a scribe for the apostle Paul and accompanied him on many ventures proclaiming the Word of Jesus to the Gentiles. The

Book of Mark is the second book of the gospels and is believed to have been written before 70 AD (*Ryrie Study Bible*). The following verses are important passages referring to our Lord and Savior, Jesus Christ.

And a voice came out of the heavens "Thou art My beloved Son, in Thee I am well pleased." (Mark 1:11)

The voice of Almighty God after the baptism of Jesus by John the Baptist.

…."The time is fulfilled, and the kingdom of God is at hand, repent and believe in the gospel." (Mark 1:15)

The proclamation by Jesus as He began His preaching.

"But in order that you may know that the Son of Man has authority on earth to forgive sins." He said to the paralytic – "I say to you, rise, take up your pallet and go home." (Mark 2:10–11)

A statement made by Jesus showing that He had both the power to heal the sick and afflicted as well as to forgive the sins of mankind.

"For nothing is hidden, except to be revealed, nor has anything been secret, but that it should come to light." (Mark 4:22)

Nothing is hidden from Jesus whether seen or secret.

And there arose a fierce gale of wind and the waves were breaking over the boat so much that the boat was already filling up. And He Himself was in the stern, asleep on the cushion, and they awoke Him and said to Him, "Teacher, do You not care that we are perishing?" And being aroused, He rebuked the wind and said to the sea, "Hush be still." And the wind died down and it became perfectly calm. And He said to them, "Why are you so timid? How is it you have no faith?" (Mark 4:37–40)

A meaningful example of the power of Jesus Christ as the wind and the sea responded to His voice. Can you imagine how you would react in this situation?

And He was saying, "That which proceeds out of the man that is what defiles the man. For from within, out of the heart of men, proceed the evil thoughts, fornications, thefts, murders, adulteries, deeds of coveting and wickedness, as well as deceit, sensuality, envy, slander, pride and foolishness. All these evil things proceed from within and defile the man." (Mark 7:20–23)

Jesus is making the point that sin comes from the heart. Does a review of these sins have resonance with you? In what way?

And Jesus went out, along with His disciples to the villages of Caesarea Philippi; and on the way he questioned His disciples, saying to them, "Who do people say that I am?" …. And He continued by questioning them "But, who do you say that I am?" Peter answered Him and said to Him "Thou art the Christ." (Mark 8:27 and 29)

Acknowledgement by Peter, a disciple, who recognized Him to be the Son of God.

And Jesus looking around, said this to His disciples "How hard it will be for those who are wealthy to enter the kingdom of God!" And the disciples were amazed at his words. But Jesus answered again and said to them Children, how hard it is to enter the kingdom of God! "It is easier for a camel to go through the eye of a needle than for a rich man to enter the kingdom of God." (Mark 10:23–25)

Christ does not say that a rich person cannot enter heaven. But, due to their wealth, it is more difficult for them, than it is for a poor person, to understand the need for God.

"But it is not so among you, but whoever wishes to become great among you shall be your servant; and whoever wishes to be first among you shall be slave of all. For even the Son of Man did not come to be served, but to serve, and to give His life as a ransom for many." (Mark 10:43–45)

Jesus emphasizes to His disciples the importance of service to others over self-importance.

"And whenever you stand praying, forgive if you have anything against anyone; so that your Father who also is in heaven may forgive you of your transgressions. But if you do not forgive, neither will the Father who is in heaven forgive your transgressions." (Mark 11:25–26)

Forgiveness is bound together with faith and without it there are consequences.

Have you not even read the Scripture, "The stone which the builders rejected, this has become the cornerstone." (Mark 12:10)

Here, Jesus is relating that His rejection by the Jewish hierarchy did not prevent Him from establishing His becoming the cornerstone for mankind and His heavenly kingdom

And Jesus began to say to them, "See to it that no one misleads you. But be on guard; for they will deliver you to the courts, and you will be flogged in the synagogues and you will stand before governors and kings for My sake as a testimony to them. ...And you will be hated by all on account of My name, but the one who endures to the end, he shall be saved. For those days will be a time of tribulation since has not occurred since the beginning of the creation, which God created till now, and never shall. But take heed, behold I have told you everything in advance. Now learn the parable from the fig tree: when its branch has already become tender, and puts forth its leaves; you know that summer is near. Even so, you too, when you see these things happening recognize that He is near, right at the door. Heaven and earth will pass away, but My words will not pass away. But of that day or hour no one knows, not even the angels in heaven, nor the Son, but the Father alone. Take heed; keep on the alert; for you do not know when the appointed time is." (Mark 13:5, 9, 13, 19, 23, 28-29, 31–33)

In these passages, Jesus describes to His apostles the end times, the tribulation, and the time of His coming again. With this description available to all of us, and with this information in mind, it is imperative to be conscious of our actions.

"Keep watching and praying that you do not come into temptation; the spirit is willing but the flesh is weak." (Mark 14:38)

Do you acknowledge the weakness of all flesh? When you are tempted, and you will be, pray for guidance and do not act impulsively. Remember temptation never comes from God.

And entering the tomb they saw a young man sitting at the right, wearing a white robe; and they were amazed. And he said to them "Do not be amazed; you are looking for Jesus the Nazarene, who has been crucified, He has risen; He is not here; behold here is the place where they laid Him. But go, tell His disciples and Peter, He is going before you into Galilee; there you will see Him, just as He said to you." And they went out and fled from the tomb, for trembling and astonishment had gripped them; and they said nothing to anyone, for they were afraid. (Mark 16: 5–8)

This describes the resurrection and the women going to the tomb and finding that Jesus had risen from the dead. Imagine the wonder, the fear, and the joy. Think how you would have felt, if this had happened to you.

So then, the Lord Jesus had spoken to them, He was received up into heaven, and sat down at the right hand of God. (Mark 16:19)

His ascension into heaven noted here.

Luke was a physician and a close friend and companion of Paul, but Luke was not an eyewitness of the life of Jesus Christ. His Gospel is estimated to have been written in approximately 60 AD. It should also be noted that Luke was the only writer of the Gospels that was a Gentile (*Ryrie Study Bible*).

"For nothing will be impossible with God." (Luke 1:37)

No other being can ever make this statement in truth. Never forget this as you proceed on your spiritual journey.

And the angel said to them, "Do not be afraid for, behold, I bring you good news of great joy which shall be for all the people; for today in the city of David there has been born for you a Savior, who is Christ the Lord. (Luke 2:10–11)

An angelic announcement of the birth of Jesus Christ and the assignment of three titles to Him.

Jesus answered and said to them, "It is not those who are well that need a physician, but those who are sick. I have not come to call the righteous but sinners to repentance." (Luke 5:31–32)

In this passage, Jesus responds to various "religious officials" about His purpose of evangelizing to all people.

"For nothing is hidden that shall not become evident, nor anything secret that shall not be known and come to light. Therefore, take care how you listen, for whoever has to him shall more be given; and whoever does not have, even what he thinks he has shall be taken away from him." (Luke 8:17–18)

Nothing is hidden from Jesus. He cannot be deceived but only one's self can be.

"The one who listens to you listens to Me, and the one who rejects you rejects Me; and who rejects Me rejects the One who sent Me." (Luke 10:16)

This was Jesus's message to the early church, but this also resonates for us today.

"All things have been handed over to Me by My Father, and no one knows who the Son is except the Father, and who the Father is except the Son, and anyone whom The Son wills to reveal Him." (Luke 10:22)

Jesus gave this message to His disciples.

"And I say to you, ask and it shall be given to you, seek and you shall find; knock and it shall be opened to you. For everyone who asks receives; and he who seeks, finds, and to him who knocks, it shall be opened." (Luke 11:9–10)

Open your heart to Christ our Lord and follow His advice. Why would you refuse such an opportunity?

"He who is not with Me, is against Me; and who does not gather with Me scatters." (Luke 11:23)

We all must choose whether to be believers or not. There is no halfway choice, so choose with thoughtfulness and care.

And He said to His disciples, "For this reason I say to you, do not be anxious for your life, as to what you shall eat, nor for your body, as to what you shall put on. For life is more than food, and the body than clothing. Consider the ravens, for they neither sow nor reap; and they have no storeroom, nor barn, and yet God feeds them; how much valuable you are than the birds! And which of you by being anxious can add a single cubit to his life's span. If then you cannot do even a very little thing, why are you anxious about other matters?" (Luke 12:22-26)

Be careful and keep this prudent advice in perspective.

"Strive to enter by the narrow door; for many, I tell you, will seek to enter and will not be able." (Luke 13:24)

The narrow door is Jesus Christ apart from whom there is no other way to heaven and eternal life.

"But when you give a reception invite the poor, the crippled, the lame, the blind and you will be blessed, since they do not have the means to repay you; for you will be repaid at the resurrection of the righteous." (Luke 14:13)

We should give to those who can never repay and do so without hesitation.

And He said, "A certain man had two sons; and the younger of them said to his Father, 'Father, give me the share of the estate that falls to me.' And he divided his wealth between them. And not many days later the younger son gathered everything together and went on a long journey into a distant country, and there he squandered his estate with loose living. "Now when he had spent everything, a severe famine occurred in the country and he became in need." (Luke 15:11-14)

He then decided to return to his home to work as a laborer for his father. While he was still a long way off, his father saw him, felt compassion for him, and ran and embraced him.

Are we not to do likewise to express forgiveness even when the extent of the problem is significant? What is your opinion?

...the chief priests and scribes with the elders confronted Him and they spoke, saying to Him, "Tell us by what authority You are doing these things, or who is the one who gave You this authority?" And He answered and said to them, "I shall also ask you a question, and you tell Me: "Was the baptism of John from heaven or from men?" And they reasoned among themselves, "if we say from heaven," He will say, "Why did you not believe him?" "But if we say, from men, all the people will stone us to death, for they are convinced that John was a prophet." And they answered, "that they did not know where it came from." And Jesus said to them. "Neither will I tell you by what authority I do these things." (Luke 20:1-8)

Think of the wisdom in His answer to their question. Either way, they were boxed in so they had to back off.

"But He looked at them and said, "What then is this that is written, The stone which the builders rejected this became the chief cornerstone?" "Everyone who falls on that stone will be broken to pieces; but on whomever it falls, it will scatter him like dust." (Luke 20:17-18)

Jesus speaks on the consequences of His rejection.

"Now He is not the God of the dead, but of the living; for all live to Him." (Luke 20:38)

Jesus is the living God, now and forever!

"Truly I say to you this generation will not pass away until all things take place. Heaven and earth will pass away, but My words will not pass away. Be on guard that your hearts will not be weighted down with dissipation and drunkenness and the worries of life, and that day will come on you suddenly like a trap; for it will come upon all those who dwell on the face of all the earth. But keep on the alert at all times, praying in order that you may have strength to escape all these things that are to come about to take place, and to stand before the Son of Man." (Luke 21:32–36)

Here, Jesus warns of the end times and of the judgment to come.

And He came out and proceeded as was His custom to the Mount of Olives and the disciples all followed Him. And when He arrived at the place, He said to them, "Pray that you may not enter into temptation." And He withdrew from them about a stone's throw, and He knelt and began to pray saying, "Father, if Thou art willing, remove this cup from Me; yet not My will, but Thine be done." (Luke 22: 39–42)

The cup that Jesus speaks of was all the suffering that was to be involved in the act of the sinless Son of God taking upon Himself the sins of mankind including the necessary, though temporary, separation from God. This took place in the Garden of Gethsemane.

While He was still speaking, behold, a multitude came, and the one called Judas, one of the twelve, was preceding them; and he approached Jesus to kiss Him. But Jesus said to him, "Judas, are you betraying the Son of Man with a kiss?" And Jesus said to the chief priest and officers of the temple and elders that had come against Him, "Have you come out with swords and clubs as against a robber? While I was with you daily in the temple, you did not lay hands on Me, but this hour and the power of darkness are yours." (Luke 22: 47–48, 52–53)

Judas betrayed and identified Jesus with his kiss and, at that point, Jesus was arrested.

"If you are the Christ, tell us." But He said to them, "If I tell you, you will not believe and if I ask a question, you will not answer. But from now on the Son of Man will be seated at the right hand of the power of God." And they all said, "Are you the Son of God then?" And He said to them, "Yes I am." And they said, "What further need do we have of testimony? For we have heard it ourselves from His own mouth." (Luke 22:67–71)

Jesus responds to members of the Sanhedrin (the Jewish Council) that He is the Son of God. At this point, they bring Him before Pilate, the Roman Governor, so that Pilate may pass a sentence upon Him. Afterwards, Pilate sent Him before King Herod. Jesus was returned, and after questioning, Pilate sentenced Jesus to be crucified.

And two others also, who were criminals, were being led away to be put to death along with Him. And when they came to the place called The Skull, there they crucified Him and the criminals, one on the right and the other on the left. But Jesus was saying, "Father, forgive them for they know not what they are doing." And they cast lots, dividing up His garments among themselves. And it was now about the sixth hour, and darkness fell over the whole land until the ninth hour, the sun being obscured; and the veil of the temple was torn in two. And Jesus, crying out with a loud voice said, "Father, into Thy hands I commit My spirit." And having said this, He breathed His last. (Luke 23:32–34, 44–46)

Jesus asked for forgiveness for those crucifying Him before passing into death.

Now He said to them "These are My words which I spoke to you, while I was still with you, that all things which are written about Me in the Law of Moses and the Prophets and in the Psalms must be fulfilled." And He said to them, "Thus it is written that the Christ should suffer and rise again from the dead the third day; and that repentance for the forgiveness of sins should be proclaimed in His Name to all the nations beginning with Jerusalem. You are witnesses of these things." "And behold, I am sending forth the promise of My Father upon you; but you are to stay in the city until you are clothed with the power from on high." (Luke 24:44 & 46–49)

These are Jesus' instructions to His disciples prior to His ascension into heaven.

The book of John is the last of the four gospel books. John, a beloved disciple, wrote this in the late 80's, or early 90's, AD. He emphasizes Jesus' purpose throughout this book. John, one of the inner circle, was very active and played a leading role in the development of the early church in Jerusalem. Although it was the last of the four gospels written, it is the most theological of the four. John was also the longest living of the disciples and died in exile on the island of Patmos (*Ryrie Study Bible*).

In the beginning was the Word, and the Word was with God, and the Word was God. He was in the beginning with God. All things came into being by Him, and apart from Him nothing came into being that has come into being. (John 1:1–3)

Before time began, Jesus Christ was already in existence with God.

And the Word became flesh, and dwelt among us and we beheld His glory, glory as of the only begotten from the Father, full of grace and truth. (John 1:14)

Jesus was unique for He was God from all eternity and yet joined Himself to sinful humanity in the incarnation. The God-man possessed all the attributes of the deity and the all the attributes common to humanity except sin. He will live forever as the God-man in His resurrection body.

For the Law was given through Moses, grace and peace were realized through Jesus Christ. (John 1:17)

Grace is the unmerited favor of God and is the basis of our salvation.

...and because He did not need anyone to bear witness concerning man for He Himself knew what was in man. (John 2:25)

Many believed in Jesus and in the words that He spoke but there were also many skeptics. There are many skeptics in the world today. Are you one? I hope not.

Now there was a man of the Pharisees, named Nicodemus, a ruler of the Jews; this man came to Him by night, and said to Him, "Rabbi, we know that You have come from God as a teacher; for no one can do these signs that You do unless God is with him." Jesus answered and said to him, "Truly, truly I say to you unless one is born again, he cannot see the kingdom of God." (John 3:1-3)

Jesus explains the necessity of being born again into a new life with Christ and what this accomplishes.

"For God so loved the world, that He gave His only begotten Son, that whoever believes in Him shall not perish, but have eternal life. For God did not send the Son into the world to judge the world, but that the world should be saved through Him." (John 3:16-17)

Carefully consider this powerful passage. There has never been one as meaningful as this nor will there ever be one to match it.

"He who comes from above is above all, he who is of the earth is from the earth, and speaks of the earth. He who comes from heaven is above all. "For He whom God has sent speaks the words of God, for He gives the Spirit without measure. The Father loves the Son and has given all things into His hand. He who believes in the Son has eternal life; but he who does not obey the Son does not see life, but the wrath of God abides on him." (John 3:31 & 34–36)

Plain and direct. Pay attention.

"For not even the Father judges anyone, but He has given all judgment to the Son. In order that all may honor the Son, even as they honor the Father. He who does not honor the Son, does not honor the Father who sent Him. Truly, truly, I say to you, he who hears My word, and believes Him who sent Me, has eternal life, and does not come into judgment, but has passed out of death into life. Truly, truly, I say to you an hour is coming and now is, when the dead shall hear the voice of the Son of God; and those who hear shall live." (John 5:22–25)

Christ's authority is seen in the spheres of resurrection and judgment. Those who believe will escape a negative judgment.

"I can do nothing on My own initiative. As I hear I judge, and My judgment is just, because I do not seek My own will, but the will of Him who sent Me." (John 5:30)

Whose will you obey as you proceed along life's path; your own or God's? Consider this very carefully.

"Do not work for the food that perishes, but for the food which endures to eternal life, which the Son of Man shall give to you, for on Him the Father, even God has set His seal." (John 6:27)

To be spiritually fed a man must fully believe.

"For this is the will of My Father, that everyone who beholds the Son and believes in Him, may have eternal life; and I Myself will raise him up on the last day." (John 6:40)

Pause and consider the power and impact of this. Praise our merciful God!

Jesus said therefore to the twelve, "You do want to go away also, do you?" Simon Peter answered Him, "Lord to whom shall we go? You have the words of eternal life and we have believed and have come to know that You are the Holy One of God." Jesus answered them, "Did I Myself not choose you, the twelve, and yet one of you is a devil?" Now He meant Judas the son of Simon Iscariot, for he, one of the twelve, was going to betray Him. (John 6:67–71)

Jesus asked this of His disciples after some of His followers had left Him.

"He who believes in Me, as the Scripture said, From His innermost being shall flow rivers of living water." (John 7:38)

Belief in Christ will provide peace of mind in the heart of the believer and also the willingness to witness their commitment to others.

Again therefore Jesus spoke to them saying, "I am the light of the world, he who follows Me shall not walk in darkness, but shall have the light of life." (John 8:12)

Do not forget this dynamic fact.

And He was saying to them, "You are from below, I am from above; you are of this world, I am not of this world. I said therefore to you that you shall die in your sins; for unless you believe that I am He, you shall die in your sins." (John 8:23–24)

This statement by Jesus doubtlessly infuriated Jewish authorities since this included them along with the sinners.

Jesus therefore saying to those Jews who had believed Him, "If you abide in My word, you are truly disciples of Mine; and you know the truth and the truth shall make you free." (John 8:31–32)

Thanks be to God.

Jesus answered, "If I glorify Myself, My glory is nothing; it is My Father that glorifies Me of whom you say, He is our God, and you have not come to know Him, but I know Him; and if I say I do not know Him, I shall be a liar like you, but I do know Him and keep His word." (John 8:54–55)

Being pressed again by the unbelieving Pharisees, Jesus expresses who He is and that Almighty God has sent Him.

Jesus said to them, "Truly, truly, I say to you before Abraham was born, I am." (John 8:58)

Jesus very plainly states that He is the Son of God and was before creation.

"For this reason the Father loves Me, because I lay down My life and take it up again. No one has taken it away from Me, but I lay it down on My own imitative; I have authority to lay it down and I have authority to take it up again. This commandment I received from My Father." (John 10:17–18)

Keep this in perspective to better understand His reason for His action.

"I and the Father are One." (John 10:30)

Thoughtfully consider the power and meaningfulness of this statement. Bear in mind that the Father and the Son are in perfect unity in both their natures and their actions.

PEACE WITHIN THROUGH GOD'S WAY

..."Lazarus, is dead and I am glad for your sakes that I was not there, so that you may believe; but let us go to him." ...Martha, therefore, when she heard that Jesus was coming, went to meet Him; but Mary still sat in the house. Martha therefore, said to Jesus, "Lord, if You had been here, my brother would not have died."...Jesus said to her, "I am the resurrection and the life; he who believes in Me shall live even if he dies, and everyone who lives and believes in Me shall never die. Do you believe this?" Therefore, when Mary came where Jesus was, she saw Him, and fell at His feet, saying to Him, "Lord, if you had been here, my brother would not have died." ...."Where have you laid him? They said to him, "Lord, come and see." Jesus wept. Jesus therefore, being deeply moved within, came to the tomb. Now it was a cave, and a stone was lying against it. Jesus said, "Remove the stone." Martha the sister of the deceased, said to Him, "Lord, by this time there will be a stench, for he has been dead four days." Jesus said to her, "Did I not say to you, if you believe, you will see the glory of God?" And so they removed the stone. And Jesus raised His eyes and said, "Father, I thank Thee that Thou heardest Me. And I know that Thou dost hearest Me always; but because of the people standing around I said it, that they may believe that Thou didst send Me." And when He had said these things, He cried out with a loud voice, "Lazarus come forth." He who had died came forth, bound hand and foot with wrappings; and his face was wrapped around with a cloth. Jesus said to them, "Unbind him, and let him go." (John 11:14-15, 20-21, 25-26, 32, 34-35, 38-44)

Like Martha, we must have faith in Jesus. The resurrection of Lazarus is a vivid example for all of us of the validity and the power of Jesus and of the fact of eternal life for His believers.

"Truly, truly, I say to you, he who receives whomever I send receives Me, and he who receives Me, receives Him who sent Me." (John 13:20)

It should be understood that He is sending the apostles to seek others.

"A new commandment I give to you, that you should love one another, even as I have loved you, that you love one another. By this all men will know that you are my disciples, if you love one another." (John 13:34–35)

Without love in your heart, you will have an almost impossible time reaching Jesus Christ, our Lord and Savior.

Jesus said to him, "I am the way, and the truth and the life; no one comes to the Father but through Me." (John 14:6)

Jesus is the doorway to salvation. There is no other.

"He who has My commandments and keeps them, he it is who loves Me; and he who loves Me shall be loved by My Father, and I will love him, and will disclose Myself to him." (John 14:21)

The measure of one's love is the extent to which one keeps Christ's commandments.

"Peace, I leave with you; My peace I give to you; not as the world gives, do I give to you. Let not your heart be troubled nor let it be fearful." (John 14:27)

Can you imagine receiving more peace than this?

"I am the vine and you are the branches; he who abides in Me and I in him, he bears much fruit for apart from Me you can do nothing." (John 15:5)

A sound message to His disciples to maintain their close personal relationship with Him as they take His message to the world.

"But I tell you the truth, it is to your advantage that I go away; for if I do not go away, the Helper shall not come to you; but if I go, I will send Him to you." (John 16:7)

Jesus explains to the disciples that it is important for the Holy Spirit to come to them, but the Holy Spirit cannot come until He is no longer with them.

"But when He, the Spirit of truth, comes, He will guide you into all the truth; for He will not speak on His own imitative, but whatever He hears, He will speak; and He will disclose to you what is to come." (John 16:13)

Jesus explains to his disciples how the Holy Spirit will provide guidance and truth to them.

These things I have spoken to you, that in Me you may have peace. In the world you have tribulation, but "Take courage; I have overcome the world." (John 16:33)

In other words, by His resurrection, Jesus has overcome the afflictions, chastisements, and sins of mankind.

In Chapters 18 and 19, John tells us of the arrest of Jesus, His appearance before the high priest and the Sanhedrin (the Pharisee council) and also before Pilate, the Roman Governor, prior to His crucifixion. We shall begin with the appearance before Pilate.

Pilate therefore said to Him, "So you are a king?" Jesus answered, "You say correctly that I am a king. For this I have been born, and for this I have come into the world, to bear witness to the truth. Everyone who is the truth, hears My voice." (John 18:37)

At this point, we hear a question from Pilate that we have heard many times before, "What is truth?" He was both frustrated and irritated with the answer Jesus gave to him and did not really understand the meaning of Jesus' response.

Pilate therefore said to Him, "You do not speak to me? Do you not know that I have the authority to release You, and I have authority to crucify You?" Jesus answered, "You have no authority over Me, unless it had been given to you from above; for this reason he who delivered Me up to you has the greater sin." (John 19:10-11)

Caiaphas, the high priest, is the one who delivered Jesus to Pilate.

When Pilate therefore heard these words, he brought Jesus out, and sat Him down on the judgment seat at a place called The Pavement, but in Hebrew, Gabbatha. Now it was the day of preparation of the Passover; it was about the sixth hour. And he said to the Jews, "Behold your King!" They therefore cried out "Away with Him, away with Him, crucify Him!" Pilate said to them, "Shall I crucify your King?" The chief priests answered, "We have no king but Caesar." So he then delivered Him to them to be crucified. They took Jesus therefore, and He went out, bearing His own cross to the place called the Place of a Skull, which is called in Hebrew, Golgotha. There they crucified Him, and with Him two other men one on either side, and Jesus in between. (John 19:13-18)

Pilate sarcastically called Jesus "King". The Pharisees responded with jealousy and hostility that Jesus should be crucified; and then this horrific act was done.

After this, Jesus knowing all things had already been accomplished, in order that the Scripture might be fulfilled, said "I am thirsty." A jar full of sour wine was standing there; so they put a sponge full of sour wine upon a branch of hyssop, and brought it up to His mouth. When Jesus therefore had received the sour wine, He said "It is finished!" And He bowed His head and gave up His spirit. (John 19:28–30)

These passages retrace for us the tragic circumstances of His suffering and death on the Cross. By His sacrifice, He has redeemed mankind from the sins of the world. Consider the pain and suffering He endured for us. Are you willing to suffer for Him?

Now on the first day of the week, Mary Magdalene came early to the tomb, while it was still dark, and saw the stone already taken away from the tomb. And so she ran and came to Simon Peter and to the other disciple whom Jesus loved, and said to them, "They have taken away the Lord out of the tomb, and we do not where they have laid Him." Peter therefore went forth, and the other disciple, and they were going to the tomb. And the two were running together; and the other disciple ran faster than Peter, and came to the tomb first; and stooping and looking in, he saw the linen wrappings lying there; but he did not go in. Simon Peter therefore also came, following him, and entered the tomb, and he beheld the wrappings lying there, and the face-cloth, which had been on His head, not lying with the linen wrappings, but in a place rolled up by itself. So the other disciple who had first come to the tomb entered then also, and he saw and believed. For as yet they did not understand the Scripture, that He first must rise again from the dead. So the disciples went away again to their own homes. But Mary was standing outside the tomb weeping; and so as she wept, she stooped and looked into the tomb; and she beheld two angels in white sitting, one at the head and the other at the feet, where the body of Jesus had been lying. And they said to her, "Woman, why are you weeping?" She said to them, "Because they have taken away my Lord, and I do not know where they have laid Him." When she had said this, she turned around, and beheld Jesus standing there, and did not know that it was Jesus. Jesus said to her, "Woman, why are you weeping? Whom are you seeking?" Supposing Him to be the gardener, she said to Him, "Sir, if you have carried Him away, tell me where you have laid Him, and I will take Him away." Jesus said to her, "Mary!" She turned and said to Him in Hebrew, "Rabboni!" (which means, Teacher) Jesus said to her, "Stop clinging to Me, for I have not yet ascended to the Father, but go to My brethren, and say to them, I ascend to My Father, and your Father, and My God and your God." Mary Magdalene came announcing to the disciples, "I have seen the Lord" and He had said these things to her. (John 20:1–18)

Can you imagine the astonishment and wonder of being present at this awesome event? How do think you would have reacted had you been there?

When therefore it was evening, on that day, the first day of the week, and when the doors were shut where the disciples were, for the fear of the Jews, Jesus came and stood in their midst, and said to them, "Peace be with you." And when He has said this, He showed both His hands and His side. The disciples therefore rejoiced when they saw the Lord. (John 20:19–20)

These dramatic circumstances took place after His resurrection. He showed his disciples, and all mankind, that He has power over death.

I ask that you be patient and try to understand that, though Jesus Christ is the focus of this book, *He is the most important element in your life.*

The Book of Acts was written by Luke, a physician and a companion of Paul, in approximately 61 AD. This book focuses on the spread of the Christian message throughout the northern Mediterranean and areas of the Middle East. The apostle, Peter, the strongest of His disciples, became the spokesman for the Christian community. He was largely responsible for the growth of the community in the early days.

At a later date, Paul joined the community in Antioch which commissioned him, along with Barnabas, to undertake and spread the gospel throughout Asia Minor. This became the basis of Paul's first missionary journey. This initial trip began on the island of Cyprus, went from one end of the island to the other and then proceeded to Pamphylia on the southern coast of what today is Turkey. From there, it proceeded inland to multiple towns before returning to the point of departure, Antioch, Syria (from *The Bible Gateway*).

The time covered in the Book of Acts is approximately 30 years. It is important to understand how the Word and the life of Jesus, our Lord, was spread throughout the known world at that time. This remarkable spread of the teachings of Jesus was accomplished without telephone, television, internet, auto, or any motorized vehicles.

"...but you shall receive power when the Holy Spirit has come upon you; and you shall be My witnesses both in Jerusalem and in all Judea and Samaria, and even to the remotest part of the earth." (Acts 1:8)

Jesus tells His disciples what He expects of them after they receive the Holy Spirit.

...this Man, delivered up by the predestined plan and foreknowledge of God, you nailed to a cross by the hands of godless men and put Him to death. And God raised Him up again, putting an end to the agony of death, since it was impossible for Him to be held by its power. (Acts 2:23–24)

The apostle Peter explains that God's plan was ordained and followed exactly.

"Therefore let all the House of Israel know for certain that God has made Him both Lord and Christ – this Jesus whom you crucified." (Acts 2:36)

The acknowledgment that Jesus is both Lord and Christ and that repentance through Him brings salvation.

Now when Simon saw that the Spirit was bestowed through the laying on of the apostles hands, he offered them money saying, "Give this authority to me as well, so that everyone on whom I lay my hands on will receive the Holy Spirit." But Peter said to him, "May your silver perish with you, because you thought you could obtain the gift of God with money! You have no part or portion in this matter, for your heart is not right before God. Therefore repent of the wickedness of yours, and pray for the Lord that if possible, the intention of your heart may be forgiven you." (Acts 8:18-22)

No one, at any time, may ever buy, at any price, salvation, the gift of God.

Now Saul, still breathing threats and murder against the disciples of the Lord, went to the high priest, and asked for letters from him to the synagogues at Damascus, so if he found any belonging to the Way, both men and women, he might bring back bound to Jerusalem. And it came about as he journeyed, he was approaching Damascus, and suddenly a light from heaven flashed around him; and he fell to the ground and heard a voice saying to him, "Saul, Saul, why are you persecuting Me?" And he said, "Who art Thou, Lord? And He said, "I am Jesus whom you are persecuting, but rise, and enter the city, and it shall be told you what you must do." (Acts 9:1-6)

Before his conversion, Saul was a vigorous persecutor of Christians. But, after this encounter with Jesus on the road to Damascus, he became a powerful, enthusiastic follower of Jesus and he changed his name to Paul. He was largely responsible for taking the message of Jesus to the Mediterranean area; not just Syria, Turkey and Palestine but also to the northern part as far west as Spain through Greece and Italy.

And opening his mouth, Peter said: "I most certainly understand that God is not one to show partiality; but in every nation the man who fears Him and does what is right, is welcome to Him."... While Peter was still speaking these words, the Holy Spirit fell upon all those who were listening to the message. And all the circumcised believers who had come with Peter were amazed, because the gift of the Holy Spirit had been poured out upon the Gentiles also. For they were hearing them speaking with tongues and exalting God. Then Peter answered, "Surely no one can refuse the water for these to be baptized who have received the Holy Spirit just as we did, can he?" And he ordered them to be baptized in the name of Jesus Christ. Then they asked him to stay on a few days. (Acts 10:34-35, 44-48)

There are several points to consider regarding these verses. First, Jesus shows no partiality towards any individual or race. Secondly, these barriers were cast down due to the healing exhibited by the Holy Spirit.

...And it came about that for an entire year they met with the church, and taught considerable numbers; and the disciples were first called Christians in Antioch. (Acts 11:26)

The word "Christians" means followers of Christ.

"Therefore let it be known to you, brethren, that through Him forgiveness of sins is proclaimed to you; and through Him everyone who believes is freed from all things which could not be freed through the Law of Moses." (Acts 13:38-39)

Although this was first expressed centuries ago, it is accurate and true today.

At this point, Paul leaves Greece and journeys back to Jerusalem. Here he encounters various groups who speak out against him.

The Roman commander intercedes and takes him to be scourged. Paul says to the centurion standing by, "Is it lawful to scourge a man who is a Roman and uncondemned?" And the commander responds, "Tell me, are you a Roman?" And he answers, "Yes." From this point, Paul is taken before the Council (which was called the Sanhedrin) and after he is struck by the high priest, an argument ensues. (Both Pharisees and Sadducees comprised the Sanhedrin, however, they shared different outlooks and practices.) After more dissension, he is taken to the barracks.

But on the night immediately following, the Lord stood at his side and said, "Take courage; for as you have solemnly witnessed to My cause at Jerusalem so you must witness at Rome also." (Acts 23:11)

At this point, the Jews plot to kill Paul. Paul is, once again, taken charge of by the Roman guard and taken to appear before Felix, the Roman governor. His appearance before the governor drags on for two long years and then he has to appear before the new governor, Porcius Festus. He appeals to Festus that he should appear before Caesar, as he was a Roman. Festus grants this request.

I ask that you consider the stress and strain of such a frustrating procedure. Do you feel you could have endured such or would you have been willing to do it for Jesus? However, before he was sent to Rome, Paul is sent to appear before King Agrippa of the Jews. Festus thought that by doing this he could establish a specific charge for sending Paul to Rome. Agrippa responds to Festus that Paul should be set free except that he had appealed to Caesar. Eventually, the vessel that was transporting Paul to Rome is shipwrecked. Paul survives being lost at sea. He finally arrives at the island of Malta. He is greeted with kindness by the natives of the island, but while in the process of lighting a fire is bitten by a poisonous viper. When Paul survives this, the locals think he is a god. They bring those who are ill to him and he heals them. Here's another example of his courage and his faith in Jesus Christ. Three months later, after leaving Malta, he arrives in Rome.

And when we entered Rome, Paul was allowed to stay by himself, with the soldier who was guarding him. And it happened after three days he called together those who were the leading men of the Jews and when they had come together, he began saying to them, "Brethren, though I had nothing against our people, or the customs of our fathers, yet I was delivered prisoner from Jerusalem into the hands of the Romans." (Acts 28:16–17)

Paul explains to those present that he has done no wrong and they, in turn, ask him to express his convictions about the Lord to them. Some believed in his description of Jesus but there were many skeptics, particularly among the Jews. During this period, he stayed in rented quarters for two years. All throughout this time, he continued to preach the message of the kingdom of God, teaching openly about Jesus Christ while being regularly harassed.

The next section of the New Testament is comprised of twenty-one epistles, or letters, to various churches providing examples of Christian teaching as well as discussions of ethical behavior and other practical matters. Regarding the composition of the twenty-one letters, thirteen are attributed to the apostle Paul.

These epistles were directed to churches in Greece, in areas of Asia Minor (Turkey, Cyprus, and Syria) and in Rome. The most prominent and longest of these is the letter to the Romans which Paul wrote while he was in Corinth. "Hebrews" was also thought by some to have been written by Paul but the actual author is unknown.

Of the seven remaining letters, two were written by the apostle Peter, three by the apostle John, one by Jude (a half-brother of Jesus), and the last was written by James (another half-brother of Jesus) who was also a member of the Council in Jerusalem. All of these letters disclose the spread of the word of God through Jesus Christ. I hope this explanation makes it easier for you to consider and bring you into a better focus. Let us now begin with Paul's letter to the Romans (from *Bible Gateway*).

For in it the righteousness of God is revealed from faith to faith; as it is written, "But the righteous shall live by faith." (Romans 1:17)

Here, Paul explains that one can be righteous in God's sight only through faith. He who is just and honest shall live. Believe in the Lord Jesus Christ and be saved.

For even though they knew God, they did not honor Him as God, or give thanks; but they became futile in their speculations and their foolish heart was darkened. Professing to be wise, they became fools.... Therefore God gave them over in their lusts of their hearts to impurity, that their bodies be dishonored among them. For they exchanged the truth of God for a lie, and worshiped and served the creature rather than the Creator, who is blessed forever, Amen. For this reason God gave them over to degrading passions; for their women exchanged the natural function for that which is unnatural, and in the same way also the men abandoned the natural function of the woman and turned in their desire toward one another, men with men committing indecent acts and receiving in their own persons the due penalty of their error. And just as they did not see fit to acknowledge God any longer, God gave them over to a depraved mind, to do those things which are not proper, being filled with all unrighteousness, wickedness, greed, evil; full of envy, murder, strife, deceit, malice; they are gossips, slanderers, haters of God, insolent, arrogant, boastful inventors of evil, disobedient to parents, without understanding, untrustworthy, unloving, unmerciful, and although they knew the ordinance of God, that those who practice those things are worthy of death, they not only do the same; but also give hearty approval to those that practice them. (Romans 1:21-22, 24-32)

At this time, sexual perversion was prevalent and sin, in general, was rampant. It is apparent that they not only practiced these things but that they encouraged and vicariously enjoyed the sins of others.

But God demonstrates His own love towards us so that while we were yet sinners, Christ died for us. (Romans 5:8)

What a blessing for mankind.

But now being freed from sin and enslaved to God, you derive your benefit, resulting in sanctification and the outcome, eternal life. For the wages of sin is death, but the free gift of God is eternal life in Jesus Christ our Lord. (Romans 6:22-23)

I ask that you be serious and consider the benefit of receiving Jesus Christ as your Lord and Savior.

Wretched man that I am! Who will set me free from the body of this death? Thanks be to God through Jesus Christ our Lord! So then, on the one hand I myself with my mind am serving the law of God, but on the other, with my flesh the law of sin. (Romans 7:24-25)

Paul expresses having mixed emotions on this due to his sincere commitment to Jesus.

... in order that the requirements of the Law be fulfilled in us, who do not walk according to the flesh, but according to the Spirit. For the mind set on the flesh is death, but the mind set on the Spirit, is life and peace. (Romans 8:4, 6)

The contrast here is between one dominated by the flesh, and its sinful nature, and one dominated by the Holy Spirit. Where do you fit?

But if we hope for what we do not see, with perseverance we wait eagerly for it. And in the same way the Spirit also helps our weakness; for we do not know how to pray as we should, but the Spirit Himself intercedes for us with groaning too deep for words. (Romans 8:25-26)

The Holy Spirit helps us in our weakness and helps us pray intelligently about various situations.

For I am convinced that neither death nor life, nor angels, nor principalities, nor things present, nor things to come, nor powers, nor height, nor depth or any other created thing, shall be able to separate us from the love of God, which is in Christ Jesus our Lord. (Romans 8:38-39)

Nothing in the universe is beyond God's control. Therefore, nothing can separate us from His eternal love. What a powerful statement.

But what does it say? The word is near you, in your mouth and in your heart – that is the word of faith which we are preaching, that if you confess with your mouth that Jesus as Lord, and believe in your heart that God raised Him from the dead, then you will be saved. (Romans 10:8-9)

This is The Way of Salvation: proclaim with your mouth and believe in your heart and confess that Jesus is Lord.

Let us behave properly as in the day, not in carousing and drunkenness, not in sexual promiscuity and sensuality, not in strife and jealousy. But put on the Lord Jesus Christ, and make no provisions for the flesh in regards to its lusts. (Romans 13:13-14)

Be sober and clean in the eyes of God, otherwise you will pay a heavy price for your inappropriate actions. Do not kid yourself.

Who are you to judge the servant of another? To his own master he stands or falls, and stand he will, for the Lord is able to make him stand. (Romans 14:4)

Never misunderstand this fact; only Jesus is the judge of all.

For not one lives for himself, and not one dies for himself, for if we live, we live for the Lord, or if we die, we die for the Lord, therefore, whether we live or die, we are the Lord's. (Romans 14:7–8)

We are always the Lord's but make it your practice to live for the Lord.

Now may the God of hope fill you with all joy and peace in believing, that you may abound in hope by the power of the Holy Spirit. (Romans 15:13)

It is my sincere desire that you and many others may find and share this with friends and family and others as well; the feeling of joy and hope that comes by committing yourself to our Lord and Savior, Jesus Christ.

Now I urge you, brethren, keep your eye on those who cause dissensions and hindrances contrary to the teaching which you learned, and turn away from them. For such men are slaves not of our Lord Christ but of their own appetites; and by their smooth and flattering speech they deceive the hearts of the unsuspecting. (Romans 16:17–18)

I trust that you will not allow yourself to be conned by the slick and smooth talk of those who advocate sin and destruction.

JOHN H. (JAN) DOLCATER, JR.

The book of 1 Corinthians was written by the apostle Paul in 50 to 55 AD when he was living in the community of Ephesus on the western coast of what is now Turkey. Earlier, Paul had had a vision from the Lord to come to Macedonia (Greece today) and he responded to the call. Paul and his companions left Galatia and arrived on the coast and proceeded by boat from Troas to Philippi where he founded the first Christian church in Europe. These events took place on his second missionary trip. From Philippi, he went to Athens where he was very unsuccessful in his efforts to preach the gospel.

From Athens, he moved on to the city of Corinth, a large city of 200,000 that had the reputation of being sinful in many ways. As an example, the large temple of Venus had a thousand prostitutes. While a significant number of the inhabitants participated in the sinful pursuits of the flesh, they also encouraged others to do so. Every evil thing of significance was available in Corinth.

Paul worked to change the sinful habits of the locals and made progress in this matter before leaving and returning to Ephesus. However, he continued to receive reports of the misdeeds of Corinth resulting in the writing of his letter of 1 Corinthians. This was a letter that rebuked the ways of Corinth and asked that the Corinthians consider two courses of action and then determine which they should follow.

The first course of action Paul mentioned was that they continued their evil approach. The second course of action was that they change and follow the ways of Almighty God and His Son, Jesus Christ. The letter was quite stern and some of the inhabitants, but not the majority, decided that the ways of God were preferable. Let us now explore the approach that Paul utilized in his mission for Corinth. He begins softly before turning to the evils in a serious manner (from *The Bible Gateway*).

For the word of the cross is to those who are perishing foolishness, but to us that are being saved it is the power of God.... Because the foolishness of God is wiser than men, and the weakness of God is stronger than men. (1 Corinthians 1:18 and 25)

Strive to gain the wisdom of God through Jesus Christ. This is simplicity, yet it is perfection. The worldly wisdom highly prized by the Corinthians is the very antithesis of the wisdom of God.

... that no man should boast before God. ...that just as it is written, "Let him who boasts, boast in the Lord." ...that your faith should not rest on the wisdom of men, but on the power of God. (1 Corinthians 1:29 & 31, also 2:5)

Paul did not want their faith to be based on clever arguments or discussions, but on God's power.

I wrote you in my letter not to associate with immoral people; ...But actually I wrote to you not to associate with any so-called brother if he should be an immoral person, or covetous, or an idolater, or a reviler, or a drunkard, or a swindler – not even to eat with such a one. ... But those who are outside God judges. Remove the wicked man from among yourselves. (1 Corinthians 5:9, 11, 13)

It is not realistic to have no contact with those who are evil but avoid having fellowship or close relations with those who are evil.

Food is for the stomach and the stomach is for food, but God will do away with both of them. Yet the body is not for immorality, but for the Lord, and the Lord is for the body. (1 Corinthians 6:13)

Some of the Corinthians were suggesting that sexual indulgence and the body needing food are the same. Not so, said Paul, the body should always glorify the Lord.

Flee immorality. Every other sin that a man commits is outside the body, but the immoral man sins against his own body. Or do you not know that your body is a temple of the Holy Spirit who is in you, whom you have from God, and that you are not your own? For you have been bought for a price; therefore glorify God in your body. (1 Corinthians 6:18–20)

Make a firm commitment to avoid immorality.

But take care lest this liberty of yours somehow become a stumbling block to the weak. ...And thus, by sinning against the brethren and wounding their conscience, when it is weak, you sin against Christ. (1 Corinthians 8:9 &12)

Do not tempt others to sin. This applies to all things in our daily lives.

No temptation has overtaken you but such as is common to man; and God is faithful, who will not allow you to be tempted beyond what you are able; but with the temptation will provide the way of escape also, that you may be able to endure it. (1 Corinthians 10:13)

Trust God to give you the power to overcome temptation.

Test all conduct to see whether or not it manifests the character of God. To test yourself on this subject, utilize the four following questions as to the temptation.

First, is it beneficial? Second, is it enslaving? Third, does this in any way edify you? And, lastly, will it hinder or impede the spiritual growth of others? After doing this, I believe your determination of what the proper decision should be will be far easier.

Therefore whoever eats the bread or drinks the cup of the Lord in an unworthy manner, shall be guilty of the body and blood of the Lord. (1 Corinthians 11:27)

If you come to the altar of the Lord with unconfessed sin, or in an unworthy manner, one is subject to judgment.

Love is patient, love is kind, and is not jealous, love does not brag and it is not arrogant, does not act unbecomingly; it does not seek its own, is not provoked, does not take into account wrong suffered, does not rejoice in unrighteousness, but rejoices with the truth; bears all things, believes all things, hopes all things, endures all things. Love never fails, but if there are gifts of prophecy, they will be done away; if there are tongues, they will cease; if there is knowledge it will be done away. ... When I was a child, I used to speak as a child, think as a child, reason as a child, when I became a man I did away with childish things. ...But now abide faith, hope, love, these three, but the greatest of these is love. (1 Corinthians 13:4–8, 11, 13)

The first part defines the perfection of love. All of these attributes should be pursued diligently, but love is the greatest since it is expressed by God.

...for God is not a god of confusion, but of peace, as in all the churches of the saints. (1 Corinthians 14:33)

Peace flows through Him and our Lord Jesus Christ.

Do not be deceived; Bad company corrupts good morals. (1 Corinthians 15:33)

Good and simple advice. Consistently pay attention to this.

"O death, where is your victory? O death, where is your sting?" The sting of death is sin, and the power of sin is the law; but thanks be to God who gives us the victory through our Lord Jesus Christ. Therefore, my beloved brethren, be steadfast, immovable, always abounding in the work of the Lord, knowing that your toil is not in vain in the Lord. (1 Corinthians 15:55–58)

Remember, the sting of death is sin because it is by sin that death gains authority over man. Also, remember the powerful promise that a firm belief in the resurrection and a solid hope for the future creates incentive for service in the present.

The apostle Paul wrote the letter which became the book of 2 Corinthians approximately a year after his first letter to them. He initially made a return visit to Corinth to attempt to get the church to change from its former devious ways. He heard later that the church had again reverted to its previous evil practices and the second letter was written at that time. This letter was both sorrowful and stern and the letter was delivered by Titus. While he was in Macedonia, Titus arrived and told Paul the church had finally repented of its rebellious behavior (*Ryrie Study Bible*).

For God who said, "Light shall shine out of darkness" is the One who is shone in our hearts to give the light of knowledge of the glory of God in the face of Christ. (2 Corinthians 4:6)

May the light of Christ shine through you to others.

Therefore we do not lose heart, but though our outer man is decaying, yet our inner man is being renewed day by day....while we look not at the things that are seen, but at the things that are not seen; for the things which are seen are temporal, but the things that are not seen are eternal. (2 Corinthians 4:16 & 18)

Maintain your focus on the things that are eternal.

For we walk by faith, not by sight. (2 Corinthians 5:7)

Assurance is found in Jesus rather than in things of a temporal nature.

For we must all appear before the judgment seat of Christ, that each one may be recompensed for the deeds in the body, according to what he has done, whether good or bad. (2 Corinthians 5:10)

Believers will be judged, in a review of their lives, for the purpose of rewarding their good and evil deeds, while the unbeliever will be dealt with according to his evil deeds.

Therefore if any man is in Christ, he is a new creature; the old things passed away; behold new things have come. (2 Corinthians 5:17)

This demonstrates the decisive change that salvation brings.

He made Him who knew no sin to be sin on our behalf, that we might become the righteousness of God in Him. (2 Corinthians 5:21)

This tells us that the sinless Savior has taken our sins upon Himself that we might have God's righteousness. This certainly emphasizes the heart of the gospel.

Do not be bound together with unbelievers; for what partnership have righteousness and lawlessness, or what fellowship has light with darkness. (2 Corinthians 6:14)

This applies to marriage as well as to business and other personal relationships.

For the sorrow that is according to the will of God produces a repentance without regret, leading to salvation; but the sorrow of the world produces death. (2 Corinthians 7:10)

A proper definition or reflection of sorrow.

For you know the grace of our Lord Jesus Christ, that though He was rich, yet for your sake He became poor, that you through His poverty might become rich. (2 Corinthians 8:9)

Jesus gave His all for mankind.

The Book of Galatians was written by the apostle Paul in either 53 AD or 55 AD and directed to the churches that were established there on his first missionary trip. Galatia was located in what is now central Turkey (*Ryrie Study Bible*).

Grace to you and peace from God the Father and the Lord Jesus Christ, who gave Himself for our sins, that He might deliver us out of this present evil age, according to the will of our God and Father, to whom be the glory forevermore. Amen. (Galatians 1:3–5)

Here, the apostle Paul summarizes his whole preaching message.

"I do not nullify the grace of God; for if righteousness comes through the Law, then Christ died needlessly." Galatians 2:21

It was the Galatians, and not Paul, who nullified the grace of God by wanting to retain the Law. If God wanted obedience through the Law, why would He send His Son to suffer and die on a cross?

Now that no one is justified by the Law before God is evident for "The righteous man shall live by faith." (Galatians 3:11)

One can be justified in Jesus's sight only by faith and commitment to Him.

But the scripture has shut all men under sin, that the promise by faith in Jesus Christ might be given to those who believe. (Galatians 3:22)

Believe in the Lord Jesus Christ and you will be saved.

But when the fullness of the time came, God sent forth His Son, born of a woman, born, under the Law in order that He might redeem those who are under the Law, that we might receive adoption as sons. And because you are sons, God has sent forth the Spirit of His Son into our hearts, crying, "Abba Father!" Therefore you are no longer a slave, but a son; and if a son, then an heir through God. (Galatians 4:4–7)

The Holy Spirit in the heart of the believer shows his acceptance of God as a son and heir.

But I say, walk by the Spirit, and you will not carry out the desire of the flesh. For the flesh sets its desire against the Spirit, and the Spirit against the flesh; for those are in opposition to one another, so that you may not do the things you please. (Galatians 5:16–17)

The Spirit will provide victory over the flesh and its works.

The fruit of the Spirit is love, joy, peace, patience, kindness, goodness, faithfulness, gentleness, self-control; against such things there is no law. Now those who belong to Christ Jesus have crucified the flesh with its passions and desires. If we live by the Spirit, let us also walk by the Spirit. (Galatians 5:22–25)

Please make every effort to memorize this very meaningful passage.

Do not be deceived, God is not mocked; for whatever a man sows, this he will also reap. For the one who sows to his own flesh shall from the flesh reap corruption, but the one who sows to the Spirit shall from the Spirit reap eternal life. (Galatians 6:7–8)

Never make the error of mocking God as it is a surety that this will bring very serious consequences.

But may it never be that I should boast, except in the cross of our Lord Jesus Christ, through which the world has been crucified to me and I to the world. (Galatians 6:14)

The apostle Paul exclaims his commitment to Jesus Christ.

The Book of Ephesians was written by the apostle Paul about 60 AD while he was in prison in Rome. This was primarily a letter of encouragement to the church in Ephesus. This church was established on his second missionary trip. My wife and I had the privilege of seeing the front of this old church several years ago while on a cruise of the Greek Isles (from *The Bible Gateway*).

In Him we have redemption through His blood, the forgiveness of our trespasses, according to the riches of His grace. (Ephesians 1:7)

We are released from the bondage of our sins by the grace of Jesus.

Among them we too all formerly lived in the lusts of our flesh, indulging the desires of the flesh and of the mind, and by nature children of wrath, even as the rest. But God, being rich in mercy, because of His great love with which He loved us, even when we were dead in our transgressions, made us alive together with Christ. (by grace you have been saved). (Ephesians 2:3–5)

Salvation is available to us by grace through Jesus Christ. Be ever thankful for this.

…and to know the love of Christ which surpasses knowledge, that you may be filled up to all the fullness of God. (Ephesians 3:19)

Allow the completeness of this to soak into your soul and be ever thankful.

...but speaking the truth in love, we are to grow up in all aspects into Him, who is the head, even Christ. (Ephesians 4:15)

There is no greater love than to share love with Jesus Christ.

But do not let immorality or any impurity or greed ever be named among you, as is proper among saints; and there must not be filthiness and silly talk, or coarse jesting, which are not fitting, but rather giving of thanks. For this you know with certainty that no immoral or impure person or covetous man, who is an idolater, has an inheritance in the kingdom of Christ and God. Let no one deceive you with empty words, for because of these things the wrath of God comes upon the sons of disobedience. (Ephesians 5:3–6)

Many of the things mentioned in these verses are sins of the tongue. Do you engage in any of them? Do you identify with this? Do you need to make any changes?

And do not get drunk with wine, for that is dissipation, but be filled with the Spirit. ...always giving thanks for all things in the name of our Lord Jesus Christ to God, even the Father. (Ephesians 5:18 & 20)

Paul teaches in this epistle that all believers are sealed with the Spirit when they believe, but not all are filled, since this depends on your yielding to God's will.

For our struggle is not against flesh and blood, but against the rulers, against the powers, against the world forces of darkness, the spiritual forces of wickedness in the heavenly places. (Ephesians 6:12)

The believers' enemies are the demonic hosts of Satan always assembled for mortal combat.

The apostle Paul wrote the letter to the Philippians while either in Rome or in Caesarea where he was imprisoned. The date of the letter is also in question, but this was written, most probably, in 60-62 AD. Paul had received a gift from the church in Philippi, which he had founded on his second missionary trip. As this was the first church established in Europe, Paul had an affectionate feeling for the Philippians and this letter expressed his appreciation to the church for their thoughtfulness (*Ryrie Study Bible*).

For me to live in Christ and to die is gain. (Philippians 1:21)

Paul found all of life's meaning by living in Christ, and by dying there would be union with Him without the limitations of life.

Do nothing from selfishness or empty conceit, but with humility of mind let each of you regard of one another as more important than himself; do not merely look out for your own personal interests, but also for the interests of others. (Philippians 2:3–4)

Paul recommends humility and the right deposition that Christ Himself demonstrated.

…that at the name of Jesus every knee should bow, of those who are in heaven and on earth and under the earth, and that every tongue should confess that Jesus Christ is Lord, to the glory of God the Father. (Philippians 2:10–11)

Keep this always in mind.

More than that, I count all things to be loss in view of the surpassing value of knowing Christ Jesus my Lord, for whom I have suffered the loss of all things, and count them but rubbish in order that I may gain Christ, and may be found in Him not having a righteousness of my own derived from the Law, but that which is through faith in

Christ the righteousness which comes from God on the basis of faith. (Philippians 3:8–9)

Paul contrasts works-righteousness, which is based on the law, with faith-righteousness which is from God through Christ.

I press on toward the goal for the prize of the upward call of God in Christ Jesus. (Philippians 3:14)

We should strive, as Paul did, on our own pilgrimage through life.

Be anxious for nothing, but in everything by prayer and supplication with thanksgiving let our requests be known to God. And the peace of God, which surpasses all comprehension, shall guard your hearts and your minds in Christ Jesus. (Philippians 4:6–7)

I can do all things through Him who strengthens me. (Philippians 4:13)

We should always have faith in God and our Lord Jesus Christ as we confront our trials.

The Book of Colossians was written by Paul about 61 AD while he was imprisoned in Rome. The church of Colossae was approximately 100 miles east of Ephesus in central Turkey. This letter was to the church, as they had deviated from Paul's teachings and were involved with various heresies that were far away from the emphasis on Jesus Christ (*Ryrie Study Bible*).

And He is before all things and in Him all things hold together. He is also the head of the body, the church; and He is the beginning, the firstborn from the dead; so that He Himself might come to have first place in everything. For it was the Father's good pleasure for all the fullness to dwell in Him, and through Him to reconcile all things to

Himself, having made peace with the blood of His cross; through Him, I say, whether things on earth or things in heaven. (Colossians 1:17–20)

The full essence of deity dwells in Christ.

As you therefore have received Christ Jesus the Lord, so walk in Him. (Colossians 2:6)

The believer is to walk by faith.

See to it that no one takes you captive through philosophy and empty deception, according to the tradition of men, according to the elementary principles of the world, rather than according to Christ. For in Him all the fullness of Deity dwells in bodily form, and in Him you have been made complete, and He is the head over all rule and authority. (Colossians 2:8–10)

In Jesus Christ, deity dwells in His body. By all means avoid the deceptions so prevalent in the world today.

And so, as those who have been chosen of God, holy and beloved, put on a heart of compassion, kindness, humility, gentleness and patience; bearing with one another and forgiving each other, whoever has a complaint against anyone; just as the Lord forgave you, so also should you. And beyond, all these things put on love, which is the perfect bond of unity. And let the peace of Christ rule in your hearts, to which you were called in one body, and be thankful. Let the word of Christ richly dwell within you; with all wisdom teaching and admonishing one another with psalms and hymns and spiritual songs, singing with thankfulness in your hearts to God. And whatever you do in word or deed do all in the name of the Lord Jesus, giving thanks through Him to God the Father. (Colossians 3:12–17)

Do nothing that interferes with your loyalty to God. Our purpose is to be always loyal to Him and to His Son in thanks and praise.

The first letter to the Thessalonians was written by Paul in about 51 AD. The city of Thessalonica was the second place in Europe where the gospel was preached, and it is believed that Paul was only in this location for three weeks. Yet, he was successful in reaching a significant number of Gentiles to turn from idol worship to the teachings of Jesus. His letter expressed thankfulness for their acceptance of his preaching and also counseled them regarding issues of church life (*Ryrie Study Bible*).

For this is the will of God, your sanctification; that is that you abstain from sexual immorality; that each of you know how to possess his own vessel in sanctification and honor, not in lustful passion, like the Gentiles who do not know God. (1 Thessalonians 4:3–5)

It was the will of God that everyone maintain mastery over their own body and keep it pure.

For God has not destined us for wrath, but for obtaining salvation through our Lord Jesus Christ. (1 Thessalonians 5:9)

The believer is to be delivered from the anguish and tribulation associated with the day of the Lord.

Now may the God of peace Himself sanctify you entirely; and may your spirit and soul and body be preserved complete, without blame at the coming of Lord Jesus Christ. (1 Thessalonians 5:23–24)

A closing two-verse prayer.

The second letter to the Thessalonians was written fairly soon after the first. Word had reached Paul that there had been a misunderstanding or a misrepresentation of the time of the coming of the Lord. Needless to say, this caused confusion which Paul attempted to rectify with this letter (*Ryrie Study Bible*).

Let no one in any way deceive you, for it will not come unless the apostasy comes first, and the man of lawlessness is revealed, the son of destruction, who opposes and exalts himself above every so-called god or object of worship, so that he takes the seat in the temple of God, displaying himself as being God. (2 Thessalonians 2:3-4)

Apostasy is a climactic revolt against God and the lawless one is an individual of the future who will come during the tribulation days. However, the Thessalonians thought that time was happening in their presence, which Paul attempted to clarify.

Finally brethren, pray for us that the word of the Lord may spread rapidly and be glorified, just as it did also with you; and that we may be delivered from perverse and evil men; for not all have faith. But the Lord is faithful and He will strengthen and protect you from the evil one. (2 Thessalonians 3:1-3)

A comparison between those who believed and those of wickedness.

For even while we were with you, we used to give you this order; if anyone will not work, neither let him eat. For we hear that some among you are leading an undisciplined life, doing no work at all, but acting like busybodies. Now such persons we command and exhort in the Lord Jesus Christ to work in quiet fashion and eat their own bread. (2 Thessalonians 3: 10-12)

Some of their group thought that the end of the world was near and, so, they no longer needed to work. However, Paul was explicit in clearing away that misconception. I believe these verses have relevance in our society today. What about you?

The first letter to Timothy was written by Paul while he was in Macedonia in approximately 63 AD. Timothy was associated with Paul since Paul's second missionary trip. Timothy had been left in charge at

Ephesus and this letter was for his guidance while Paul journeyed on. It emphasized the law, prayer, and the last days, as well as money, its uses and pitfalls. This letter also dealt with the appearances of individuals and the care of widows. This letter as well as 2 Timothy and Titus are referred to as the pastoral letters (*Ryrie Study Bible*).

But the goal of our instruction is love from a pure heart and a good conscience and a sincere faith. (1 Timothy 1:5)

This goal is most certainly one that should be attained.

...realizing the fact that law is not made for a righteous man, but for those who are lawless and rebellious, for the ungodly and sinners, for the unholy and profane, for those who kill their fathers or mothers, for murderers, and immoral men and homosexuals, and kidnapers, and liars and perjurers, and whatever else is contrary to sound teaching. (1 Timothy 1:9–10)

Sound teaching is in reference to healthy or wholesome doctrine.

For there is one God and one mediator also between God and men, the man Christ Jesus, who gave Himself as a ransom for all, the testimony borne at the proper time. (1 Timothy 2:5–6)

Jesus suffered on the cross for mankind.

But the Spirit explicitly says that in later times some will fall away from the faith, paying attention to deceitful spirits and doctrines of demons, men who forbid marriage, abstaining from food, which God has created to be gratefully shared in by those who truly believe and know the truth. For everything created by God is good and nothing is to be rejected, if it is received with gratitude. (1 Timothy 4:1 & 3–4)

Christians should live affirmatively, neither renouncing the world for a life of self-denial nor plunging into indulgence.

But have nothing to do with worldly fables fit only for old women. On the other hand discipline yourself for the purpose of godliness; for bodily discipline is for only of little profit, but godliness is profitable for all things, since it holds promise of the present life and also the life to come. (1 Timothy 4:7-8)

The benefits of bodily discipline are limited but the benefits of godliness are extensive and permanent.

If anyone advocates a different doctrine, and does not agree with sound words, those of our Lord Jesus Christ, and with doctrine conforming to godliness, he is conceited and understands nothing; but he has a morbid interest in controversial questions and disputes about words, out of which arise envy, strife, abusive language, evil suspicions. (1 Timothy 6:3-4)

Heretical teachers were distorting the truth of Christ. The same situation is present today as well.

But those who want to get rich fall into temptation and a snare and many foolish and harmful desires which plunge men into ruin and destruction. For the love of money is the root of all sorts of evil, and some by longing for it have wandered away from the faith, and pierced themselves with many a pang. But flee from these things, you man of God, and pursue righteousness, godliness, faith, love, perseverance and gentleness. Fight the good fight of faith, take hold of the eternal life to which you were called, and you made the good confession in the presence of many witnesses. (1 Timothy 6:9-12)

The pursuit of money must be measured. Restraint should be exercised. Also, consider the virtues listed in these verses.

O Timothy, guard what has been entrusted to you, avoiding worldly and empty chatter and the opposing arguments of what is falsely called "knowledge"– which some have professed and gone astray from the faith. Grace be with you. (1 Timothy 6:20–21)

Keep your faith regardless of the circumstances surrounding you.

The Second Letter of Timothy was written about 66 AD while Paul was imprisoned in Rome. Paul was keenly aware of his fate and was sending this very personal letter to his young contemporary to encourage and strengthen him (*Ryrie Study Bible*).

Retain the standard of sound words which you have heard from me, in the faith and love which we are in Christ Jesus. (2 Timothy 1:13)

Never lose your faith regardless of the adversity that you face.

Suffer hardship with me as a good soldier of Christ Jesus. No soldier in active service entangles himself in the affairs of everyday life, so that he may please the one who enlisted him as a soldier. (2 Timothy 2:3–4)

Make it a priority on your calling and be dedicated to it. By so doing, you are fulfilling your commitment to Christ.

It is a trustworthy statement: for if we died with Him, we shall also reign with Him; If we endure, we shall also reign with Him; if we deny Him, He will also deny us; If we are faithless, He remains faithful for He cannot deny Himself. (2 Timothy 2:11–13)

May the eyes of your soul be in sync with the eyes of God. When they are in focus, worry disappears as God is with us.

All Scripture is inspired by God and profitable for teaching, for reproof, for correction, for training in righteousness. (2 Timothy 3:16)

The Bible came from God through the men who wrote it.

For the time will come when they will not endure sound doctrine; but wanting to have their ears tickled, they will accumulate for themselves teachers in accordance with their desires and will turn away their ears from the truth and will turn aside to myths. But you, be sober in all things, endure hardship, do the work of an evangelist, fulfill your ministry. (2 Timothy 4:3–5)

Men, then and now, have turned away from the truth to pursue things of every nature. Never allow your faith and trust in Jesus Christ to drift or to be diminished.

I have fought the good fight, I have finished the course, I have kept the faith; in the future there is laid up for me a crown of righteousness, which the Lord, the righteous Judge, will award to me on that day; and not only to me, but also to all who have loved His appearing. (2 Timothy 4:7–8)

Paul recognizes that his time is near. Not too long after this, Paul was beheaded by the proclamation of the Emperor Nero. Paul, a man for all seasons, passes to his Lord.

When you consider that Paul wrote this very meaningful and thoughtful letter from a dungeon while awaiting his execution, the clarity and heart expressed is astounding

The Letter to Titus was written by Paul to his associate Titus, a gentile by birth, who had been left in charge of the church on the island of Crete about 65 AD. He sends forward his guidance and encouragement to Titus in this letter (*Ryrie Study Bible*).

For the overseer must be above reproach as God's steward, not self-willed, not quick tempered, not addicted to wine, not pugnacious, not fond of sordid gain, but hospitable, loving what is good, sensible, just, devout, self controlled. (Titus 1:7–8)

In the first century AD, the vices noted above were quite common as they are today. So, this is sound advice for all times.

He saved us not on the basis of our deeds which we have done in righteousness, but according to His mercy, by the washing of regeneration and renewing of the Holy Spirit. ...that being justified by His grace we might be made heirs according to the hope of eternal life. (Titus 3:5 & 7)

Personal salvation is not achieved by good deeds. Salvation is by God's grace and not a reward for man's worthwhile acts.

But shun foolish controversies and genealogies and strife and disputes about the Law; for they are unprofitable and worthless. Reject a factious man after a first and second warning knowing that such a man is perverted and is sinning, being self-condemned. (Titus 3:9–11)

An individual who chooses both willfully and primarily for themselves is to be avoided.

The letter of Paul to Philemon, the last of Paul's letters, was written in 61 AD and was also written from his imprisonment in Rome. It was written to Philemon, who was a slaveholder in Colossae, asking him to accept a former slave. Onesimus, the former slave, was a convert of Paul's in Rome and was going back to his former owner and looked for release and redemption from that former owner (*Ryrie Study Bible*).

...and I pray that the fellowship of your faith may become effective through the knowledge of every good thing which is in you for Christ's sake. (Philemon 1:6)

Paul praises the change in Onesimus and hopes this will be favorably received by Philemon.

"I, Paul, am writing this with my own hand. I will repay it (lest I should mention to you that you owe to me even your own self as well.") (Philemon 1:19)

Philemon was also a convert of Paul's and he is asking for Philemon to receive his former slave as a free man.

The Letter to the Hebrews was written in 64-66 AD by an individual unknown to anyone but God. It was sent to Jews believed to be in Italy and was meant for these converts to readily accept the superiority of Jesus Christ and thus of Christianity (*Ryrie Study Bible*).

God, after He spoke long ago to the fathers in the prophets in many portions and in many ways, in these last days has spoken to us in His Son, whom He appointed heir of all things, through whom also He made the world. (Hebrews 1:1–2)

We should pay attention to God's will through our Lord Jesus Christ in all thoughts and plans that we initiate.

But of the Son He says, "Thy throne O God is forever and ever, and the righteous scepter is the scepter of His kingdom. Thou hast loved righteousness and hated lawlessness. Therefore God, Thy God, hath anointed Thee with oil of gladness above Thy companions. (Hebrews 1:8–9)

By virtue of his understanding, the writer of Hebrews visualizes the recognition of Jesus above all others.

For every house is built by someone, but the builder of all things is God. (Hebrews 3:4)

The buildings of man are temporary but God, the builder of all things, builds with permanence.

For the word of God is living and active and sharper than any two edged sword, and is piercing as far as the division of and soul and spirit, of both joints and marrow, and able to judge the thoughts and intentions of the heart. (Hebrews 4:12)

Only the word of God has the power to reach the inmost parts of one's personality and be able to judge their innermost thoughts.

...how much more the blood of Christ, who through the eternal Spirit offered Himself without blemish to God, cleanse your conscience from dead works to serve the living God? (Hebrews 9:14)

What a significant measure!

Otherwise, He would have needed to suffer since the foundation of the world; but now once at the consummation of the ages He has been manifested to put away sin by the sacrifice of Himself. And inasmuch as it is appointed for men to die once after this comes judgment, so Christ also, having been offered once to bear the sins of many, shall appear a second time for salvation without reference to sin, to those who eagerly await Him. (Hebrews 9:26-28)

In the first coming of Christ, he dealt with sin once for all. In His second coming, He will take redeemed sinners to Himself in the consummation of their salvation.

How much severer punishment do you think he will deserve, who has trampled under foot the Son of God, and has regarded as unclean the blood of the covenant by which he was sanctified, and has insulted the Spirit of grace? (Hebrews 10:29)

The three indictments specified in this verse describe the enormity of the sin of unbelief.

Now faith is the assurance of things hoped for, the conviction of things not seen. ...By faith we understand that the worlds were prepared by the word of God, so that what is seen was not made out of things which are visible. (Hebrews 11:1 & 3)

Faith gives reality and proof of things unseen treating them as if they were already objects of sight rather than of hope.

Therefore, since we have so great a cloud of witnesses surrounding us, let us also lay aside every encumbrance and the sin which so easily entangles us, and let us run with endurance the race that is set before us, fixing our eyes on Jesus the author and perfecter of faith, who for the joy set before Him endured the cross, despising the shame, and has sat down at the right hand of the throne of God. (Hebrews 12:1–2)

It is critical to keep focused on Jesus and put aside all distractions.

Jesus Christ is the same yesterday and today, yes and forever. (Hebrews 13:8)

What a comforting thought to consider.

The book of James is believed to be written by Jesus' half-brother, James, in the period of 45 to 49 AD. James became the primary leader of the church in Jerusalem. This letter by James was written to the members of the twelve tribes who believed in Jesus but were scattered throughout other parts of the world. The letter's key subjects include the measure of faith and works as well as the difficulty some individuals have with the power of the tongue (*Ryrie Study Bible*).

There is a significant amount of sound learning and principles in this brief but very meaningful letter. I encourage you to dig in and read this very intently.

Consider it all joy my brethren, when you encounter various trials, knowing that the testing of your faith produces endurance. (James 1:2–3)

Have you ever looked at a trial you are facing in a joyful manner? I doubt it but I promise you that if you try this approach you will definitely find your strength and faith will increase. Accept this challenge with determination.

But if any of you lacks wisdom, let him ask of God, who gives to all men generously and without reproach, and it will be given to him. (James 1:5)

Think of the opportunity being offered here. The magnitude of it is enormous. I encourage you to humble yourself to ask Him for guidance in any trial you face.

Let no one say when he is tempted, "I am being tempted by God," for God cannot be tempted by evil, and He Himself does not tempt anyone. But each one is tempted when he is carried away and enticed by his own lust. Then when lust has conceived it gives birth to sin, and when sin is accomplished, it brings forth death. Do not be deceived, my beloved brethren. (James 1:13–16)

To be tempted is to be tested and when this occurs in your life take a moment to reflect and ask for His help to overcome the temptation.

Every good thing bestowed and every perfect gift is from above, coming down from the Father of lights, with whom there is no variation or shifting shadow. (James 1:17)

The point is clear: all good things come from above.

This you know, my beloved brethren. But let everyone be quick to hear, slow to speak, and slow to anger; Therefore putting aside all filthiness and all the remains of wickedness, in humility receive the word implanted, which is able to save your souls. But prove yourselves doers of the word and not merely hearers who delude themselves. (James 1:19, 21–22)

Sound advice to be adhered to.

If anyone thinks himself to be religious, and yet does not bridle his tongue but deceives his own heart, this man's religion is worthless. (James 1:26)

Vanity is on full display here.

My brethren, do not hold your faith in our glorious Lord Jesus Christ with an attitude of personal favoritism. (James 2:1)

Jesus shows no favoritism to people of wealth or position.

For judgment will be merciless to one who has shown no mercy, mercy triumphs over judgment. (James 2:13)

Recognize this fact and act accordingly.

What use is it, my brethren, if a man says he has faith, but he has no works? Can that faith save him? (James 2:14)

Here, James is not saying that we are saved by works but that a faith without good works is a dead faith.

So also the tongue is a small part of the body, and yet it boasts of great things. Behold now how great a forest is set aflame by such a small fire. (James 3:5)

It is very important to control the tongue as it can cause enormous problems.

For where jealously and selfish ambition exist, there is disorder and every evil thing. But wisdom from above is first pure, then peaceable, gentle, reasonable, full of mercy, and good fruits, unwavering without hypocrisy. (James 3:16–17)

Utilize godly wisdom and not selfish ambition and your pathway will avoid many bumps in the road.

What is the source of quarrels and conflicts among you? Is not the source your pleasures that wage war in your members? You lust and you do not have; so you commit murder. And you are envious and cannot obtain; so you fight and quarrel. You do not have because you do not ask. You ask and you do not receive, because you ask with wrong motives, so that you may spend it on your pleasures. You adulteresses, do you not know the friendship with the world is hostility toward God? Therefore whoever wishes to be a friend of the world makes himself an enemy of God. Or do you not think that the Scripture speaks to no purpose; "He jealously desires the Spirit which He has made to dwell in us?" (James 4:1–5)

All too often, lust is the cause of many poor outcomes and we should turn away from the things of the world and towards God.

Submit therefore to God. Resist the devil and he will flee from you. Draw near to God and He will draw near to you. Cleanse your hands, you sinners; purify your hearts, you double minded. Humble yourselves in the presence of the Lord and He will exalt you. (James 4:7, 8 & 10)

You cannot be half-hearted in your commitment to God. As I stated earlier, you cannot walk with God and run with the devil. You may try to, but it will never work.

Yet, you do not know what life will be like tomorrow. You are just a vapor that appears for a little while and then vanishes away. Instead, you ought to say, if the Lord wills, we shall live and also do this or that. But as it is, you boast in your arrogance; all such boasting is evil. Therefore, to one who knows the right thing to do, and does not do it, to him it is sin. (James 4:14–17)

The folly of forgetting God in your business or personal life is another manifestation of worldliness.

But above all my brethren, do not swear, either by heaven or by earth or with any other oath; but let your yes, be yes and your no, no; so that you may not fall under judgment. (James 5:12)

Flippant, obscene, or blasphemous oaths are all forbidden.

…Let him know that he who turns a sinner from the error of his way will save his soul from death, and will cover a multitude of sins. (James 5:20)

James is referring to Christians who turn someone to Christ and will, by their efforts, cover a significant amount of their own sins and receive eternal life.

The first epistle of Peter was written by the apostle in about 63-65 AD. The theme of the letter is expressed in 5:12 where Peter refers to "the true grace of God" in the life of a believer. This letter, written in Rome, was addressed to believers who were scattered throughout what was then the Roman Empire (*Ryrie Study Bible)*.

Blessed be the God and Father of our Lord Jesus Christ, who according to His great mercy has caused us to be born again to a living hope through the resurrection of Jesus Christ from the dead. (1 Peter 1:3)

Be happy and content that God has created you and be ever willing and thankful to do His will. How much do you think you do on your own without the help and guidance of God? You may be successful, for a while but in time you will probably fail and, perhaps, fail very badly. I know this all too well as that was my pattern; to work hard, be consistent, and be innovative…and, still, it did not come out right. I encourage you to learn from my errors in judgment.

…that the proof of your faith, being more precious than gold which is perishable, even though tested by fire, may be found to result in praise and glory and honor at the revelation of Jesus Christ; and though you have not seen Him, you love Him and although you do not see now, but believe in Him, you greatly rejoice with joy inexpressible and full of glory, obtaining as the outcome of your faith the salvation of your souls. (1 Peter 1:7–9)

Faith in Christ is priceless no matter the extent of pressures or persecutions you face or endure.

As obedient children do not be conformed to the former lusts which were yours in ignorance, but like the Holy One who called you, be holy yourselves also in your behavior; because it is written "You shall be holy for I am holy." (1 Peter 1:14–16)

Be obedient to God and avoid impulsive behavior and poor judgment.

…and while being reviled, He did not revile in return; while suffering He uttered no threats but kept entrusting Himself to Him who judges righteously. (1 Peter 2:23)

The death of the sinless Jesus was the perfect substitute for the sins of mankind. Jesus offers you life. Are you willing to accept it? If not, why not?

JOHN H. (JAN) DOLCATER, JR.

To sum up, let all be harmonious, sympathetic, brotherly kindhearted and humble in spirit; not returning evil for evil or insult for insult, but giving a blessing instead; for you were called for the very purpose that you might inherit a blessing. For, let him who means to love life and see good days, restrain the tongue from evil and his lips from speaking guile. And let him turn away from evil and do good; Let him seek peace and pursue it. For the eyes of the Lord are upon the righteous, and his ears attend to their prayer. But the face of the Lord is against those who do evil. (1 Peter 3:8–12)

These words expressed above are an echo of the words of Christ.

But even if you should suffer for the sake of righteousness, you are blessed. And do not fear their intimidation, and do not be troubled, but sanctify Christ as Lord in your hearts, always being ready to make a defense to everyone who asks you to give an account for the hope that is in you, yet with gentleness and reverence. (1 Peter 3:14–15)

Whatever the challenges you face, always show reverence to Christ with peace in your heart.

Therefore since Christ has suffered in the flesh, arm yourselves with the same purpose, because he who has suffered in the flesh has ceased from sin, so as to live the rest of time in the flesh no longer for lusts of men, but for the will of God. (1 Peter 4:1–2)

As Christ suffered in the flesh, take on for yourselves the same attitude of living your life free of sin. Remember that God's way is best.

The letter of 2 Peter was written about 66 AD not long before his martyrdom in Rome, where he was crucified upside down. This letter is a reminder of the truth of Christianity as it was being opposed by heresies that were popping up throughout the areas where the Christian philosophy had flourished (*Ryrie Study Bible*).

Grace and peace be multiplied to you in the knowledge of God and of Jesus our Lord. (2 Peter 1:2)

It is hard to comprehend how, without any significant mode of transportation or communication, the Word of God was spread throughout the majority of the known world by men who had so little formal training prior to becoming followers of Jesus Christ.

Now for this very reason also, applying all diligence in your faith, supply moral excellence, and in your moral excellence, knowledge and in your knowledge, self-control, and in your self-control, perseverance and in your perseverance, godliness, and in your godliness, brotherly kindness, and love. For if these qualities are yours and are increasing they render you neither useless nor unfruitful in the true knowledge of our Lord Jesus Christ. For he who lacks these qualities is blind or short sighted, having forgotten his purification from his former sins. Therefore, brethren be all the more diligent to make certain about His calling and choosing you, for as long as you practice these things, you will never stumble; for in this way the entrance into the eternal kingdom of our Lord and Savior Jesus Christ will be abundantly supplied to you. (2 Peter 1:5–11)

Please pay attention to this wisdom as it clearly and emphatically shows you the road map of the highway to heaven. What is your opinion of the road map that Peter has laid out? Does it make sense to you? Try it and discover a life changing experience.

But know this first of all that no prophecy of Scripture is a matter of one's own interpretation, for no prophecy was ever made by an act of human will, but men moved by the Holy Spirit spoke from God. (2 Peter 1:20–21)

When someone implies that the Bible is out of date, I ask that you ponder the two passages of the letter of 2 Peter that you have just read.

Think on it. All Scripture is inspired by God. Many centuries ago, Peter plainly but eloquently described the pathway that each of us needs to follow if we truly love our Lord Jesus Christ.

...then the Lord knows how to rescue the godly from temptation, and to keep the unrighteous under punishment for the day of judgment, and especially those who indulge the flesh and its corrupt desires and despise authority. Daring, self-willed, they do not tremble when they revile angelic majesties. (2 Peter 2:9–10)

Be on notice as these verses lay reality on the line for you to either accept or ignore. Pay attention because the consequences of not doing so are an unpleasant fact waiting for you around the corner.

For if after they have escaped the defilements of the world by the knowledge of the Lord and Savior Jesus Christ, they are then entangled in them and are overcome, the last state has become worse for them than the first. It has happened to them according to the true proverb. "A dog returns to its own vomit" and "a sow after washing returns to wallowing in the mire." (2 Peter 2:20 & 22)

This is a graphic description of a person returning to sin after experiencing Christ and then regressing even more deeply than before. Commitment to Christ must be a full and unwavering one or the result is failure and a return to a sinful fate.

But do not let this one fact escape your notice, beloved, that with the Lord one day is as a thousand years and a thousand years as one day. The Lord is not slow about His promise, as some people count slowness, but is patient toward you, not wishing any to perish but for all to come to repentance. (2 Peter 3:8–9)

Christ's return is not happening as quickly as some would like but this leaves more time for more people to repent. But will they?

Therefore, ...beloved, since you look for these things, be diligent to be found by Him in peace, spotless and blameless, and regard the patience of the Lord to be salvation; just as our beloved brother Paul, according to the wisdom given him, wrote to you. (2 Peter 3:14-15)

Bear in mind that on the day of the return of the Lord, the time for deciding about your salvation is in the past. Delay in your decision will have very negative consequences.

You therefore, beloved, knowing this beforehand, be on your guard lest, being carried away by the error of unprincipled men, you fall from your own steadfastness, but grow in the grace and knowledge of our Lord and Savior Jesus Christ. To Him be the glory, both now and to the day of eternity. Amen. (2 Peter 3:17-18)

All of us have free will to make choices. It is my prayer for each of you that you choose wisely and with your eyes on Our Lord and Savior, Jesus Christ.

The letter of first John was written around 90 AD while the apostle was in Ephesus. With this letter, he was appealing to the churches to recognize that they should not stray into other practices or teachings that were in conflict with the teaching of Jesus Christ (*Ryrie Study Bible*).

And this is the message we have heard from Him, and announce to you, that God is light and in Him there is no darkness at all. If we say that we have fellowship with Him and yet walk in darkness, we lie and do not practice the truth; but if we walk in the light as He Himself is in the light, we have fellowship with one another, and the blood of Jesus His Son cleanses us from all sin. (1 John 1:5-7)

To walk in the light is to live in obedience of God's commandments.

If we say we have no sin, we are deceiving ourselves, and the truth is not in us. If we confess our sins, He is faithful and righteous to forgive us our sins and to cleanse us from all unrighteousness. (1 John 1:8–9)

This is a reference to the indwelling principle of sin rather than the act of sin. Never hesitate to confess your sin to Jesus and ask for forgiveness.

My little children, I am writing these things to you that you may not sin. And if anyone sins, we have an Advocate with the Father, Jesus Christ the righteous, and He Himself is the propitiation for our sins and not for ours only, but also for those of the whole world. (1 John 2:1–2)

He is our helper by offering to satisfy our confession.

Do not love the world, nor the things in the world. If anyone loves the world, the love of the Father is not in him. For all that is in the world, the lust of the flesh and the lust of the eyes and the boastful pride of life is not from the Father, but is from the world. And the world is passing away, and also its lusts, but the one who does the will of God abides forever. (1 John 2:15–17)

The love of the world revolves around the things of Satan and not of God. Two of these things are vain glory and the boasting about possessions.

Who is the liar but the one who denies that Jesus is the Christ? This is the antichrist, the one who denies the Father and the Son. Whoever denies the Son does not have the Father; the one who confesses the Son has the Father also. (1 John 2:22–23)

The supreme liar is the one who denies that Jesus Christ came in the flesh and that He was both man and God.

No one who abides in Him, sins; no one who sins has seen Him or knows Him. Little children, let no one deceive you, the one who practices righteousness is righteous, just as He is righteous; the one who practices sin is of the devil; for the devil has sinned from the beginning. The Son of God appeared for this purpose, that He may destroy the works of the devil. No one who is born of God practices sin, because His seed abides in him; and he cannot sin, because he is born of God. By this the children of God and the children of the devil are obvious; anyone who does not practice righteousness is not of God, nor the one who does not love his brother. (1 John 3:6–10)

Habitual actions indicate one's character. The nature of the relationship of God and His Son prevent the Christian from habitual sinning.

We are from God; he who knows God listens to us; he who is not from God does not listen to us. By this we know the spirit of truth and the spirit of error. Beloved, let us love one another, for love is from God; and everyone who loves is born of God and knows God. (1 John 4:6–7)

This is one of the greatest passages declaring God is love.

No one has beheld God at any time; if we love one another God abides in us, and His love is perfected in us. (1 John 4:12)

Think on this; love is God's supreme quality. God says He is known only by those who live in love.

Whoever confesses that Jesus is the Son of God, God abides in him and he in God. (1 John 4:15)

Thank You, Lord, Amen.

Words from the booklet *Our Daily Bread* are appropriate here. "Jesus Christ is not valued at all until He is valued above all."

There is no fear in love; but perfect love casts out fear, because fear involves punishment and the one who fears is not perfected in love. (1 John 4:18)

How does this passage make you feel? Think; do not neglect this opportunity to commit your life to Christ.

The one who believes in the Son of God has the witness in himself; the one who does not believe God has made Him a liar, because he has not believed in the witness that God has borne concerning His Son. And the witness in this that God has given us eternal life and this life is in His Son. He who has the Son has the life; but who does not have the Son of God does not have the life. (1 John 5:10–12)

A very challenging thought is brought forward here. Where do you stand regarding this? Your response is exceptionally important so think this through with care.

And this is the confidence which we have before Him, that if we ask anything according to His will, He hears us. And if we know that He hears us in whatever we ask, we know that we have the requests which we have asked from Him. (1 John 5:14–15)

Never forget that His will is always best for us.

The second letter of John was also written approximately in 90 AD from Ephesus to a church of unknown origin in regard to walking in the commandments of God (*Ryrie Study Bible*).

Grace, mercy and peace will be with us, from God the Father and from Jesus Christ the Son of the Father, in truth and love. (2 John 1:3)

I pray that we all will share in these blessings.

Anyone who goes too far and does not abide in the teachings of Christ, does not have God; the one who abides in the teaching, he has both the Father and the Son. (2 John 1:9)

This passage really gets down to the nitty-gritty. No halfway response will cut it.

The third letter of John was also written from Ephesus about 90 AD. It was written to an individual called Gaius regarding a disagreement between individuals in as to the practice of their faith (*Ryrie Study Bible*).

Beloved, do not imitate what is evil, but what is good. The one who does what is good is of God; the one who does what is evil has not seen God. (3 John 1:11)

Sound advice to follow at all times. Do you agree? I hope so.

The letter of Jude was written somewhere between 70 and 80 AD by another half-brother of Jesus. I find it interesting that two of Jesus' half-brothers, sons of Joseph and Mary, were very strongly influenced to follow Jesus and His teaching. This letter dealt with the false teachers who had arisen in the churches and were promoting immoral, covetous and divisive reactions (*Ryrie Study Bible*).

For certain persons have crept in unnoticed, those who were long beforehand marked out for this condemnation, ungodly persons who turn the grace of our God into licentiousness and deny our only Master and Lord Jesus Christ. (Jude 1:4)

To deny Jesus as Lord is to disbelieve the most basic Christian tenet.

Just as Sodom and Gomorrah and the cities around them, since they in the same way as these indulged in gross immorality and went after strange flesh, are exhibited as an example, in undergoing the punishment of eternal fire. (Jude 1:7)

God dealt with the behavior of these two communities by destroying them.

……..in the last time there shall be mockers, following after their own ungodly lusts. These are the one who cause divisions, worldly-minded devoid of the Spirit. (Jude 1:18–19)

The worldly-minded were false teachers that taught heresy. Is it possible to believe that similar false teachers are also among us today? Not sure how you feel about this, but I believe the probability is real.

…keep yourselves in the love of God, waiting anxiously for the mercy of our Lord Jesus Christ to eternal life. (Jude 1:21)

I encourage you to open your heart and allow the love of God and the mercy of Jesus Christ to surround you.

Now to Him who is able to keep you from stumbling, and to make you stand in the presence of His glory blameless with great joy, to the only God our Savior, through Jesus Christ our Lord, be glory majesty dominion and authority, before all time and now and forever. Amen. (Jude 1:24–25)

This is one of the greatest benedictions in the New Testament.

The Revelation to John, the beloved disciple, came from Jesus Christ while John was imprisoned on the isle of Patmos. It was written at some point during the 80's to 90's AD. Christians were being persecuted by Rome from the time of Nero to Diocletian. They were being encouraged to recant their faith in Jesus and accept the cult of emperor worship.

This revelation was from Jesus and He is the center of this entire book. It begins with John's vision of the risen Christ and His risen glory in chapter one. In chapters two and three, Jesus directs His churches on earth, and, then, in the next two chapters, He is the risen Lamb to whom all worship is directed. Chapters 6-19 describe the judgments of the coming seven-year period of the rapture, the tribulation on this earth, and the display of the wrath of the Lamb. This is particularly the case in chapters 16-17. Christ's return to earth is emphasized in chapter 19:11-21. Christ's millennial reign is described in chapter 20. In conclusion, the description of the new heaven and the new earth are shown in the final chapters 21-22 (*Ryrie Study Bible*).

There is much in this book of the Bible that is difficult to comprehend, as it is apocalyptic. I encourage you, as you read any part of this, to exercise thoughtful and prayerful care to gain the most meaning for yourself, as somewhere in the future of the earth the events described in this chapter will become reality. Make a concerted effort to read each chapter and not just the passages and thoughts that I have noted and emphasized. My goal is to describe, as best as possible, what this means to me, a committed lay person, but there is much that is beyond my ability to analyze. For that reason, I encourage you to speak to your preacher or priest or a learned individual with a theological background regarding the parts that you find difficult. Let us now explore what lies ahead.

Blessed is he who reads and those who hear the words of prophecy, and heed the things that are written in it; for the time is near. (Revelation 1:3)

This is the first of seven beatitudes in Revelation. The number 7 appears fifty-four times in this book, which is more than any other number mentioned in the Bible. There is no question that this number has significance, but it is not explainable at this time.

I am the Alpha and the Omega, says the Lord God, who is and who was, and who is to come, the Almighty. (Revelation 1:8)

Alpha and Omega are the first and last letters of the Greek alphabet indicating that the Lord God is the beginning and end of all things.

And when I saw Him, I fell at His feet as a dead man. And He laid His right hand on me, saying, "Do not be afraid, I am the first and the last, and the living One; and I was dead and behold, I am alive forevermore, and I have the keys of death and of Hades." (Revelation 1:17-18)

God is called the Alpha and the Omega. Here Christ gives Himself a similar title. The "keys" denote the authority of Christ over physical death and Hades, the place that temporarily holds the innermost part of the unbeliever between death and the ultimate casting into the lake of fire (Revelation 20:14).

The vision of Jesus to the churches is the next area to explore.

I know your deeds and your toil and perseverance, and that you cannot endure evil men, and you put to the test those who call themselves apostles, and they are not, and you found them to be false; and you have perseverance and have endured for My name's sake, and have not grown weary. But I have this against you, that you have left your first love. Remember therefore from where you have fallen, and repent and do the deeds you did at first; or else I am coming to you, and will remove your lampstand out of its place – unless you repent. (Revelation 2:2–5)

This was the content of His message to the church of Ephesus. He would remove the usefulness of that church, due to their straying from their original commitment, unless they repented and again followed Jesus as they had done previously.

I know your tribulation and your poverty (that you are rich), and the blasphemy by those who say they are Jews and are not, but are a synagogue of Satan. Do not fear what you are about to suffer. Behold, the devil is about to cast some of you into prison, that you may be tested, and you will have tribulation ten days. Be faithful until death, and I will give you the crown of life. (Revelation 2:9-10)

This was the content of His message to the church of Smyrna; that they would have ten days of a trial of intense persecution and that they should be faithful unto death. The reward for those who were faithful was to be spared from the eternal separation from God in the lake of fire.

I know where you dwell, where Satan's throne is, and you hold fast my name and you did not deny My faith, even in the days of Antipas. My witness, My faithful one, who was killed among you, where Satan dwells. But I have a few things against you, because you have there some who hold the teaching of Balaam, who keeps teaching Balak to put a stumbling block before the sons of Israel, to eat things sacrificed to idols, and to commit acts of immorality. Thus you also have some who in the same way hold the teaching of the Nicolaitans. ...He that has an ear let him hear what the Spirit says to the churches. To him who overcomes, to him I will give some of the hidden manna, and I will give him a white stone, and a new name written on the stone which no one knows but he who receives it. (Revelation 2:13-15 & 17)

This was the content of His message to the church of Pergamum. It is apparent that this church was located in the midst of a sinful community. The manna referred to is the sufficiency of Christ for the believers' needs. The white stone indicates the believer is assured of his acquittal before God by his repentance.

I know your deeds and your love and faith and service and perseverance, and that your deeds of late are greater than at first. But I have this against you, that you will tolerate the woman Jezebel, who calls herself a prophetess, and she teaches and leads my bond-servants astray, so that they commit acts of immorality and eat things sacrificed to idols. And I gave her time to repent; and she does not want to repent of her immorality. ...Nevertheless, what you have, hold fast until I come. And he who overcomes, and he who keeps My deeds until the end, to him I will give authority over the nations; ...and I will give him the morning star. (Revelation 2:19–21 & 25–26 &28)

This was the content of His message to the church of Thyatira; to not be led astray by anyone teaching a false doctrine. The morning star referred to is either Christ, Himself, or the immortal life that one will receive from Christ. No greater gift could anyone hope to receive.

And to the angel of the church in Sardis: He who has the seven Spirits of God and the seven stars says this; I know your deeds, that you have a name that you are alive but you are dead. Wake up, and strengthen the things that remain, which were about to die; for I have not found your deeds completed in the sight of My God. Remember therefore, what you have received and heard; and keep it, and repent. If therefore you will not wake up, I will come like a thief, and you will not know at what hour I will come upon you. He who overcomes shall thus be clothed in white garments; and I will not erase his name from the book of life, and I will confess his name before My Father, and before His angels. (Revelation 3:1–3 & 5)

This was the content of His message to the church of Sardis; that their church had become dead in its worship and that it needed to repent or there would be the serious consequence of their removal from the book of life.

I know your deeds. Behold, I have before you an open door which no one can shut, because you have a little power, and have kept My word, and have not denied My name. Behold, I will cause those of the synagogue of Satan, who say they are Jews, and are not, but lie – behold I will make them come and bow down at your feet, and to know that I loved you. …He who overcomes, I will make him a pillar of the temple of My God and he will not go out from it anymore; and I will write upon him the name of My God, and the name of the city of My God, the new Jerusalem, which comes down out of heaven from My God, and My new name. (Revelation 3:8-9 & 12)

This was the content of His message to the church in Philadelphia; that their believers would be delivered from the tribulation that is to come. It appears this church had been more successful in maintaining the Christian life than the other churches. The reference to the pillars was to let the believers know that they would be honored in the New Jerusalem. The people of faith need to avoid being tempted.

I know your deeds that you are neither cold nor hot. I would that you were cold or hot. So because you are lukewarm, and neither hot nor cold, I will spit you out of My mouth. Because you say I am rich and have become wealthy and have need of nothing, and you do not know that you are wretched and miserable and poor and blind and naked. … Those whom I love, I reprove and discipline; be zealous therefore, and repent. Behold, I stand at the door and knock; if anyone hears My voice and opens the door, I will come into him, and will dine with him, and he with Me. He who overcomes, I will grant to him to sit down with Me on My throne as I also overcame and sat down with My Father on His throne. (Revelation 3:15-17 & 19-21)

This was the content of His message to the church in Laodicea; that it appeared that they were simply content with their prosperity and were not sharing this with others. If they remained with that attitude, He would throw them out from His presence. However, they were offered an opportunity to receive Him into their presence in a rightful manner and, by so doing, could have a positive reception.

All seven of these churches were located in an area to the east of Ephesus in what is now Turkey. It is apparent that they had slipped into half-hearted or misguided habits that Jesus could not accept, and it was His intent to get them to shape up or face the consequences.

My personal belief is that the weaknesses, perversions, and difficulties described here regarding the churches in this vision could well apply to churches throughout the world today. It is reasonable to recognize that far too many have drifted away from the direction that Jesus would prefer for us. What is your opinion?

The description of Jesus's throne in heaven and all of the circumstance around it covered in chapters four and five should be read carefully. The judgments of the seals and the trumpets in chapters six through twelve are most graphic and are also frightening for all to consider.

All of these elements of the vision of Jesus are both profound and are certain to come to pass at some point in the life of humanity. However, no one in humankind, currently or from the past, knows the timetable for these occurrences. Only God knows the timing. However, we're all on notice that all of this lies in the future of the world as we know it. As we proceed in our search in this book, the revelation revealed to us should always bring questions and concerns to the heart of a child of God.

In chapter 13, the antichrist, who receives his power from Satan, the beast, and the false prophet are a trio who will lead a large percentage of the population astray to worship the antichrist. During the last 42 months, or 3 ½ years, of the tribulation the power of the antichrist is almost unrestrained. The saints of God, who have endured, heard from heaven the second beatitude in chapter 14:13:

"Blessed are the dead who die in the Lord from now on!" "Yes," says the Spirit, "that they may rest from their labors, for their deeds follow with them."

As we go forward through chapters 15 through 17, the devastation and destruction that is experienced is truly beyond our intellects to absorb. In the midst of this is the third beatitude in chapter 16:15:

"Blessed is the one who stays awake and keeps his garments, lest he walk about naked and men see his shame."

A verse that further describes the chaotic situation is in chapter 18:14:

"And the fruit that you long for has gone from you and all things that were luxurious and splendid have passed away from you, and men will no longer find them."

As the tribulation winds down from its heights, the fourth beatitude is shown in chapter 19:9-10:

"Blessed are those who are invited to the marriage supper of the Lamb." And He said to me, "These are true words of God." ... the testimony of Jesus is the spirit of prophecy.

The next portion concerns the Advent of Christ, from chapter 19:11–15:

"And I saw a heaven opened, and behold a white horse, and He who sat upon it is called Faithful and True; and in righteousness He judges and wages war. And His eyes are a flame of fire, and upon His head are many diadems; and He has a name written upon Him which no one knows except Himself. And he is clothed with a robe dipped in blood;

and His name is called The Word of God. And the armies which are in heaven, clothed in fine linen, white and clean were following Him on white horses. And from His mouth, comes a sharp sword, so that with it He may smite the nations; and He will rule them with a rod of iron; and He treads the wine press of the fierce wrath of God, the Almighty."

At this point, the scene shifts to the struggle at Armageddon shown in chapter 19:17-21:

"And I saw an angel standing in the sun; and He cried out with a loud voice, saying to all the birds which fly in the midheaven, "Come, assemble for the great supper of God; in order that you may eat the flesh of kings and the flesh of commanders and the flesh of mighty men and the flesh of horses, and of those who sit on them, and the flesh of all men, both free men and slaves, and small and great." And I saw the beast and the kings of the earth and their armies assembled to make war against Him who sat upon the horse and against His army. And the beast was seized, and with him the false prophet who performed the signs in his presence, by which he deceived those who had received the mark of the beast and those who worshiped his image; those two were thrown alive into the lake of fire which burns with brimstone. And the rest were killed with the sword which came from the mouth of Him who sat upon the horse, and all the birds were filled with their flesh."

The description of the millennium, the thousand-year period that Christ will rule on earth, begins in chapter 20. In chapter 20:1-3:

'And I saw an angel coming down from heaven, having the key of the abyss and a great chain in his hand. And he laid hold of the dragon, the serpent of old, who is the devil and Satan, and bound him for a thousand years, and threw him into the abyss, and shut it up and sealed it over him, so he should not deceive the nations any longer, until the thousand years were completed; an after these things he must be released for a short time.'

During this period, righteousness will flourish; peace will be universal, and the presence of all the earth will be greatly enhanced. At the conclusion of this time, Satan will be loosed to make one final attempt to overthrow Christ, but without success.

Now begins the resurrection of the saints of God. In chapter 20: 4–5:

'And I saw thrones and they sat upon them, and judgments were given to them. And I saw the souls of those who had been beheaded because of the testimony of Jesus and because of the word of God, and those who had not worshiped the beast or his image, and had not received the mark upon their forehead and upon their hand; and they came to life and reigned with Christ for a thousand years. The rest of the dead did not come to life until the thousand years was completed. This is the first resurrection. In verse six is the fifth beatitude, Blessed and holy is the one who has apart in the first resurrection over these the second death has no power, but they will be priests of God and of Christ and will reign with Him for a thousand years.'

At this point, the sinners rebel as shown now in chapter 20:7–9:

"And when the thousand years are completed, Satan will be released from his prison, and he will come out to deceive the nations, which are in the four corners of the earth, Gog and Magog, to gather them together for the war; the number of them is like the sand of the seashore. And they came up on the broad plain of the earth, and surrounded the camp of the saints and the beloved city and fire came down from heaven and devoured them. In verse 10 Satan is doomed. And the devil that deceived them was thrown into the lake of fire and brimstone, where the beast and the false prophet are also; and they will be tormented day and night forever and ever."

Sinners are now judged in chapter 20:11–15:

"And I saw a great white throne and Him who sat upon it from whose presence earth and heaven fled away, and no place was found for them. And I saw the dead the great and the small standing before the throne and books were opened: and another book was opened, which is the book of life; and the dead were judged from the things which were written in the books according to their deeds. And the sea gave up the dead which were in it and death and Hades which were in them; and they were judged, every one according to their deeds. And death and Hades were thrown into the lake of fire. This is the second death, the lake of fire. And if anyone's name was not found in the book of life, he was thrown into the lake of fire."

Here is pictured the judgment of the unbelieving dead. It occurs at the close of the millennium. It is based on works, in order to show that the punishment is deserved. The unsaved people are, first of all, in the judgment because they rejected Christ as Savior during their lifetimes; this is the resurrection of judgment. It needs to be understood that Christ was on the throne before the judgment.

What follows is the descent of the New Jerusalem and the Eternal State beginning in chapter 21:1:

"And I saw a new heaven and a new earth; for the first heaven and the first earth passed away, and there is no longer any sea."

In other words, the present creation will be destroyed so that it may be cleansed from all the effects of sin.

Moving forward into chapter 21:2:

"And I saw the holy city, new Jerusalem coming down from heaven from God, made ready as a bride adorned for her husband."

This heavenly city will be the abode for all the saints and is the place Christ is preparing for His people. During the millennium, the New Jerusalem apparently will be suspended over the earth and it will be the dwelling place for all believers during eternity. We proceed forward to the description of what transpires in the next phase in chapter 21:3-8:

"And I heard a loud voice from the throne saying, "Behold, the tabernacle of God is among men, and He shall dwell among them, and they shall be His people, and God, Himself shall be among them, and He shall wipe away every tear from their eyes and there shall no longer be any death; there shall no longer be any mourning or crying, or pain; the first things have passed away." And He who sits on the throne said, "Behold, I am making all things new." And He said, "Write for these words are faithful and true." And He said to me, It is done, I am the Alpha and the Omega, the beginning and the end. I will give to the one who thirsts from the spring of the water of life without cost. "He who overcomes shall inherit these things, I shall be his God and he will be My son." But for the cowardly and unbelieving and abominable and murderers and immoral persons and sorcerers and idolaters and all liars, their part will be in the lake of fire and brimstone which is the second death."

The fate of those described above is plainly stated for all to fully comprehend and understand. I believe it would be a wise decision for all to read and reread this several times and give very thoughtful consideration to all that was said.

Now follows the description of the New Jerusalem as shown in chapter 21:9-27:

"Come here, I shall show you the bride, the wife of the Lamb." And he carried me away in the Spirit to a great and high mountain, and showed me the holy city, Jerusalem, coming down from heaven from God, having the glory of God, Her brilliance was like a very costly stone, as a stone of crystal-clear Jasper. It had a great and high wall with twelve gates, and at the gates twelve angels; and names were written on them which are those of the twelve tribes of the sons of Israel. There were three gates on the east, and three gates on the north, and three gates on the south and three gates on the west. And the wall of the city had twelve foundation stones, and on them were the twelve names of the twelve apostles of the Lamb. And the one who spoke with me had a gold measuring rod to measure the city and its gates and its wall. And the city is laid out as a square, and its length is as great as its width; and he measured the city with the rod, fifteen hundred miles, its length and width and height are equal. And he measured the wall seventy-two yards according to human measurements, which are also angelic measurements. And the material of the wall was jasper; and the city was pure gold, like clear glass. The foundation stones of the city wall were adorned with every kind of precious stone. The first foundation stone was jasper; the second, sapphire; the third, chalcedony; the fourth, emerald; the fifth, sardonyx; the sixth, sardius; the seventh, chrysolite; the eighth, beryl; the ninth, topaz; the tenth, chrysoprase; the eleventh, jacinth: the twelfth, amethyst. And the twelve gates were twelve pearls; each one of the gates was a single pearl. And the street of the city was pure gold, like transparent glass. And I saw no temple in it for the Lord God, the Almighty, and the Lamb, are its temple. And the city has no need of the sun or the moon to shine upon it, for the glory of God, has illumined it, and its lamp is the Lamb. And the nations shall walk by its light and the kings of the earth shall bring their glory into it. And in the daytime (for there shall be no night there) its gates shall never be closed; and they shall bring the glory and the honor of the nations into it; and nothing unclean, and no one who practices abominations and lying shall ever come into it, but only those whose names are written in the Lamb's book of life."

The entirety of this description is overwhelming to me, and I believe will be for you as well. Before going into the final chapter, I ask that you take several minutes and reread all that has been described to us and do your best to visualize the scope and vastness of the New Jerusalem. Do not forget that all of this vision will become fact and reality, as it is simply a matter of time for all believers in Jesus Christ. Are you ready?

Chapter 22 is the last chapter in the book of Revelation and also of the Bible. Pay full attention to all that is presented. The description and delights of the New Jerusalem are now front and center.

And he showed me a river of the water of life, clear as crystal, coming from the throne of God and of the Lamb, in the middle of its street. And on either side of the river was the tree of life, bearing twelve kinds of fruit, yielding its fruit every month, and leaves of the tree were for the healing of the nations. (Revelation 22:1–2)

These descriptive phrases indicate the fullness of life and continuous blessing in the New Jerusalem.

And there shall no longer be any curse; and the throne of God and of the Lamb shall be in it; and His bond-servants shall serve Him; and they shall see His face, and His name shall be on their foreheads. And there shall no longer be any night; and they shall not have need of the light of a lamp nor the light of the sun, because the Lord God shall illumine them; and they shall reign forever and ever. (Revelation 22:3–5)

Words of comfort are expressed from *verses 6-17* as follows:

"And he said to me, 'These words are faithful and true,' and the Lord, the God of the spirits of the prophets, sent His angel to show to His bond-servants the things which must shortly take place. 'And behold, I am coming quickly. Blessed is he who heeds the prophecy of this book.' And I, John, am the one who heard and saw these things. And when I heard and saw, I fell down to worship at the feet of the angel who showed me these things. And he said to me, 'Do not do that; I am a fellow servant of yours and of your brethren, the prophets and those who heed the words of this book; worship God.' And he said to me, 'Do not seal up the words of the prophecy of this book, for the time is near. Let the one who does wrong still do wrong, and the one who is filthy still be filthy and let the one who is righteous still practice righteousness; and let the one who is holy, still keep himself holy.'"

It should be plainly understood that when Christ comes there will no longer be the opportunity for a man to change his destiny. What he is then, he will be forever. I have no idea if you or any of your contemporaries have ever paid any serious attention to this fact, but if not, please do so now.

Continuing in verse 12:

"Behold, I am coming quickly, and My reward is with Me, to render to every man according to what he has done. 'I am the Alpha and the Omega, the first and the last, the beginning and the end.'"

Here is noted the final beatitude, in verse 14:

"Blessed are those who wash their robes, that they may have the right to the tree of life and may enter by the gates into the city."

The "those" noted here are those who believe in Jesus Christ as their Lord and Savior.

In the closing passages, beginning in verse 15, we see that Outside are the dogs and sorcerers, the immoral persons, the murderers and the idolaters and everyone who loves and practices lying.

"'I, Jesus have sent my angel to testify to you these things for the churches. I am the root and the offspring of David, the bright morning star.' And the Spirit and the bride say, 'Come,' and let the one who hears say, 'Come.' And let the one who is thirsty come; let the one who wishes take the water of life without cost."

Prophetic words of caution are offered in verses 18–19.

"I testify to everyone who hears, the words of the prophecy of this book, if anyone adds to them, God shall add to him the plagues that are written in this book; and if anyone takes away the words of the book of prophecy, God shall take away his part from the tree of life and from the holy city, which are written in this book."

Do not ever consider additions or omissions to this book.

We now have the closing benediction in verses 20–21:

"He who testifies to these things says, 'Yes, I am coming quickly.' Amen. Come, Lord Jesus. The grace of our Lord Jesus be with all. Amen."

This dynamic book of the revelation of Jesus should always be a cornerstone and a vivid remembrance for you as you move forward in your spiritual life. With the conclusion of Revelation, we have now completed all the elements in relation to our course of travel through the scriptures in the Bible that relate to the life, purpose, and future of Jesus Christ. Now, let us move forward and review the other elements of the Bible that have significant importance for you. Remember, let the Bible always be your anchor so you will remain well grounded.

JOY

A pure expression of happiness. This is often expressed throughout the Bible by individuals as they encounter the blessings and love of our Almighty God.

Have you ever been out of our beloved country for an extended period of time? When I was ordered to report for active duty in the Air Force, I had an unusual experience. My orders were to report to the port of embarkation rather than to go to a stateside duty station for indoctrination to begin my service. After fifteen days at three locations in the northeast, I landed in Frankfurt Germany.

The six of us who reported together waited several days for future assignment and at that point I asked the others, if they thought we could get a three-day pass rather just sitting around twiddling our thumbs. They agreed it was a good idea and, since it was my idea, I was elected to see the Colonel for permission. I asked, and he asked me where we wanted to go, and I told him "Garmisch Partenkirshen" in the Alps. He said to be back on Monday. We spent several days there skiing on the Zugspitze, the tallest mountain in Germany. Being a Florida native, this was only the second time in my life that I had even seen snow much less skied on it.

After arriving back in Frankfurt, we got our permanent duty stations. By the grace of God, I drew the best location; Bushy Park AFB in London. My wife June and I spent almost 2 years there with our little girl. We were most fortunate to be able to explore London, as well as Oxford, Cambridge, the midlands, and Edinburgh. We also had the opportunity on leave to go to the continent and visit Belgium, the Netherlands, Denmark, Germany, Austria, Switzerland, Italy, Monaco, and France.

We headed back home on the SS United States, at that time the world's largest ocean liner. We all had a genuine feeling of joy coming into New York harbor and passing the Statue of Liberty. That concluded my service career and although we thoroughly enjoyed our adventure, it was good to be home again. I was blessed again because at that time, while I was in Europe, the war was going full tilt in Korea.

For his anger is but for a moment, His favor is for a lifetime; Weeping may last for the night, But a shout of joy comes in the morning. (Psalms 30:5)

Be ever thankful that our Lord is a forgiving God.

Restore me to the joy of Thy salvation, and sustain me with a willing spirit. (Psalms 51:12)

Allow the Lord to bless and to keep you in His hands.

Shout joyfully to the Lord all the earth. (Psalms 100:1)

A close relationship with God brings happiness, joy, and peace.

Those who sow in tears shall reap with joyful shouting. (Psalms 126:5)

Very often, sorrow and hardship bring strength and joy to us. "Sorrow comes to stretch spaces in our hearts so that joy can be found." (A meaningful comment to ponder from *Streams in the Desert.*)

Folly is joy to him who lacks sense, but a man of understanding walks straight. (Proverbs 15:21)

A reminder for us: be careful how and where we walk and with whom.

And the angel said to them, " Do not be afraid, for behold, I bring you good news of a great joy which shall be for all the people; for today in the city of David has been born for you a Savior, who is Christ the Lord. (Luke 2:10–11)

An angelic announcement of the birth of Jesus Christ.

But the fruit of the Spirit is love, joy, peace, patience, kindness, goodness, faithfulness, gentleness, and self control; against such things there is no law. Now those who belong to Christ Jesus have crucified the flesh with its passions and desires. If we live by the Spirit, let us also walk by the Spirit. (Galatians 5:22–25)

This jewel of verses expresses the fruits of the spirit in such a beautiful manner.

Therefore, since we have so great a cloud of witnesses surrounding us, let us also lay aside every encumbrance and the sin which so easily entangles us and let us run with endurance the race that is set before us, fixing our eyes on Jesus, the author and perfecter of faith who for the joy set before Him endured the cross, despising the shame, and has sat down at the right hand of the throne of God. (Hebrews 12:1–2)

Excellent advice urging us to maintain fixing our vision on Jesus and what He wishes us to do in our lives.

Consider it all joy my brethren, when you encounter various trials… (James 1:2)

Do you respond in this manner when confronted by trials? My guess is… probably not. However, I ask you to think for a moment and recognize that when you face trials do so with an open mind. If you do, you will recognize that the trial may well be, in reality, an opportunity to explore something new and for you to grow in the process. Here's hoping this works for you.

...though you have not seen Him, you love Him, and though you do not see Him now, but believe in Him you greatly rejoice with joy inexpressible and full of glory. (1 Peter 1:8)

Belief and faith in Jesus are priceless.

JUDGMENT

We must understand that each of us will experience the judgment of Jesus Christ regarding all of the deeds, both good and evil, that we have committed in our lives. With this caution in mind, it behooves each of us to make every effort to both maintain and keep His commandments and to live righteously.

The Lord judges the people; Vindicate me, O Lord, according to my righteousness and my integrity that is in me. (Psalms 7:8)

Be slow to judge others but quick to judge yourself.

And He will judge the world in righteousness. He will execute judgment for the peoples with equity. (Psalms 9:8)

Our God is just in all things.

If we are to be accountable to God, how do we prepare for judgment? Dr. Charles Stanley offers these recommendations:

1. Be saved
2. Review your lifestyle
3. Reevaluate your priorities
4. Renew a daily commitment
5. Consider what you can do to be pleasing to God.

I encourage you to take a little time and give these recommendations your thoughtful attention.

He is the Lord our God; His judgments are in all the earth. (Psalms 105:7)

God's word is always faithful. Should man ask for anything more than that as we are judged?

The conclusion when all has been heard, is fear God and keep His commandments, because this applies to every person.

For God will bring every act to judgment, everything which is hidden, whether it is good or evil. (Ecclesiastes 12:13-14)

Be aware that each of us will face judgment before Jesus.

"I can do nothing on My own initiative. As I hear, I judge; and My judgment is just, because I do not seek My own will, but the will of Him who sent Me." (John 5:30)

Jesus acknowledges that the judgment that He expresses is, in fact, the will of God.

"Do not judge according to appearance, but judge with righteous judgment." (John 7:24)

Do not be severe in judging others but utilize that measure of discipline in judging yourself.

…The Lord knows how to rescue the godly from temptation, and to keep the unrighteous under punishment for the day of judgment. (2 Peter 2:9)

Straightforward advice regarding how to deal with temptation. Use it. When the day of judgment occurs, God will decide about mankind and not mankind about God.

Before moving forward to explore another topic, I want to explain an example of my own poor judgment and how it almost cost me my life. In the years following my filing for my business Chapter 11 bankruptcy, I continued to call on the network of customers who had agreed to continue to do business with me and help me with the rigors of paying off my creditors.

On this particular evening, I had finished my last call of the day in Williston and was driving back toward Ocala where I could pick up the interstate to head for home. It was late, and I carelessly decided to pass another car as we were proceeding up a hill on this two-lane road. Pressing the accelerator down hard, I had just pulled even with the car I was passing when suddenly a car loomed over the crest of the hill headed right for me at a very fast clip. The other driver, by the grace of God, took to the shoulder and the three cars maintained their course without a collision.

I was a fool to have taken such a risk, particularly when you consider my prior head-on collision with the tractor trailer. Not to justify my foolish error, but during that seven-year ordeal, and even after, my average work week was 70 to 80 hours plus a week and this definitely clouded my reasoning. I mention this to you to remind you that no matter how you may be proceeding in any of your activities never take foolish chances. If you do, and survive as I did, stop and thank God that He looked out for you and allowed you to survive a frightful peril. After this happened, I could not help but wonder why He had let me escape death again. A phrase frequently used in the Rev. Scott Davis' book, *The Odds Are Too Great*, certainly applies to me in this instance:

JOHN H. (JAN) DOLCATER, JR.

"Seek the forgiveness of the Lord regardless of your lack of judgment in the trial you face."

When you are faced with a puzzling situation and are unsure what to do, try this suggestion from *Streams in the Desert*: "Submit your problem to God and ask Him to shut every door but the right one for you." I am confident this will produce positive results for you if this is done in confident faith.

KINDNESS

This trait is perhaps best expressed by the Golden Rule: do unto others as you would have them do unto you. Put simply, each of us has options of behavior to exhibit. Remember, kindness does not depend on how others treat us nor is it a manipulation to get what we want. Kindness is a selfless quality that always considers what is best for others whether they deserve it or not. The best course to follow is to be kind to family, friend, and foe whenever possible. The results will be fruitful in the majority of instances. I also remind you that one of God's kindnesses is to lead people to repentance.

Do not let kindness and truth leave you; Bind then around your neck, write them on the tablet of your heart. So you will find favor and good repute in the sight of God and man. (Proverbs 3:3–4)

If you follow this advice, you will be pleasing to God.

But the fruit of the Spirit is love, joy, peace, patience, kindness, goodness, faithfulness, gentleness, and self control; against such things there is no law. Now those who belong to Christ Jesus have crucified the flesh with its passions and desires. If we live by the Spirit, let us also walk by the Spirit. (Galatians 5:22–25)

Kindness is one of the fruits of the Spirit. Try and keep it always in your demeanor.

Now for this very reason also, applying all diligence in your faith, supply moral excellence, and in your moral excellence, knowledge, and in your knowledge, self-control, and in your self-control, perseverance and in your perseverance, godliness, and in your godliness, brotherly kindness, and in your brotherly kindness, love. For if all these qualities are yours and are increasing, they render you neither useless nor unfruitful in the true knowledge of our Lord Jesus Christ. (2 Peter 1:5–8)

Please pay attention to this sound advice. It will lead you to the highway to heaven.

Before proceeding to the next topic, I want to ask you, what is the most important kindness that has been done for you by either another individual or by God? Far too often, kindnesses that are done for us are taken for granted.

I want to tell you about an event in my life after I had become a manufacturer's rep. I was in Orlando for a meeting with the principal of an important vendor. After our meeting concluded, the owner suggested we have dinner. This sounded great and we headed to Freddie's Steak House. His daughter, an officer of the company, was also present. After a libation, our steaks were presented, and as usual, they were excellent. We were talking and laughing and enjoying our time together and, all of a sudden, I could not breathe. I had swallowed a piece of steak and was choking terribly. In panic, I stood up and held my arms above my head since I could not speak.

My vendor, a man in his seventies at that time, rushed around the table and put the Heimlich grip on me and, fortunately, I coughed up the piece of steak I was choking on. If he had not had the presence of mind to respond as he did, there is no question in my mind I would have choked to death in a fairly short time. It was a very close encounter with cashing it in. I had heard of people having this type of experience, but never thought this would happen to me. If this should ever happen to you, I hope and pray a Good Samaritan will be there for you with an act of kindness.

"If you are kind, people may accuse you of selfish, ulterior motives; be kind anyway." – Mother Teresa, Calcutta, India

KNOWLEDGE

As we proceed through life, we have opportunities to gain useful information that is important to our welfare and well-being. The accumulation of this information is categorized as "knowledge." It is critical to glean as much as possible from Biblical instruction in order to achieve peace of mind and lead a productive life.

The fear of the Lord is the beginning of knowledge; fools despise wisdom and instruction. (Proverbs 1:7)

Pay attention and gain wisdom and understanding.

Whoever loves discipline loves knowledge; he who hates reproof is stupid. (Proverbs 12:1)

Straightforward and easy to understand. Pay attention to this.

The mind of the intelligent seeks knowledge. But the mouth of fools feeds on folly. (Proverbs 15:14)

What do you feed on? Where is your trough?

...All the world may become accountable to God, because by the works of the law, no flesh will be justified in His sight; for through the law comes the knowledge of sin. (Romans 3:19–20)

Do not make the error of not fully comprehending this. All are accountable to God for their actions, thoughts, and deeds.

For God, who said, "Light shall shine out of darkness is the One who shone in our hearts to give light of the knowledge of the glory of God in the face of Christ." (2 Corinthians 4:6)

Please allow the light of Christ to penetrate into you and illumine your soul.

...to know the love of Christ which surpasses knowledge that you may be filled up to all the fullness of God. (Ephesians 3:19)

The key to having the right kind of relationship with Jesus Christ is having His love in your heart while caring for others.

That their hearts may be encouraged having been knit together in love, and attaining to all wealth that comes from the full assurance and understanding resulting in a true knowledge of God's mystery, that is Christ Himself. (Colossians 2:2)

The apostle Paul explains that love and understanding will lead you to the realities of God and to Jesus Christ.

O Timothy, guard what has been entrusted to you, avoiding worldly and empty chatter and opposing the argument of what is falsely called "knowledge"...which some have professed and thus gone astray from their faith. (1 Timothy 6:20–21)

The apostle Paul instructs young Timothy in his assignment of being head of the church in Ephesus as to where he should place his trust.

Maintain your faith regardless of the circumstances surrounding you.

...if we go on sinning willfully after receiving the knowledge of the truth, there no longer remains a sacrifice for sins. (Hebrews 10:26)

Don't discard your relationship with God in a careless and foolish manner.

LOVE

This topic is exceptionally important to understand as it embraces three different aspects. The first is the love that God has for each of us, the second is the love that we have for God, and, thirdly, the love we have for our family, friends, and fellowman.

Let us begin with the love that God has for us. Keep in mind all three are of the utmost importance.

"For God so loved the world, that He gave His only begotten Son, that whoever believes in Him should not perish, but have eternal life." (John 3:16)

This is perhaps the most well-known to us of all verses in the Bible. Please commit this to memory and make a consistent effort to gain for yourself the goal of eternal life.

For the Father Himself loves you, because you have loved Me, and believed that I came forth from the Father. (John 16:27)

Take a moment to consider the significance of this statement by our Lord Jesus Christ.

...God demonstrates His own love towards us in that we were yet sinners, Christ died for us. (Romans 5:8)

An explicit example of God's love for us.

For I am convinced that neither death, nor life, nor angels, nor principalities, nor things present, nor things to come, nor powers, nor height, nor depth, nor any other created thing, shall be able to separate us from the love of God which is in Christ Jesus our Lord. (Romans 8:38–39)

I do not know of any more powerful statement of God's love for us than this one so plainly stated by the apostle Paul. *Streams of the Desert* shares this from Paul's remarkable quote: "Those who are readiest to trust God without evidence with nothing other than His word always receive the greatest evidence of His love."

...God, being rich in mercy, because of His great love with which He loved us, even when we were dead in our transgressions, made us alive together with Christ. (By grace you have been saved.) (Ephesians 2:4–5)

Unworthy as we are, I encourage you to take time and thank our Almighty God who loves us.

...when the kindness of God our Savior and His love for mankind appeared, He saved us, not on the basis of deeds which we have done in righteousness, but according to His mercy, by the washing of regeneration and renewing of the Holy Spirit. (Titus 3:4–5)

His love for us plus our commitment to Him brings salvation.

See how great a love the Father has bestowed upon us, that we should be called children of God; and such we are. (1 John 3:1)

Know Him as your father.

Beloved, let us love one another, for love is from God; and every one who loves is born of God and knows God. The one who does not love does not know God, for God is love. By this the love of God is manifested in us that God has sent His only begotten Son into the world that we might live through Him. In this is love, not that we loved God, but that He loved us and sent His Son to be the propitiation for our sins. (1 John 4:7–10)

God is love. He can be known only by those who live in love.

There is no fear in love; but perfect love casts out fear because fear involves punishment and the one who fears is not perfected in love. We love because He first loved us. If someone says, "I love God" and hates his brother, he is a liar, for the one who does not love his brother whom he has seen, cannot love God whom he has not seen. (1 John 4:18-20)

Understand that God has loved us all from the beginning and we have a responsibility to love one another.

Keep yourselves in the love of God, waiting anxiously for the mercy of our Lord Jesus Christ to eternal life. (Jude 1:21)

Be ever patient in the love of God.

Think on this thought as we move on in our understanding of God's love for us. One of the most devastating failures a Christian can experience is the inability to embrace the pure love of God. Can you think of any reason that would prevent someone from not accepting a blessing such as this? Could this be happening to you or has this already occurred? If so, open your heart and soul to Him if you have felt like this. If you are aware that this may have happened with a friend or associate, please encourage them to do so as well. When you fully accept and experience the unconditional love of God there is no question in your mind that you will be filled with overwhelming joy. God's love has no boundaries and the love of God is alive and filled with joy. God's love for us is unconditional and when it is accepted by us our lives experience significant change. Trouble and worry become peace. Fear is exchanged for confidence. Are you willing to love like that? I definitely hope so.

Let us now consider the scripture that shows our love for God knowing that, unlike other expressions of love, His love for us is constant and unchanging.

…You shall love the Lord your God with all your heart, and with all your soul, and with all your might. (Deuteronomy 6:5)

Jesus called this the first and greatest commandment and later added to it "with all your mind."

O love the Lord all you His godly ones! The Lord preserves the faithful. And fully recompenses the proud doer. (Psalm 31:23)

Maintain an expectant outlook in your life and work diligently to have a positive loving relationship with the Lord.

…If anyone loves God, he is known by Him. (1 Corinthians 8:3)

What is *your* feeling about God? Do you have a genuine feeling of love for Him? If not, why not?

We love, because He first loved us. (1 John 4:19)

How fortunate we are.

Whoever believes that Jesus is the Christ is born of God; and whoever loves the Father loves the child born of Him. By this we know that we love the children of God, when we love God and observe His commandments. For this is the love of God, that we keep His commandments, and His commandments are not burdensome. (1 John 5:1–3)

If we truly love God, then we will, without hesitation, make every effort to keep His commandments.

Now let us examine other scripture that relates to our loving one another.

"But I say to you, love your enemies, and pray for those who persecute you in order that you may be sons of your Father who is in heaven; for He causes His sun to rise on the evil and the good, and sends rain on the righteous and the unrighteous." (Matthew 5:44–45)

For many this may be difficult to do. However, think on this and I know it will make good sense for you to follow this advice.

"This is my commandment, that you love one another, just as I have loved you. Greater love has no one than this, that one lay down his life for his friends." (John 15:12–13)

This was expressed by Jesus to others.

A thought from the booklet *Our Daily Bread* is worth considering here. "Be an expression of the love of Jesus."

Let love be without hypocrisy. Abhor what is evil, cling to what is good. (Romans 12:9)

Make every effort to maintain this attitude in your dealings with everyone.

Owe nothing to anyone except to love one another; for he who loves his neighbor has fulfilled the law. (Romans 13:8)

Love is a debt that no one can fully discharge.

For the whole law is fulfilled in one word, in the statement, "You shall love your neighbor as yourself." (Galatians 5:14)

As the Lord said, this is the first and greatest commandment.

Little children, let us not love with word or with thought, but in deed and truth. (1 John 3:18)

The apostle John frequently addressed others with the words "little children" and here he encourages us to not just talk about loving others but to do so in action.

I believe a quotation from 1 Corinthians 13:13 is appropriate to consider here. "Now abide faith, hope, love, these three; but the greatest of these is love." Nothing surpasses love and nothing places more emphasis on it than this does. However, I do feel it is appropriate to add these additional scriptures as sound advice for you to consider.

Those who love Thy law have great peace. And nothing causes them to stumble. (Psalms 119:165)

Regardless of your age, live life with a purpose with both love and humility in your heart and being. Life, indeed, is full for you if lived with love and purpose with guidance from the Lord.

Love does no wrong to a neighbor; love therefore is the fulfillment of the law. (Romans 13:10)

Straightforward and to the point. Please remember this; some things are more important than how we feel about them at the moment they first cross our minds. Make every effort to not let your feelings push you to something that is hurtful and not expressed in love.

"A new commandment I give to you, that you love one another, even as I have loved you, that you also love one another. By this all men will know that you are my disciples, if you have love for one another" (John 13:34–35)

Mutual love should be one of the strongest possible reasons for the Christian faith.

And we know that God causes all things to work together for good to those who love God, as those who are called according to His purpose. (Romans 8:28)

This verse is a repetition but please keep this close to your heart. I strongly believe in the realism of this verse. Does it have a significant meaning to you? I hope so.

Love is patient, love is kind, and is not jealous, love does not brag and it is not arrogant, does not act unbecomingly, it does not seek its own, is not provoked, does not take into account wrong suffered, does not rejoice in unrighteousness, but rejoices with the truth; bears all things, believes all things, hopes all things, endures all things. Love never fails. When I was a child, I used to speak as a child, think as a child, reason like a child; when I became a man I did away with childish things. But now abide faith, hope, love these three, but the greatest of these is love. (1 Corinthians 13: 4-8, 11, 13)

This passage defines the perfection of love. All three of these attributes should be pursued diligently but love is the greatest since it is expressed by God.

But the fruit of the Spirit is love, joy, peace, patience, kindness, goodness, faithfulness, gentleness, and self control; against such things there is no law. Now those who belong to Christ Jesus have crucified the flesh with its passions and desires. If we live by the Spirit, let us also walk by the Spirit. (Galatians 5:22–25)

Love is one of the fruits of the Spirit.

There is no fear in love; but perfect love casts out fear, because fear involves punishment, and the one who fears is not perfected in love. We love because He first loved us. (1 John 4:18–19)

We can appreciate and cherish this beautiful expression of love.

I like this notation from the booklet, *Our Daily Bread*: "Loving Father, may I not let my fear stop me from following You, for I know that You will always love me and will never leave me alone."

LOVINGKINDNESS

Compassion and mercy are shown to mankind in the most meaningful manner by God the Father Almighty. This extension of understanding indicates His steadfast love for mankind. All of this is bound together with love in faith and trust.

Do not remember the sins of my youth or my transgressions. According to Thy lovingkindness remember Thou me... (Psalms 25:7)

I read this one frequently as it has much meaning for me.

All the paths of the Lord are lovingkindness and truth. To those who keep His covenant and His testimonies. (Psalms 25:10)

Do not waver in your commitment to God.

Many are the sorrows of the wicked, but he who trusts in the Lord, lovingkindness shall surround him. (Psalms 32:10)

Perhaps one may attain a short-term gain but, without God, a long-term loss is a certainty.

Psalms 33:5 He loves righteousness and justice; The earth is full of the lovingkindness of the Lord.

God is dependable in all things.

The Lord will command His lovingkindness in the daytime; And His song will be with me in the night. A prayer to the God of my life. (Psalms 42:8)

Be thankful that the lovingkindness of the Lord is always with us as we follow Him.

The Lord is compassionate and gracious, slow to anger and abounding in lovingkindness. (Psalms 103:8)

However, I caution you – do not test the Lord.

Who is wise? Let him give heed to those things; And consider the lovingkindness of the Lord. (Psalms 107:43)

Make every effort to be humble and to praise the Lord.

Some thoughtful advice from *Our Daily Bread*. "Each day we need to be still and listen to the Lord." Be patient and listen well as this is often not done. I am curious; when you pray, do you listen for the Lord to respond to you? If not, be still and listen quietly.

The earth is full of Thy lovingkindness, O Lord; Teach me Thy statutes. (Psalms 119:64)

JOHN H. (JAN) DOLCATER, JR.

We cannot know God without knowing His Word.

The Lord's lovingkindness never ceases for His compassion never fails. (Lamentations 3:22)

How meaningful is this to you? Think about it.

MERCY

Thoughtful caring and compassion shown to those in need of help, comforting, or understanding. Mercy should be expressed by us all as we minister to those in need.

The Lord is gracious and merciful. Slow to anger and great in lovingkindness. The Lord is good to all... (Psalms 145:8-9)

Be ever grateful for this.

...so we, who are many, are one body in Christ, and individually members one of another. And since we have gifts that differ according to the grace given to us, let each exercise them accordingly, if prophesy according to the proportion of faith; if service, in his serving; or he who teaches in his teaching; or he who exhorts in his exhortation; he who gives with liberality; he who leads with diligence; he who shows mercy with cheerfulness. (Romans 12:5-8)

We all have a purpose in our lives for Christ. What do you think yours is? How recently have you thought about it?

Let me tell you about two instances where God was merciful to me as I traveled northern Maine on business. In that area, it is not uncommon to see moose, but I promise you that you do not want to see them unexpectedly at night when you are on the road. When you consider their weight, which is 900 to 1200 pounds, you can understand the devastation they can inflict.

My first encounter with one was late one evening between Houlton and Presque Isle. Out of nowhere, I saw the legs of one and just barely missed having contact. When you see only the legs, either you just missed one or you have one through the windshield.

Immediately after this, I pulled off onto the shoulder and sat quietly for about 10 minutes to regain my composure from the shock and fear. Without question, I had just had a near-death experience. A friend of ours on his way home from Bangor was not as fortunate as he collided with one and the "jaws of life" could not remove him before he died.

Several months later, as I traveled one evening on my way to St Johns, New Brunswick I just missed a large bull moose. Believe me, there is nothing quite as intimidating. Was I just plain lucky or perhaps God has a purpose for me? I offer a suggestion for you to consider; whatever problem may exist in your life, put all in the hands of God and walk in faith with peace in your heart, and be thankful for His mercy.

…we too all formerly lived in the lusts of the flesh, indulging in the desires of the flesh and of the mind and were by the nature children of wrath, even as the rest. But God being rich in mercy, because of His great love with which He loved us even when we were dead in our transgressions made us alive with Christ. (by grace you have been saved) (Ephesians 2:3–5)

Be ever thankful for the mercy shown to us by our Almighty God.

He saved us not on the basis of deeds, which we have done in righteousness, but according to His mercy, by the washing of regeneration and renewing of the Holy Spirit. (Titus 3:5)

Personal salvation is not a reward for good deeds but for our commitment to Jesus Christ.

...judgment will be merciless to one who has shown no mercy: mercy triumphs over judgment. (James 2:13)

Be merciful to others at all times.

But the wisdom from above is first pure, then peaceable, gentle, reasonable, full of mercy and good fruits, unwavering, without hypocrisy. (James 3:17)

This key point is made not only for the time when this transpired but also for all times.

Blessed be the God and Father of our Lord Jesus Christ who according to His great mercy has caused us to be born again to a living hope through the resurrection of Jesus Christ from the dead. (1 Peter 1:3)

Thoughtful consideration of this will enable us to understand that all things come from Him. Thanks be to God.

Grace, mercy and peace will be with us from God the Father and from Jesus Christ the Son of The Father, in truth and love. (2 John 1:3)

The apostle John explains the gifts of God.

MORALITY

This is demonstrated by the pure in heart as they keep their pathway away from evil in their thoughts, words and deeds. Flee from lust; seek truth and honesty in all your dealings. Desire to obey God and allow this feeling in you to become intense. As a result, you will find sinful inclinations of less or no interest to you.

"You shall not commit adultery." (Exodus 20:14)

One of the ten commandments noted here.

You shall not lie with a male as one lies with a female it is an abomination. (Leviticus 18:22)

Thus, says the Lord in regard to an unnatural act.

…Can a man walk on hot coals and not be burned and his feet not be scorched? So is the one, who goes into his neighbor's wife. Whoever touches her will not go unpunished. (Proverbs 6:28–29)

Do not deceive yourself with fleshly impulses.

The man who commits adultery with a woman is lacking sense… (Proverbs 6:32)

Do not allow the pursuit of flesh to overcome you.

Harlotry, wine and new wine take away understanding. (Hosea 4:11)

The party is over and, now, where do you really stand? Always avoid harlotry and be prudent and cautious with wine. If you are not careful, the "party" will bite you.

Finally, brethren, whatever is true, whatever is honorable, whatever is right, whatever is pure, whatever is lovely, whatever is of good repute, if there is any excellence and if anything worthy of praise, let your mind dwell on these things. (Philippians 4:8)

Utilize these thoughts when you are tempted in any way.

For this is the will of God your sanctification; that is that you abstain from sexual immorality. (1 Thessalonians 4:3)

A message to Thessalonica which at the time was wide open to all kinds of sexual practices. However, I suggest that this applies to all of us today as well.

NURTURING

Reaching out in both a caring and helpful manner to those who are in need of guidance and understanding.

Then Jesus said to His disciples, "If anyone wishes to follow Me, let him deny himself and pick up his cross and follow Me. For whoever wishes to save his life shall lose it; but whoever loses his life for My sake will find it. For will a man profit if he gains the whole world and forfeits his soul? For what will a man give in exchange for his soul? For the Son of Man is going to come in the glory of His Father with His angels, and will then recompense every man according to his deeds." (Matthew 16:24–27)

Place your thinking in perspective with reality. What can a person possibly hope to obtain if they forfeit their soul?

And He was saying, "For this reason I have said to you, that no one can come to Me, unless it has been granted him from the Father." (John 6:65)

Jesus is explaining to His disciples the need for them to express this nurturing to others as they reach out as witnesses on His behalf.

We must all be spiritually fed and nurtured.

And, fathers, do not provoke your children to anger, but bring them up in the discipline and instruction of the Lord. (Ephesians 6:4)

Provide your children with guidelines but do so with thoughtfulness and consistency and help them in a nurturing manner.

See how great love the Father has bestowed upon us, that we should be called children of God; and such we are. (1 John 3:1)

As God nurtures each of us, it is imperative to extend this same caring to our own children as well.

OBEDIENCE

I believe that all of us know that children are to be obedient to their parents. However, I ask you, as an adult, is it our responsibility to be obedient to the laws of man? I believe you will answer affirmatively, but are we obedient to the laws of God? If not, why not? Make it your practice to exercise efforts each day to obey the precepts and commandments of God. Let's consider the various elements of obedience that are important in relation to our commitment to God.

The advice noted here is from *In Touch Ministries:*

1. Have courage. "Have I not commanded you? Be strong and courageous! Do not tremble or be dismayed for the Lord your God is with you wherever you go." (Joshua 1:9)
2. Learn to wait for the Lord and not get ahead of Him. "For from of old they have not heard or perceived by ear. Neither has the eye seen a God besides Thee. Who acts in behalf of the one who waits for Him?" (Isaiah 64:4)
3. Meditate on His word. "The book of the law shall not depart from your mouth, but you shall meditate on it day and night, so that you may be careful to do according to all that is written in it; for then you will make your way prosperous, and then you will have success." (Joshua 1:8)

4. Listen to God. "Take care what you listen to. By your standard of measure it shall be measured to you; and more shall be given to you besides." (Mark 4:24)
   5. Forsake sin and surrender your will to Him.

I want to relate to you an experience of what the word "obedience" reminds me of. One morning years ago, as I was leading my Sunday School class of ninth-graders, I asked the group "How many of you feel you have enough discipline at home?" A total of two children raised their hands. I wonder how obedience and discipline would apply to this age group today? What do you think? My guess is not one of a group like this would raise their hands.

Then the Lord God took the man and put him into the garden of Eden to cultivate it and keep it. And the Lord God commanded the man, saying "From any tree of the garden you may eat freely, but from the tree of the knowledge of good and evil you shall not eat, for in the day that you eat from it you shall surely die." (Genesis 2:15–17)

This is the initial guideline regarding obedience.

When you make a vow to God, do not hesitate in paying it for He takes no delight in fools. Pay what you vow. (Ecclesiastes 5:4)

Obey God and fulfill your commitments in obedience to Him

It is not part of our faith to question but to obey.

For He whom God has sent speaks the words of God for He gives the Spirit without measure. The Father loves the Son, and has given all things into His hand. He who believes in the Son has eternal life, but he who does not obey the Son shall not see life, but the wrath of God abides on him. (John 3:34–36)

Please pay attention to this solemn message. If you choose to not obey and commit to Jesus, the Son of God, you will not see eternal life and the wrath of God will be upon you.

"Our obedience to God will guide us through the unknown and draw us closer to Him" – a thoughtful message from *Our Daily Bread*.

Let no one deceive you with empty words, for because of these things the wrath of God comes upon the sons of disobedience. (Ephesians 5:6)

Empty chatter by allegedly knowledgeable individuals can lead one astray. Do not let it be you.

As obedient children, do not be conformed to the former lusts which you were yours in ignorance., but like the Holy One who called you, be holy also in your behavior; because it is written "You shall be holy for I am holy." (1 Peter 1:14–16)

You are being called by the Lord to be holy.

Since you have in obedience to the truth purified your souls for a sincere love of the brethren, fervently love one another from the heart. (1 Peter 1:22)

Avoid obeying in a half-hearted manner but obey with feelings of truth with all you have in you.

I offer this suggestion for you to think over. Walking in obedience and trust is the only way to find true peace.

OPPORTUNITY

We must exercise care and thoughtful prayer if we are to attain the best results from the opportunities that come our way.

Have you ever faced an opportunity that made you feel a bit overwhelmed? Did you question whether it was beyond your ability or whether you were up to it? Did it make you feel inadequate? How did you handle this situation? Were you impulsive or did you fret and stew about it? This type of crossroads situation could have a profound effect on the rest of your life. With that in mind, I encourage you, if such an occurrence happens again, do not try to solve it on your own or with just the input of friends or family.

Do not be intimidated by any of the potential perils or uncertainties. Always remember to place your decisions regarding your opportunities in the hands of God for His approval and guidance. Never forget that God has a purpose for your life. Do not feel uneasy when He alters your steps or your pathway? He will replace your awkward feelings with the courage needed to achieve whatever is necessary. If you do this, you will be pleased with the results as there is no better source to rely on, and you will not miss out on the benefits. Remember that God has all the resources you need to grow and be fruitful.

Here are four principles from Dr. Charles Stanley regarding adversity. After reviewing them please consider how each may help you.

1. Adversity is one of God's most effective tools to strengthen our faith.
2. When God sends us adversity, He never sends it to hurt us but to help us.
3. Thanks be to God we are never alone in adversity.
4. Adversity, if received with the best outlook, can be a precious gift from God.

I will bless the Lord who has consulted me; Indeed my mind instructs me in the night. (Psalms 16:7)

Sleepless nights provide an opportunity for receiving instruction or for facing hard facts. I am keenly aware of this situation as I had many of those restless nights while struggling to keep my business afloat in an extremely demanding situation.

I feel that the following quotation by Alexander Graham Bell, the inventor of the telephone, is appropriate. Bell said, "When one door closes, another opens; but we often look so long and so regretfully upon the closed one that we do not see the one which has been opened to us."

Don't be shy; see what opportunity is behind the new closed door. Most things worth doing are difficult so always do the best you can at all times and maximize your opportunities.

Conduct yourselves with wisdom towards outsiders, making the most of the opportunity. Let your speech always be with grace, seasoned, as it were with salt, so that you may know how you should respond to each person. (Colossians 4:5-6)

Temper your speech so it is neither insipid nor corrupt.

In closing this section, I want to remind you that when your opportunities come be cautious as you consider them. Some may be outstanding while others may lead down a very disastrous path. Remember these words; take time to prayerfully ask God to lead you in making the right decision as it may affect the rest of your life.

Doing things my way and not God's way affected the remainder of my life. I want you to understand the sincerity of my feelings as I did not do what I have proposed for you to do. This will take a few minutes but let me tell you my story and one opportunity that I blew.

When I got out of the Air Force, I went to work in my father's business. After working in the warehouse and in the yard loading and unloading trucks and boxcars, I was asked to manage a sales territory. My dad took great pains to give me the poorest territory that our company serviced. I took the challenge and after one year I had the most productive territory in the company. I really applied myself in learning as much as I could about all aspects of the business and after several years I was made Sales Manager.

In many ways, I changed the way the company did business. Although we were in the lumber and building business, we had never had a forklift until I forced the issue. Later, I disposed of the old method of stock record keeping and we became computerized. My Dad was getting along age-wise and after a conference he agreed to retire. Our business really took off as the economy was in high gear.

When I took over, our annual sales were about $2 million. Six or seven years later, we were over $7 million. In today's dollars, that would be approximately $35 million. Achieving this increase took significantly more capital than we had available and I chose the path of borrowing from the bank. I found out later that it was far easier to borrow a million than to pay it down…or back.

At the age of thirty-seven, I was elected president of the Tampa Rotary which was the largest and most prestigious service club in the city. I was also recognized by my peers by being elected to the wholesale advisory committee for Armstrong Cork, representing the southeast. In fact, I held that position for three different terms. It seemed that everything I touched was turning out favorably.

Then, I, along with sixteen others, was invited to attend the second Armstrong Wholesale Distributor Management Seminar, a weeklong meeting in Hershey, PA. I was the youngest person in attendance, and this was very meaningful to me. When I returned home, I contacted

Andy Armstrong to initiate the first Armstrong Retail Management Seminar series which our company sponsored several months later.

Later, I came up with an innovative approach to more effectively ship bulk material such as lineal moulding. My idea was to have lineal moulding (in sixteen-foot pieces) palletized for forklift unloading in shipping from the west coast to the east coast. By doing it this way, one person could unload a boxcar in one-two hours when previously it took two or three men at least two full days to do the same thing. I was able to make this innovative plan a reality with the help of a mill in California. My idea became the rule for the industry, rather than the exception, for shipments of this type of material from the west to the east coast.

At this point, I convinced our redwood lumber supplier, Pacific Lumber Company, the largest producer of redwood, to ship palletized lumber to us and we had the first one ever shipped by them to any customer.

During this time period, I had been aware of opportunities in the home center business and introduced throughout the southeast, a large number of home improvement and decorator products, which had not been in the marketplace previously. During that period, whenever a national building material convention was held, Raford Cade from Texas, Joe Jentis from New Jersey and I were the three most sought-after attendees as we were the most successful innovators and promoters.

As a result of this success, I became way too full of myself and made a series of dumb, impulsive decisions. My lifestyle was also out of whack and, although I went to church regularly, I definitely did not have anything close to having a right relationship with the Lord. When you assemble the elements I just went over, it was not whether I was in for a fall but just when it would happen. Things were looking very bright as we were now doing business all over a wide section of the southeast and not just in Florida. However, my errors were huge. Instead of doing things God's way, I felt that if I worked hard enough on a consistent basis, and was clever in making deals and in promotion, it was inevitable that I would be successful.

Then came my accident with the tractor-trailer which I barely survived. But, fortunately, God really got my attention. Before that event, I made decisions and did things my way instead of God's way and fell very hard on my rear end as a result. I've often wondered what might have been if I had only done it His way rather than my own ill-advised one. Well, so much for that melancholy.

I have previously mentioned the rigors I had with my Chapter 11 bankruptcy. I really do not know how I survived those seven years of hell. Only by the grace of God and His guidance, and the never-to-be-forgotten love, patience, and sacrifice of my precious wife could I have ever made it through that nightmare. I definitely want to emphasize that in spite of the apparent opportunity wasted and the financial loss suffered, it was a turning point in my life. I am thoroughly convinced that it was the biggest benefit I've ever experienced as I learned the importance of doing things God's way and not my way.

In finalizing your decisions, *do not*, let me repeat, *do not* do it in an impulsive manner and *do not* get ahead of God as I did. Please, please don't mess up as I did. In closing this section, I ask that you consider this thought from a booklet called *In Touch*. "God's plan for every Believer is made up of a lifetime of small opportunities. We should seek to serve the Lord daily in fulfilling these opportunities. Ask yourself, can God use me? Then tell God you are available to work for Him in any way He desires. Peace and joy await you. His way, not ours, is Always best."

A final thought from *Our Daily Bread* is quite meaningful to me and I want to share it with you. "Take every opportunity to serve the Lord."

PATIENCE

How many of you reading this have ever said "I want to be more patient and I want to be more patient right now?" Patience is one of the fruits of the Spirit and I hope that each of you will strive to be more patient with others on a consistent basis. When you follow this suggestion, I believe you will be surprised by how many things are more positive in your affairs.

Rest in the Lord and wait patiently for Him... (Psalms 37:7)

Be still and listen for Him to guide you. And from *Streams in the Desert*: "Nothing but seeing God in everything will make us patient and loving with those who annoy and trouble us."

But the fruit of the Spirit is love, joy, peace, patience, kindness, goodness, faithfulness, gentleness, and self control; against such things there is no law. Now those who belong to Christ Jesus have crucified the flesh with its passions and desires. If we live by the Spirit, let us also walk by the Spirit. (Galatians 5:22–25)

I encourage you to memorize these verses and to review them on a daily basis. They'll provide a sound foundation for your life.

I therefore, the prisoner of the Lord, entreat you to walk in a manner worthy of the calling with which you have been called, with all humility and gentleness, with patience, showing forbearance of one another in love, being diligent to preserve the unity of the Spirit in the bond of peace. (Ephesians 4:1–3)

Regardless of the burdens you bear, exercise patience.

And so, those who have been chosen of God, holy and beloved, put on a heart of compassion, kindness, humility, gentleness and patience. (Colossians 3:12)

If you will follow this profound advice, your life will be full.

And we urge you, brethren, admonish the unruly, encourage the fainthearted, help the weak, be patient with all men. (1 Thessalonians 5:14)

In today's fast-paced world, it is often difficult to exercise patience. However, if you will make the effort to utilize it, you will find your life much more in focus and peaceful.

The Lord is not slow about His promise as some count slowness, but is patient toward you, not wishing for any to perish but for all to come to repentance. (2 Peter 3:9)

His delay is for the purpose of allowing more people to repent.

PEACE

It should be our mission to seek peace and well-being with others. However, there may come a time when your efforts may falter or fail. At that point, ask Almighty God which course you should follow. Do this, and follow His guidance, and be careful not to act impulsively.

Lovingkindness and truth have met together; Righteousness and peace have kissed each other. Truth springs from the earth and righteousness looks down from heaven. Indeed the Lord will give what is good. (Psalms 85:10-12)

Read and reread this and understand the real meaning of peace.

Those who love Thy law have great peace, and nothing causes them to stumble. (Psalms 119:165)

Think of the comfort and peace in this verse and praise the Lord.

"There is no peace for the wicked," says the Lord. (Isaiah 48:22)

Do you think this is true? A wicked person may have large amounts of money and property, a beautiful family, prestige in the community, and positions of respect. But do all of these things really provide peace? If you believe that, I urge you to reconsider, as peace is only found in committing yourself to Jesus Christ and loving and following Him.

"Come to Me, all who are weary and heavy laden, and I will give you rest..." (Matthew 11:28)

Jesus provides peace like no other. And, from *Streams in the Desert*: "It is such a comfort to drop the tangles of life into God's hands and leave them there and find the peace of God which passes all understanding."

"Peace I leave with you; My peace I give to you not as the world gives, do I give to you. Let not your heart be troubled nor let it be fearful..." (John 14:27)

Give God's peace as His witness to everyone we meet wherever we go. Overcome your hesitancy to be a witness for Jesus. I am curious; would you want Jesus to overlook you?

Therefore having been justified by faith, we have peace with God through our Lord Jesus Christ. (Romans 5:1)

True peace is only available through God and the acceptance of the Lord Jesus Christ. Do you really want it? You do have a choice, use it wisely.

…for God is not a God of confusion but of peace. (1 Corinthians 14:33)

Peace flows through Him and our Lord Jesus Christ.

But the fruit of the Spirit is love, joy, peace, patience, kindness, goodness, faithfulness, gentleness, and self control; against such things there is no law. Now those who belong to Christ Jesus have crucified the flesh with its passions and desires. If we live by the Spirit, let us also walk by the Spirit. (Galatians 5:22–25)

Peace never goes out of favor.

Be anxious for nothing, but in everything by prayer and supplication with thanksgiving let your requests be known to God. And the peace of God which surpasses all comprehension shall guard your hearts and mind in Christ Jesus. (Philippians 4:6–7)

A very powerful statement. Open your heart and allow this to sink into your soul as this is the only way to experience perfect peace.

And let the peace of Christ rule in your hearts, to which indeed you were called in one body, and be thankful. (Colossians 3:15)

What rules in your heart? Pleasure and good times? If that is the case, I suggest that you spend a little quiet time and do a reappraisal.

"The music of life is in your soul, if peace is in your heart." Another pearl from *Streams in the Desert*.

But the wisdom from above is first pure, then peaceable, gentle, reasonable, full of mercy and good fruits, unwavering without hypocrisy. And the seed whose fruit is righteousness is sown in peace by those who make peace. (James 3:17–18)

I believe this passage is a magnificent expression to live by.

Grace, mercy and peace will be with us, from God the Father and from Jesus Christ, the Son of the Father, in truth and love. (2 John 1:3)

This is a fitting time to include this offering from *Our Daily Bread*: "God's grace is immeasurable, His mercy, inexhaustible, and His peace inexpressible." Endeavor to utilize all of these traits and virtues practically in your life.

…He shall wipe away every tear from their eyes, and there shall no longer be any death; there shall no longer be any mourning or crying or pain; the first things have passed away. (Revelation 21:4)

At this time, Jesus will bring true peace to all of His believers.

Let's close this topic with this thought from *Our Daily Bread*: "Prayer with thanksgiving produces peace."

PERSEVERENCE

This means to continue firmly on course regardless of the problems or obstacles that confront you. Many people do not have a real understanding of what perseverance really means. I learned it under very difficult circumstances. From 1976 until 1983, as I worked my way through a chapter 11 bankruptcy, I had to stretch myself as I had never done previously. During most of those years, I generally worked seventy to eighty hours per week to meet expenses and also develop enough return to repay creditors. After the Chapter 11 was first filed, my employees who once numbered over fifty were now down to five. Our fleet of large trucks was reduced to one fourteen-foot flatbed. And, on top of all that, we had only a total of $13,500 of working capital. However, with this meager assortment of resources, in seven years I paid off over $1,643,000 of obligations. This was exhausting but I simply had to do all that I could do. Without a doubt, there is no way that I could have endured and been successful in reaching my goals without the power that God gave me to sustain myself. This could not have been achieved without significant love and patient understanding from my wife. I trust that you will not have to push yourself that severely but I encourage you to always make the effort to be both consistent and persistent in everything you do.

When you encounter serious decisions or problems, how do you approach or deal with them? Which do you think is best, to do it on your own or with the guidance of Almighty God? There is only one correct answer.

Remember difficulty challenges energy and perseverance. Are you up to the challenge?

...exult in our tribulations, knowing that tribulation brings about perseverance; and perseverance, proven character; and proven character, hope, and hope does not disappoint, because the love of God has been poured out within our hearts, through the Holy Spirit who was given to us. (Romans 5:3–5)

Always remember that God is at work during any trial you may encounter. Always keep in touch with Him for guidance. Trust in Him no matter what you may face. And from *Streams in the Desert*: "The road to triumph is successful when you persevere through the waste land of tribulation."

...not lagging behind in diligence, fervent in spirit, serving the Lord; rejoicing in hope, persevering in tribulation, devoted to prayer. (Romans 12:11-12)

When you have a trial or problem, do you approach it in the manner expressed in the passage above? If not, why? Let your zeal to succeed in this never slacken.

Pay close attention to yourself and in your teaching; persevere in these things, for as you do this you will insure salvation both for yourself and for those who hear you. (1 Timothy 4:16)

Are you eager to share with others what Christ is doing in your life? If not, why?

Here's one additional thought I want you to think about in terms of how it may apply to you. What is your opinion of this quotation from Thomas Edison? "Our greatest weakness is in giving up. The most certain way to success is to try one more time."

PLANNING

All plans should be formulated in two distinct ways. First, consider them with the aid of trusted associates and prudent financial advisors. Get their advice on your mission and the best method to achieve it. However, prior to actually moving forward, submit your full and complete plans to God. Ask for His directions *every day*. Listen well for His direction as He leads you to modify or eliminate aspects of your plan. Then act with determined consistency. One last point; if God ever extends a plan for you to act upon, do not hesitate but do it right away regardless of whether it seems realistic to you or not. His way is *always* best.

Without consultation plans are frustrated, but with many counselors they succeed. (Proverbs 15:22)

This may be both true and also incorrect. It is a wise move to consult individuals who are knowledgeable on the subject. However, when there are too many consultants, the outcome can often become spoiled. I encourage you to make the final consultant Almighty God as He never makes mistakes. However, remember His schedule is not the same as yours so exercise patience.

The plans of the heart belong to man, but the answer of the tongue is from the Lord. (Proverbs 16:1)

Always consider this before moving forward in whatever you do.

"For this reason the Father loves Me, because I lay down My life that I may take it again, No one has taken it away from Me, but I lay it down of My own initiative, I have authority to lay it down, and I have authority to take it up again. This commandment I received from My Father." (John 10:17–18)

The plan of God, the Father Almighty, was in place prior to the entrance of Jesus Christ into the world. It was His plan from the beginning that Jesus would come into this world to take away the sins of the world through His sacrifice, death and resurrection.

Do not seek what you shall eat, and what you shall drink, and do not keep worrying. For all these things the nations of the world eagerly seek; but your Father knows that you need these things. But seek for His kingdom, and these things shall be added unto to you. (John 12:29-31)

Always remember this as you plan your life.

I ask you to consider this thoughtful passage:

The mind of a man plans his way, but the Lord directs his steps. (Proverbs 16:9)

Let this be the way that you follow through with your plans.

In closing this section, I have a thought for you to consider regarding your planning. God has a plan for each of us. He never makes mistakes. Any road will get there, but if you do not have a good plan, it is more than likely you will not end up where you want to be.

PRAISE

Never hesitate to lift up praise and thanksgiving to our Lord God. Be sure that you do this without any doubts or questions and be positive that this is expressed with respectful enthusiasm. We should also extend our praise to others as we encourage them to achieve and fulfill their dreams and ambitions. And, never forget to praise your children as they gain in understanding and perception.

We will not conceal them from their children, but tell to the generation to come the praises of the Lord, and His strength and His wondrous works that He has done. (Psalms 78:4)

History repeats itself again and again. Far too many generations do not seem to understand the importance of explaining to our children our responsibilities in obeying God.

With my mouth I will give thanks abundantly to the Lord; And in the midst of many I will praise Him. (Psalms 109:30)

How recently have you done exactly this? Are you out of the habit? Better shape up!

Let my soul live that I may praise Thee, and let Thine ordinances help me. (Psalms 119:175)

Always open yourself to praise the Lord.

Let everything that has breath praise the Lord… (Psalms 150:6)

All should pay heed to this.

Do not boast about tomorrow, for you do not know what a day may bring forth. Let another praise you and not your own mouth. (Proverbs 27:1–2)

Put this advice in your memory box and keep it handy at all times.

Finally, brethren, whatever is true, whatever is honorable, whatever is right, whatever is pure, whatever is lovely, whatever is of good repute, if there is any excellence and if anything is worthy of praise, let your mind dwell on these things. (Philippians 4:8)

This is a very thoughtful and meaningful message for all of to remember.

PRAYER

It is exceptionally important for you to make prayer a priority in your life. When you pray, open yourself up to fully explain your thoughts to God. It should be remembered that prayer is not just making a list of requests of needs and wants. Prayer should open with thanksgiving for all the blessings that have been received. Thanksgiving should be followed by the asking of forgiveness for our transgressions of thought, word, and deed. At that point, you should ask for His guidance and direction on how and what to do in addressing your frustrations and your trials. Waiting for His response requires discipline.

Do not allow impulsive inclinations to lead you astray. Be fully alert and listen well for His direction in all things. Remember, prayer is a two-way exercise as you are actually having a conversation with God. Be still, wait quietly, and listen. You may feel an emotional nudge or perhaps a feeling like static. This is likely God responding. It is critical to understand that for a prayer to be answered by our Almighty God, you must first commit yourself to His Son, Jesus Christ. Without this commitment, your prayer will never be answered.

...According to the greatness of Thy compassion blot out my transgressions. Wash me thoroughly from any iniquity and cleanse me from my sin. (Psalms 51:1-2)

Every individual needs to use this refreshing prayer, from their heart, to cleanse themselves.

Create in me a clean heart, O God and renew a steadfast spirit within me Do not cast me away from Thy presence, and do not take Thy Holy Spirit from me. Restore to me the joy of Thy salvation, and sustain me with a willing spirit. (Psalms 51:10-12)

This is a beautiful and truly remarkable prayer. I suggest that you consider committing it to memory.

I listened recently to a sermon by Dr. Charles Stanley that covered a significant number of things that I want to review with you regarding your prayer life. I suggest that you take time for prayer (preferably at the beginning of each day.) And, don't hesitate to pray all throughout the day.

1. "You may be struggling with grief, and if this is your situation you will find comfort from God in prayer.
2. Utilize your time with God to build a relationship with Him.
3. There will be occasions when you are tempted by someone or something that you recognize as a potential problem. Ask God to strengthen you to avoid the temptation.
4. Open yourself to Him and confess all of your sins and be cleansed from all unrighteousness.
5. Use your prayer for guidance on any or all uncertainties that you encounter.
6. Conscientious prayer will help in dealing with anxiety or worry.
7. Prayer faithfully offered can strengthen your courage and your confidence.
8. Prayer is a healer of both emotional and physical distress.
9. When we pray, we must ask that our petitions be granted by His will. When we are obedient to the Lord, His Spirit will guide us and provide the wisdom we need in order to pray according to His will.
10. Pray as a family and remember the family that prays together stays together."

Life is uncertain and, as you proceed through it, do not hesitate to ask God to provide you with the proper direction. Remember this and make it a priority.

Give ear to my prayer, O God; and do not hide Thyself from my supplication. (Psalms 55:1)

How often do you pray? What do you pray for? Do you feel the presence of God when you pray? There are two things I encourage you to do when you pray. First, to persevere in your prayers as God answers prayer on His time and not on our own. Secondly, to be confident He will answer your prayer; just exercise patience and wait for His response and while waiting be still and feel His presence.

The sacrifice of the wicked is an abomination to the Lord, but the prayer of the upright is His delight. (Proverbs 15:8)

Never shy away from praising the Lord in your prayers.

Ask, and it shall be given to you, seek, and you shall find, knock, and it shall be opened to you. For everyone who knocks it shall be opened to you. For everyone who asks receives, and he who seeks finds, and to him who knocks it shall be opened. (Matthew 7:7-8)

Remember that prayer can gain access to a proud spirit, to the hardened heart, to the unbelieving mind; there are no walls too high or too thick to thwart God. Always pray fervently that God's will be done. You will see lives changed before you.

"All things you ask in prayer believing, you shall receive." (Matthew 21:22)

True faith and prayer have no bounds.

And it came about as He was praying in a certain place, after He had finished, one of his disciples said to Him, "Lord teach us to pray just as John also taught his disciples." And He said to them, "When you pray, say Father, hallowed be Thy name. Thy kingdom come. Give us each day our daily bread. And forgive us our sins. For we ourselves also forgive everyone who is indebted to us, and lead us not into temptation." (Luke 11:1-4)

This is the first recitation of the Lord's Prayer. When you say this prayer, I encourage you to say it slowly and, as you ponder the words, think of the meaning they convey.

...not lagging behind in diligence, fervent in spirit, serving the Lord; rejoicing in hope, persevering in tribulation, devoted to prayer. (Romans 12:11–12)

Do not let your zeal slacken as you pray.

I came across this prayer recently from an *In Touch* booklet and I ask that you consider using this in the next few days. "Father, I want to be like You. I want to love with abandon, to be courageous, to resist anger, to hold true to my convictions, to live with immense compassion. Teach me to follow the example of Jesus. Amen."

Devote yourselves to prayer, keeping alert in it with an attitude of thanksgiving. (Colossians 4:2)

Thoughtful words of advice regarding prayer.

For everything created by God is good and nothing is to be rejected, if it is received in gratitude; for it is sanctified by means of the word of God and prayer. (1 Timothy 4:4–5)

Christians should live affirmatively, neither renouncing the world for a life of self-denial nor plunging headlong into indulgence. Believers need to trust the Lord and pray with gratitude for His guidance.

And this is the confidence which we have before Him, that, if we ask anything according to His will, He hears us. And if we know that He hears us in whatever we ask, we know that we have the requests, which we have asked from Him. (1 John 5:14–15)

Be ever grateful for this and for His will to be done in our lives.

Here are some final thoughts before moving ahead. There are two types of prayer; false prayer and true prayer. False prayer is prayer offered by someone who does not believe in Jesus and this type of prayer will never be answered. True prayer is a dialogue between you and God. When you don't know where to turn and are not really comfortable or feeling at ease talking to anyone else about your situation or trial, make the decision to pray to our Almighty God as He is always available to listen.

I cannot express the importance of prayer too strongly and I wish to include some additional thoughts regarding prayer from *Streams in the Desert*.

1. We will get victory in prayer when we surrender our will to Him.
2. Do not go blindly into this dangerous world without prayer.
3. Nothing lies beyond the reach of prayer that lies outside the will of God.
4. Successful is the day when victory is won in prayer.

And, from *Our Daily Bread*: "The highest form of prayer comes from the depths of a humble heart."

PURPOSE

It is very important to understand that God has a purpose and plan for each and every one of us. It is very important that we recognize our primary purpose is to honor Him. Please do not just drift but be open to His guidance and direction at all times. In particular, be aware of the needs of those around us. Many of us are at some time brought to low levels. At that time, we should examine the real values and purposes of life.

Make every effort to place these true values into the proper perspective. If He calls you to do something, regardless of the situation, never delay in responding affirmatively to His call. It also may be a time of testing you in your faith. Stand firmly.

Before moving forward with this topic, I have a question. What do you think is the purpose of your life? Is it to be successful in a career or in business? Is it to be a good provider for your family? Is it to consider a run for political office? In other words, are you living for your own interests of success? All of these appear to be worthy goals but are you leaving out an important element by not considering how you can be of value by doing various things for God?

Each of us is here on this earth to be utilized for a unique purpose. With that in mind, spend some quality time in prayer with our Lord and ask Him for guidance. Ask Him what you can do to better serve Him as well as achieve goals for yourself. Learn to walk with God. Unfortunately, many people drift without taking hold of God's plan for their lives. Be on guard and do not let apparent pleasures lead you away from His purpose for you.

Life is frail in so many ways and we will experience tests as we go forward. However, utilize each day as a gift from Him because it is one that will never be reopened.

For I know the plans that I have for you, declares the Lord, plans for welfare and not for calamity to give you a future and a hope. Then you call upon Me and come and pray to Me, and I will listen to you. And you shall seek Me and find Me, when you search for Me with all your heart. (Jeremiah 29:11-13)

Do not proceed carelessly and ignore the plans our Lord has for you. Utilize prayer for guidance. Take your time and be a good listener.

"Go therefore and make disciples of all the nations, baptizing them in the name of the Father and the Son and the Holy Spirit, teaching them to observe all that I commanded you and lo, I am with you always even to the end of the age. (Matthew 28:19–20)

Before ascending into heaven, Jesus lays out for his disciples their mission.

And we know that God causes all things to work together for good to those who love God, to those who are called according to His purpose. (Romans 8:28)

We should always remember this piece of advice, particularly as we face adversities or difficulties.

Draw near to God and He will draw near to you. Cleanse your hands, you sinners, and purify your hearts, you double minded. (James 4:8)

Exercise purpose in your soul as you reach out to God.

Therefore, since Christ has suffered in the flesh, arm yourselves also with the same purpose, because he who has suffered in the flesh has ceased from sin. (1 Peter 4:1)

As you proceed on your pathway through life, bear in mind that although God may conceal the purpose of His ways, His ways are not without purpose. I want to tell you about a couple of events that have made me think about what purpose God has for my life. While traveling in New Brunswick, Canada as a sales rep I experienced some unusual happenings. The first occurred as I was driving from Bangor, Maine to St John in New Brunswick. It was winter, and the weather was really freezing cold. As I approached Calais, the last stop in Maine before the border, all of a sudden, my car went completely out of control although I did nothing to make that happen.

Suddenly, I realized that I was experiencing "black ice." Once you are on it the wild ride begins. I was on a two-lane road when the car danced over both lanes doing a 360° plus spin. If anything had been coming, I would have been toast. Be cautious if you are ever in an area when it is exceptionally cold and icy. I can assure you a situation like this is both unnerving and very scary.

The other event that happened during my sales career in New Brunswick, Canada was on a day that was quite snowy. Having spent the previous night in St John, I was traveling to my first call in Petiticodiac. About ten miles from my destination, the snow was blanketing down hard and it became very difficult to see the road. Fortunately, I was on a four-lane, divided highway. But the snow increased even more. Out of nowhere, a snowplow passed me as we were both going no more that fifteen miles per hour. I thought this was fortunate as I could now just follow the plow. The bad news was that the plow evaporated into a white-out. There was no way I could stop or pull over to the shoulder as I could not see anything.

By the grace of God, I crept along going about ten miles per hour and did not drive off the highway or get struck by another vehicle. Finally, the snow slowed enough so I could see my exit. Two other drivers that morning were not that fortunate as they were killed shortly after in the same area. These two events now make thirteen times I have had a close call with unanticipated death.

Why have I survived so many of these events? They make me wonder and I try to contemplate the reason or reasons why. I do not want, in any way, to come off to you in a manner that appears pompous or self-important, as I have certainly been humbled, as I have explained earlier. I believe that God wants me to write this book in order to reach others who are struggling with their own lives and circumstances.

I hope and pray this is reality as I feel compelled to tell others about my life and, hopefully, they can profit from my fallacies and errors. With all my heart, I am hopeful that this is particularly important and meaningful to each of you who have taken the time to read this; but most of all, I want this for my family who I love very much. Meanwhile, let's continue to look over other things about God's way.

Never allow your faith to falter as God has a divine purpose for you. Please, when this purpose is exposed to you do exactly what God wants you to do without exception. God has a purpose for each of us. I wonder what yours is. Do you?

QUIETNESS

When we come before the presence of our Heavenly Father, remember the words that He says: "Be still and know that I am God."

Better is a dry morsel and quietness with it than a house full of feasting with strife. (Proverbs 17:1)

It is far more important to be able to enjoy what you have without arguing and bitterness.

The words of the wise heard in quietness are better than the shouting of a ruler among fools. (Ecclesiastes 9:17)

Raising one's voice with loud and noisy sounds is not helpful in solving problems. Please be attentive to this.

Without our quiet time with God, we will deny our dependence upon Him.

…make it your ambition to lead a quiet life and attend to your own business and work with your hands as we commanded you. (1 Thessalonians 4:11)

Some had believed that Christ was coming again soon and were working with reluctance.

Here's some advice for you that I had mentioned previously: as you begin, or continue in your prayer life, make every effort to find and establish a quiet location so that you can concentrate on your conversation with the Lord. Interruptions prevent you from both conveying your messages and thanksgivings as well as hearing the thoughts the Lord is giving you.

First of all, then, I urge that entreaties and prayers, petitions and thanksgivings be made in behalf of all men, for kings and all who are in authority, in order that we may lead a tranquil and quiet life in all godliness and dignity. This is good and acceptable in the sight of God our Savior. (1 Timothy 2:1–3)

To be able to live in a quiet atmosphere and lifestyle is desirable for all individuals.

QUESTIONING

A mind may question many things but never doubt the presence and purposes of our Almighty God. He is ever near to each of us, if we will only reach out to Him.

What shall I render to the Lord for all His benefits toward me? (Psalms 116:12)

This question needs to be answered by each individual after considerable and careful thought. Have you ever thought about this?

Another question that should be considered is this: "what does the Bible claim for itself?" It claims that all scripture is God-bred, and this question is answered in the following passage.

All scripture is inspired by God for teaching of reproof, for correction, for training in righteousness. (2 Timothy 3:16)

Here's another question raised by many: "does man corrupt the truth by recording it for or by themselves?" For the answer to this question I refer you to the following passage.

For no prophecy was ever made by an act of human will, but by the Holy Spirit spoke from God. (2 Peter 1:21)

Consider what is expressed here; the Holy Spirit is actually a co-author with the individual who wrote this portion of the scripture.

Jesus questioned the Pharisees as seen in the following.

Now while the Pharisees were gathered together Jesus asked them a question, saying, "What do you think about the Christ, whose son is He?" They said to Him, "The son of David." He said to them, "Then how does David in the Spirit call Him Lord saying The Lord said to my Lord, "Sit at my right hand until I put Thine enemies under Thy feet?" "If David then calls Him Lord, how is He his son?" And no one was able to answer Him a word, nor did dare from that day on to ask Him another question. (Matthew 22:41–45)

Without a doubt, Jesus, in His wisdom, quelled further questions about who He was to the Pharisees. How about you? Do you question whether or not Jesus is the Son of God? Please consider this, with care, as there is only one correct answer.

RECONCILIATION

This relates to our changed relationship with the Lord. Through our belief in Him our trespasses are forgiven. By our belief, all things will be changed and brought into unity with Him.

And not only this, but we also exult in God through our Lord Jesus Christ, through whom we have now received the reconciliation. (Romans 5:11)

Reconciliation is a blessing you receive in your life when you commit to Jesus Christ.

But I am speaking to you who are Gentiles. Inasmuch then as I am an apostle of Gentiles, I magnify my ministry, if somehow I might move to jealousy my fellow countrymen and save some of them. For if their rejection of the reconciliation of the world, what will their acceptance be but life from the dead? (Romans 11:13-15)

As the Jews of Israel rejected Jesus Christ, they also lost a portion of their favor as a nation.

Now all things are from God, who reconciled us to Himself through Christ, and gave us the ministry of reconciliation, namely, that God was in Christ reconciling the world to Himself, not counting their trespasses against them, and He has committed to us the word of reconciliation. Therefore, we are ambassadors for Christ, as God were entreating through us, we beg you on behalf of Christ to be reconciled to God. He made Him who knew no sin to be sin on our behalf, that we might become the righteousness of God in Him. (2 Corinthians 5:18–21)

Because of reconciliation, a significant change occurs in us with the blessing of salvation.

For it was the Father's good pleasure for all the fullness to dwell in Him, and through Him to reconcile all things to Himself, having made peace through the blood of His cross; through Him, I say whether things on earth or things in heaven. (Colossians 1: 19–20)

Christ is the remedy for alienation from God and eventually all things will be changed and brought into unity through Him.

REDEMPTION

Only through Christ Jesus does this occur, as the sinner who believes in Christ receives God's gift of grace which then enables God to pronounce him righteous.

No man by any means can redeem his brother, or give to God a ransom for him. For the redemption of his soul is costly, and he should cease trying forever. (Psalms 49:7–8)

Redemption is the power that leads to salvation and can only be achieved by committing to God through Jesus Christ.

For all have sinned and fall short of the glory of God, being justified as a gift by His grace through the redemption which is in Christ Jesus. (Romans 3:23–24)

Only through Jesus Christ can anyone be redeemed.

In Him we have redemption through His blood, the forgiveness of our trespasses, according to the richness of His grace. (Ephesians 1:7)

There are three ideas involved in the doctrine of redemption. First, paying the ransom with the blood of Christ. Second, removal from the curse of the law, and, lastly, release from the bondage of sin into the freedom of grace.

And do not grieve the Holy Spirit of God, by whom you were sealed for the day of redemption. (Ephesians 4:30)

The Holy Spirit is grieved or pained by sin, especially by sins of the tongue.

…knowing that you were not redeemed with perishable things like silver or gold from your futile way of life inherited from your forefathers, but with precious blood as of a lamb unblemished and spotless, the blood of Christ. (1 Peter 1:18–19)

Your redemption is by the sinlessness of Jesus Christ.

REPENTANCE

Repentance is the act of asking for forgiveness of our sins and, then, turning our lives around, committing to follow God through belief and faith in our Lord Jesus Christ.

He who conceals his transgressions will not prosper, but he who confesses and forsakes them will find compassion. (Proverbs 28:13)

When asking for forgiveness and redemption from the Lord, do not ever attempt to conceal your guilt. Be completely honest. Quite a few years ago, my wife and I, and several friends, attended a retreat at the Convent of St. Mary in Peekskill, New York. It was a very moving experience and during quiet time I thought back over my life. I tried to remember various things for which I had asked Jesus for forgiveness. During that time, I remembered some things that I had never asked forgiveness for and confessed them to one of the priests and he prayed for my forgiveness. I encourage you to scan your soul and ask for forgiveness for all your sins and not just part of them.

...He said to them, "Thus it is written, that the Christ should suffer and rise again from the dead the third day, and that repentance for forgiveness of sins should be proclaimed in His name to all the nations, beginning with Jerusalem." (Luke 24:46–47)

This was the plan of God; that through this sequence of events, mankind could gain forgiveness of their sins and transgressions.

Do you think lightly of the riches of His kindness and forbearance and patience, not knowing the kindness of God leads you to repentance? (Romans 2:4)

Have you ever considered this element of the kindness of God from the perspective of it leading you to bear witness to Him? Just do it.

For the sorrow that is according to the will of God produces a repentance without regret, leading to salvation; but the sorrow of the world produces death. (2 Corinthians 7:10)

Godly sorrow leads to joy. Pay attention to this, please.

The Lord is not slow about His promise, as some count slowness, but is patient towards you, not wishing for any to perish but for all to come to repentance. (2 Peter 3:9)

Understand that our timing does not coincide with His timing.

RESURRECTION

This is God's plan for the salvation of all individuals and nations. Throughout history, this event will always be recognized as perhaps the most important ever. Jesus Christ, the Son of God, was crucified and paid the penalty of death for all our sins. Three days later, He rose from the dead and fulfilled God's purpose for mankind to move from sin to salvation.

"He is not here, for He is risen, just as He said, come and see the place where He was lying…" (Matthew 28:6)

This simply-stated fact is the basis of our Christian faith.

"For this reason the Father loves Me, that I may lay down My life, that I may take it up again. No one has taken it away from Me, but I lay it down on My own initiative, I have authority to lay it down, and I have authority to take it up again. This commandment I received from My Father." (John 10:17-18)

Jesus explains the love that the Father has for Him and also His willingness to obey the will of the Father.

Jesus said to her, "I am the resurrection and the life, he who believes in Me shall live even if he dies…" (John11:25)

There should be no greater comfort for a believer than this.

...if the Spirit of Him who raised Jesus from the dead dwells in you, He who raised Christ Jesus from the dead will also give life to your mortal bodies through His Spirit that dwells in you. (Romans 8:11)

Think of the power and meaning of this verse.

Now if Christ is preached that He has been raised from the dead, how do some among you say that there is no resurrection of the dead? But if there is no resurrection of the dead, not even Christ has been raised; and if Christ has not been raised, then our preaching is vain, your faith also is vain. (1 Corinthians 15:12–14)

If the bodily resurrection is untrue then the preaching of the gospel is a lie and Christian faith is meaningless.

So also is the resurrection of the dead. It is sown a perishable body, it is raised an imperishable body; it is sown in dishonor, it is raised in glory, it is sown in weakness, it is raised in power. (1 Corinthians 15:42–43)

Recognize that the imperishable body suffers no decay. Do you comprehend the benefit?

More than that I count all things to be loss in view of the surpassing value of knowing Christ Jesus my Lord, for whom I have suffered the loss of all things but count them as rubbish in order that I may gain Christ, and may be found in Him not having righteousness of my own derived from the Law, but that which is through faith in Christ the righteousness which comes from God on the basis of faith, that I may know Him, and the power of His resurrection and the fellowship of His sufferings, being conformed to His death; in order that I may attain to the resurrection from the dead. Not that I have already obtained it, or have already become perfect, but I press on in order that I may lay hold of that for which also I was laid hold of by Christ Jesus. (Philippians 3:8–12)

Here the apostle Paul explains his commitment and faith in the resurrection of Jesus.

Blessed be the God and Father of our Lord Jesus Christ, who according to His great mercy has caused us to be born again to a living hope through the resurrection. (1 Peter 1:3)

Here the apostle Peter explains the blessing of Jesus to the children of God.

REVERENCE

An emotion that is a blend of both respect for, and fear of, Almighty God. It is important for us to exercise quietness and thoughtfulness as we move before the presence of our Omnipotent God. We should approach the altar of the church with reverence as we kneel for communion. It is understakable that you may receive communion in another manner. However, reverence should always be exhibited when receiving this.

"You shall keep My sabbaths and reverence My sanctuary; I am the Lord." (Leviticus 26:2)

A straightforward and direct statement. Pay attention and observe.

Worship the Lord with reverence, and rejoice with trembling. (Psalms 2:11)

Follow this advice with prayer and thanksgiving.

…At Thy holy temple I will bow in reverence for Thee. (Psalms 5:7)

Never fail to exhibit humility before God.

Then the Lord said, "Because the people draw near with their words and honor Me with their lip service, but they remove their hearts far from Me, and their reverence for Me consists of tradition learned by rote, therefore behold I will once again deal marvelously with these people, wondrously marvelous..." (Isaiah 29:13-14)

Neither commitment nor reverence has meaning if stated in only a half-hearted manner. Do not make an irreverent commitment to God at any time.

By faith Noah, being warned by God about things not yet seen, in reverence prepared an ark for the salvation of his household, by which he condemned the world, and became an heir of the righteousness which is according to faith. (Hebrews 11:7)

Noah responded to the Lord with fear, respect, and reverence.

Sanctify Christ as Lord in your hearts, always being ready to make a defense to everyone who asks you to give an account for the hope that is in you, yet with gentleness and reverence. (1 Peter 1:15)

To sanctify Christ means to show reverence for Him.

RIGHTEOUS

The manner in which an individual molds the pattern of his life to follow the teachings and beliefs, in moral steadfastness, of our Almighty God, as well as the keeping of His commandments.

...a bribe blinds the eyes of the wise and perverts the words of the righteous. (Deuteronomy 16:19)

Do not accept illicit gains. That will distort your integrity.

"The Rock! His work is perfect. For all His ways are just; A God of faithfulness and without injustice, righteous and upright is He…" (Deuteronomy 32:4)

The Rock is a symbol of God's power and control over all elements opposed to evil.

The Lord knows the way of the righteous, but the way of the wicked will perish. (Psalms 1:6)

The wicked are spiritually dead and guilty before God. They will not be acquitted, either in this world or the next.

I have been young and now I am old; Yet I have not seen the righteous forsaken. (Psalms 37:25)

This is a very true and accurate statement both then and today.

The mouth of the righteous utters wisdom and his tongue speaks justice. (Psalms 37:30)

The use of the mouth gives evidence of one's character.

Cast your burden upon the Lord and He will sustain you. He will never allow the righteous to be shaken. (Psalms 55:22)

I encourage each of you who are faced with a difficult or burdensome situation to follow the thoughtful and meaningful advice in this verse.

Keep in mind and understand that the wicked appear to live in prosperity and those that live in a righteous manner may not seem to have a comparable reward. Do not forget it is far better to have a short time of apparent mediocrity or loss and a long-term reward of eternity.

The righteous man will flourish like the palm tree, he will grow like a cedar in Lebanon. Planted in the house of the Lord, they will flourish in the courts of our God. They will still yield fruit in old age; They shall be full of sap and very green. (Psalms 92:12–14)

If you wish to stay young and useful as your years increase, maintain righteousness and lean on God every day.

Be glad in the Lord you righteous ones; And give thanks to His Holy name. (Psalms 97:12)

Never be slow to express thanksgiving and praise to our Almighty God.

The sum of Thy word is truth and every one of Thy righteous ordinances is everlasting. (Psalms 119:160)

There are no faults in the Word of the Lord.

The wages of the righteous is life. (Proverbs 10:16)

Not just this life, but life eternal.

A righteous man has regard for the life of his beasts... (Proverbs 12:10)

Be kind to your work animals and your pets.

The wicked flee when no one is pursuing, but the righteous are as bold as a lion. (Proverbs 28:1)

The righteous have no spirit of fear, only a spirit of confidence.

The righteous is concerned for the rights of the poor... (Proverbs 29:7)

Godless individuals, as a rule, have little knowledge with which to comprehend such things.

"God will judge both the righteous man and the wicked man, for a time for every matter and for every deed is there..." (Ecclesiastes 3:17)

No individual will escape judgment for either the good or evil that they have done, unless they have committed their lives to Jesus Christ and received forgiveness of their sins.

... law is not made for the righteous man, but for those who are lawless and rebellious, for the ungodly and sinners, for the unholy and profane, for those who kill their fathers or mothers, for murderers, and immoral men and homosexuals, and kidnapers and liars and perjurers, and whatever else is contrary to sound teaching. (1 Timothy 1:9-10)

Pay attention to sound teaching and not wishful thoughts.

If we confess our sins, He is faithful and righteous to forgive us our sins, and to cleanse us from all unrighteousness. (1 John 1:9)

Do not overlook this opportunity to be cleansed of your sin.

RIGHTEOUSNESS

The willingness and commitment of an individual to follow the loving pathway designed by God the Father in wisdom and understanding.

The Lord is righteous; He loves righteousness; the upright will behold His face. (Psalms 11:7)

God's eyelids narrow as He scrutinizes people.

He restores my soul; He guides me in the paths of righteousness for His name's sake. (Psalms 23:3)

God is always leading us towards paths which are right in His eyes and which will honor His name.

...for He is coming to judge the earth. He will judge the world in righteousness and the people in His faithfulness. (Psalms 96:13)

Jesus Christ will come again! Are you ready for this event?

...he who sows in righteousness gets a true reward. (Proverbs 11:18)

The labor of the wicked has no blessing and brings no permanent gain in contrast to the labor of the righteous which will earn an enduring reward.

To do righteousness and justice is desired by the Lord rather than sacrifice. (Proverbs 21:3)

A valid suggestion; do what pleases the Lord.

"For I say to you, that unless your righteousness surpasses that of the scribes and Pharisees, you shall not enter the kingdom of heaven..." (Matthew 5:20)

Jesus explains to the assembled crowd that their righteousness must be genuine and not like that shown by the hierarchy of the church of that period. This is applicable for us today as well.

...seek you first His kingdom and His righteousness and all these things will be added unto you. (Matthew 6:33)

Commit this verse to your memory and make it a cornerstone in your life.

I do not nullify the grace of God; for if righteousness comes through the Law, then Christ died needlessly. (Galatians 2:21)

If God wanted obedience by the law, He would not have sent His Son to suffer and die on the cross.

...flee from these things, you man of God, and pursue righteousness, godliness, faith, love, perseverance and gentleness. Fight the good fight of faith, take hold of the eternal life to which you were called and you made the good confession in the presence of many witnesses. (1 Timothy 6:11-12)

Direct your life to accomplish things God's way and do not waver in this plan.

He saved us not on the basis of deeds which we have done in righteousness, but according to His mercy, by the washing of regeneration and by renewing of the Holy Spirit. (Titus 3:5)

Personal salvation is not achieved through good deeds but by professing your faith and commitment to Jesus Christ.

...if you should suffer for the sake of righteousness, you are blessed. And do not fear their intimidation and do not be troubled... (1 Peter 3:14)

Suffering endured in this manner brings one closer to God.

SALVATION

This is granted to an individual who confesses his sins and asks for forgiveness and commits his life to Jesus Christ. Only in this manner may salvation be achieved.

Make me know Thy ways O Lord; teach me Thy paths. Lead me in Thy truth and teach me. For Thou art the God of my salvation; For I wait for Thee all the day. (Psalms 25:4–5)

It is wise to pay attention to these statements at all times.

The Lord is my light and salvation; Whom shall I fear? The Lord is the defense of my life; whom shall I dread? (Psalms 27:1)

Fear no one if you believe and trust in the Lord.

He who offers a sacrifice of thanksgiving honors me; And to him who orders his way right I shall show the salvation of God. (Psalms 50:23)

When you place these words firmly into your way of life, your life is transformed into the life that Christ wants you to live.

…His salvation is near those that fear Him. (Psalms 85:9)

Note that fear means respect as well as fear.

…Proclaim good tidings of His salvation from day to day. (Psalms 96:2)

I offer this suggestion; you should worship Our Lord with praise and thanksgiving each day, preferably at the earliest part of it and truly all throughout the day.

Salvation is far from the wicked, for they do not seek Thy statutes. (Psalms 119:155)

When one turns his back on God and only does things his way, sooner or later, consequences are coming to that individual.

I do not know why some people take so long to make their commitment to Jesus Christ and gain their salvation. As an example, during my childhood and later as an adult, I do not remember my father ever going to church with my mother or my family except to a christening of one of the children or perhaps to a funeral. Then one night I received a call from my Mom that my Dad had suffered a stroke and could not speak and was being rushed to the emergency room at Tampa General. After I arrived at the hospital, our priest, Father Canady, also arrived. He asked if we could see my Dad and we found him on a gurney in the ER. Father Canady stood over my Dad and said "John, I want to ask you a question." He said, "John, do you believe in the Lord Jesus Christ?" My father responded by saying, "Yes," but not another word. My Dad was not able to speak for several more days. After a period of recovery, he regained the ability to speak. Within a short time after that, my father was baptized and confirmed as a member of our church. Please don't wait this long. Make your commitment to love and follow Jesus as your Savior.

Our Father in heaven hears our prayers always. Be patient and listen for His words of guidance.

...I will rejoice in the God of my salvation. (Habakkuk 3:18)

This expresses complete confidence in God.

And all flesh shall see the salvation of God. (Luke 3:6)

But not all will experience it.

... if you confess with your mouth Jesus as Lord; and believe in your heart that God raised Him from the dead, you shall be saved; for with the heart man believes, resulting in righteousness, and with the mouth he confesses resulting in salvation. (Romans 10:9–10)

These verses are right on point as to what salvation means. There is no better explanation of salvation. Give your life into His hands and you will find the peace of mind that surpasses all understanding.

Therefore if any man is in Christ, he is a new creature; the old things have passed away; behold new things have come. (2 Corinthians 5:17)

Salvation brings about a change in attitude, thought, and deed.

...Christ also, having been offered once to bear the sins of many, shall appear a second time for salvation without reference to sin, to those who early await Him. (Hebrews 9:28)

At His second coming, He will take redeemed sinners to Himself to the consummation of their salvation.

SANCTIFICATION

God loves each of us and His purpose is to have us be more and more like Him and His Son. This often requires His molding of us in ways that we have never considered and frequently do not understand. This should not be resisted, although it is very possible that in this transition we may go through difficult times or experience suffering of some sort. In time, however, if we are patient and trusting, our lives will become more useful to Him as His light shines through us to those around us. From the moment a person places his trust in the Lord Jesus Christ, God's transforming work of sanctification will be ongoing throughout his or her life. It must be understood that this is accomplished only through our brokenness.

But having been freed from sin and enslaved to God, you derive your benefits resulting in sanctification and the outcome, eternal life. For the wages of sin is death but the free gift of God is eternal life in Christ Jesus our Lord. (Romans 6:22:23)

From the moment an individual places his or her complete trust in Jesus Christ, God will begin His transforming work of sanctification. This is not a temporary or intermittent situation but will be going on throughout their lives.

...do you not know that the unrighteous shall not inherit the kingdom of God? Do not be deceived; neither fornicators, nor idolaters, nor adulterers, nor effeminate, nor homosexuals, nor thieves, not the covetous, nor drunkards, nor revilers, nor swindlers shall inherit the kingdom of God. And such were some of you; but you were washed, but you were sanctified, but you were justified in the name of the Lord Jesus Christ, and the Spirit of God. (1 Corinthians 6:9–11)

Be ever grateful you've put your former participation in unrighteous activities behind you and now commit yourself to God through Jesus Christ.

...God has chosen you from the beginning for salvation through sanctification by the Spirit and faith in the truth. (2 Thessalonians 2:13)

Both the Holy Spirit's work of regeneration and man's faith are equally necessary in salvation.

For everything created by God is good and nothing is to be rejected, if it is received with gratitude; for it is sanctified by means of the word of God and prayer. (1 Timothy 4:4–5)

The apostle Paul expresses that the Christian should live affirmatively, neither renouncing the world for a life of self-denial nor plunging into indulgence.

...if we walk in the light as He Himself is in the light, we have fellowship with one another, and the blood of Jesus His Son cleanses us from all sin. If we say we have no sin, we are deceiving ourselves, and the truth is not in us. If we confess our sins, He is faithful and righteous to forgive us our sins and to cleanse from all unrighteousness. (1 John 1:7–9)

Sanctification is an on-going procedure as the sins of mankind are forgiven and we are blessed by our Savior.

SELF-CONTROL

When you are in a high-pressure situation, how do you respond? Impetuously or thoughtfully? Do you express a calm demeanor, or do you lose your temper? A person who restrains his emotions and acts in an even manner is expressing self-control. Far too often, this element is not maintained leading to poor or disastrous results. Been there, done that. Please make the effort to avoid the errors that I have made.

He who is slow to anger is better than the mighty, and he who rules his spirit than he who captures a city. (Proverbs 16:32)

Make every effort to manage your demeanor and you will enhance your success.

Like a city that is broken in to and without walls is a man that has no control over his spirit. (Proverbs 25:28)

Lack of self-control will almost always result in unpleasantness and unhappiness.

Stop depriving one another, except by agreement for a time that you may devote yourself to prayer, and come together again lest Satan tempt you because of your lack of self control. (1 Corinthians 7:5)

Constant or repeated arguing is usually worthless; avoid it without fail.

The fruit of the Spirit is love, joy, peace, patience, kindness, goodness, faithfulness, gentleness, self control; against such things there is no law. Now those who belong to Christ Jesus have crucified the flesh with its passions and desires. If we live by the Spirit let us also walk by the Spirit. (Galatians 5:22–25)

Always remember that self-control is one of the fruits of the spirit. I encourage you to read these verses and, perhaps even, commit them to memory as a cornerstone of your belief and faith in Jesus Christ.

I strongly believe that if any individual pursues the course of developing and maintaining self-control in their lives that their lives will be far less stressful and far more productive.

Never permit self-will to deter or overcome your self-control.

SIN

The transgressions committed by mankind against the Laws of God in either thought, word, or deed are plainly laid out in the

Ten Commandments. In addition, blasphemy is also sin. There are some who believe that sin has no consequences. If you believe this, you are deceiving yourself. Sin has consequences. Sometimes these consequences are immediate, but, most often, they'll show up later. Some people rationalize their behavior by saying this or that was not really a sin or just maybe a little one. You simply cannot pick and choose how to exercise obedience to the commandments of God. Partial obedience in the eyes of God is disobedience. If one deceives himself after sinning, some of the results are fear, guilt, and shame. Have you ever considered any of the circumstances discussed here? How have you handled it? Does it make you uncomfortable? If so, open your heart to Jesus and confess your sins, and not just partially as no sin is hidden from Him.

How blessed is he whose transgressions is forgiven; whose sin is covered! (Psalms 32:1)

Have you ever felt that you have committed a sin that could not be forgiven? Jesus will forgive you. If you confess with your mouth and commit to Him and follow Him your sins may be forgiven.

Transgression speaks to the ungodly within his heart; There is no fear of God before his eyes. (Psalms 36:1)

I feel pity for anyone who does not understand that God is omnipotent and does not have the knowledge or judgment to fear Him.

I said, "I will guard my ways, which I may not sin with my tongue; I will guard my mouth as with a muzzle, while the wicked are in my presence." (Psalms 39:1)

Guard the power of your tongue as words carelessly spoken will provide a severe bite to yourself.

A brief statement from the booklet *Our Daily Bread* is appropriate to consider: "God can purge our hearts of the sin that destroys our intimacy with Him and with others."

Deliver my soul, O Lord, from lying lips, from a deceitful tongue. (Psalms 120:2)

To lie is to sin against both God and yourself.

"Therefore I say to you any sin and blasphemy shall be forgiven men, but blasphemy against the Spirit shall not be forgiven." (Matthew 12:31)

Jesus has plainly said that blasphemy against the Holy Spirit is an unforgiveable sin.

"For from within, out of the heart of men, proceed the evil thoughts, fornications, thefts, murders, adulteries, deeds of coveting and wickedness, as well as deceit, sensuality, envy, pride, slander and foolishness. All these evil things proceed from within and defile the man." (Mark 7:21–23)

Have you ever examined your own thoughts to check if you are experiencing such thoughts and desires from your heart? If so, proceed with care and considerable thoughtfulness. Open your heart to Jesus and ask for forgiveness and guidance.

Jesus answered them, "Truly, truly, I say to you everyone who commits sin is a slave of sin, and the slave does not remain in the house forever; the sin does remain forever. If therefore, the Son shall make you free, you shall be free indeed." (John 8:34–36)

Make it your goal to sincerely confess your sins and allow Jesus Christ to forgive you of your sins.

But God demonstrates His own love towards us, in that while we were still sinners, Christ died for us. (Romans 5:8)

Thoughtfully consider this demonstration of love; that Jesus Christ died for each of us.

For the death that He died, He died to sin, once for all; but the life that He lives, He lives to God. (Romans 6:10)

Jesus died to fulfill God's will for the forgiveness of sin.

Therefore do not let sin reign in your mortal body that you should obey its lusts. (Romans 6:12)

There are two choices; dethrone sin or obey its evil desires. Choose with discretion.

Therefore what benefit were you then deriving from the things of which you are now ashamed? For the outcome of these things is death. But having been freed from sin and enslaved to God, you derive your benefits resulting in sanctification and the outcome, eternal life. For the wages of sin is death, but the free gift of God is eternal life in Christ Jesus our Lord. (Romans 6:21-23)

Please read and reread this verse and consider the power and meaning in it. Which do you prefer...death or eternal life?

Therefore let us not judge one another anymore, but rather determine this – not to put an obstacle or stumbling block in a brother's way. (Romans 14:13)

In other words, do not tempt others into sin.

...I urge you brethren, keep your eye on those who cause dissensions and hindrances contrary to the teaching which you learned and turn away from them. For such men are slaves not of the Lord Christ but of their own appetites; and by their smooth and flattering speech they deceive the hearts of the unsuspecting. (Romans 16:17–18)

I trust that you will not allow yourself to be conned by the slick and smooth talk of those who advocate sin and destruction.

I wrote you in my letter not to associate with immoral people... I wrote to you not to associate with any so-called brother, if he should be an immoral person, or covetous, or an idolater or a reviler, or a drunkard or a swindler – not even to eat with such a one... Remove the wicked man from among yourselves. (1 Corinthians 5:9, 11, 13)

It's not realistic to imagine having no contact with those who are evil but avoid fellowship with those who you know are evil.

Or do you not know that the unrighteous shall not inherit the kingdom of God? Do not be deceived, neither fornicators, nor idolaters, nor adulterers, nor effeminate, nor homosexuals, nor thieves, nor the covetous, nor drunkards, nor revilers, nor swindlers will inherit the kingdom of God. And such were some of you; but you were washed, but you were sanctified, but you were justified in the name of the Lord Jesus Christ and in the spirit of our God. (1 Corinthians 6:9–11)

Guilt is a heavy burden; don't let it drag you down. God promises to deal with all your needs. Why not try things His way? If you do, I believe that you will find your burdens not as heavy and some may even disappear.

Flee immorality. Every other sin that a man commits is outside the body, but the immoral man sins against his own body. Or do you not know that your body is a temple of the Holy Spirit who is in you, whom you have from God, and that you are not your own? For you have been bought with a price; therefore glorify God in your body. (1 Corinthians 6:18–20)

Avoid the adulterous person for they are guaranteed trouble.

Therefore whoever eats the bread or drinks the cup of the Lord in an unworthy manner shall be guilty of the body and blood of the Lord. (1 Corinthians 11:27)

If you approach the altar of the Lord with unconfessed sin, or in an unworthy manner, you are subject to judgment.

Do not be deceived. Bad company corrupts good morals. (1 Corinthians 15:33)

Good and simple advice. Consistently pay attention to this.

All across our society the approach is "I want it now" without any regard to what consequences there may be. Immediate gratification appears to be the goal. It should be remembered that sin always satisfies temporarily but what is the price? I encourage you to pause when you are tempted and ask God what He wants you to have and when He wants you to have it. Patience and good judgment will provide a reward.

"O death, where is your victory? O death where is your sting?" The sting of death is sin, and the power of sin is the law; but thanks be to God, who gives us the victory through our Lord Jesus Christ. Therefore, my beloved brethren, be steadfast immovable, always abounding in the work of the Lord knowing that your toil is not in vain in the Lord. (1 Corinthians 15:55–56)

The sting of death is sin because it is by sin that death gains authority over a man.

...The Scripture has shut up all men under sin, that the promise by faith in Jesus Christ might be given to those that believe. (Galatians 3:22)

This is explained in plain and simple language.

Therefore, laying aside falsehood, "speak truth each one of you, with his neighbor for we are members of one another." Be angry, and yet do not sin; do not let the sun go down on your anger, and do not give the devil an opportunity. (Ephesians 4:25–27)

Make it a personal rule never to harbor anger as it festers and gives the devil an opportunity to create sin within you.

...Do not get drunk with wine, for that is dissipation, but be filled with the Spirit; always giving thanks for all things in the name of our Lord Jesus Christ to God even the Father. (Ephesians 5:18 & 20)

A sound guideline to practice in your life.

...consider the members of your earthly body as dead to immorality, impurity, passion, evil desire and greed, which amounts to idolatry. But now also put aside anger, wrath, malice, slander, and abusive speech from your mouth. (Colossians 3:5&8)

Put aside those things that were part of your former life now that you are committed to Christ.

...he who does wrong will receive the consequences of the wrong which he has done, and that without partiality. (Colossians 3:25)

God does not show any partiality to anyone. If a person sins, he will always bear the consequences regardless of whoever he is.

The sins of some men are quite evident going before them to judgment; for others their sins follow after...Likewise also, deeds that are good are quite evident, and those which are otherwise cannot be concealed. (1 Timothy 5:24-25)

Do not deceive yourself into believing that you have concealed your sin as nothing is concealed from God.

...Those who want to get rich fall into temptation and a snare and many foolish and harmful desires, which plunge men into ruin and destruction. For the love of money is a root of all sorts of evil and some by longing for it have wandered away from the faith, and pierced themselves with many a pang. (1 Timothy 6:9-10)

Please keep this in mind as you climb the ladder of financial success. Do not lose sight of your commitment to Jesus Christ.

For if we go on sinning willfully after receiving the knowledge of the truth, there no longer remains a sacrifice for sin... (Hebrews 10:26)

Do not let this happen to you. If you do, there will be nothing but tragedy in your future.

Let marriage be held in honor among all, and let the marriage bed be undefiled, for fornicators and adulterers God will judge. (Hebrews 13:4)

Keep this always in mind as you may be tempted. Pray that lust will pass from your mind.

...Putting aside all filthiness and all that remains of wickedness, in humility receive the word implanted, which is able to save your souls. (James 1:21)

Never put aside the word of truth. It will strengthen you in times of testing.

Submit therefore to God. Resist the devil and he will flee from you. Draw near to God and He will draw near to you. Cleanse your hands, you sinners, and purify your hearts you double minded. (James 4:7–8)

Stay close to God; and not just in tumultuous times but at all times. Make every effort to be fully committed to God. Half-heartedness counts for nothing.

…Above all, my brethren, do not swear, either by heaven or by earth, or with any other oath; but let your yes be yes, and your no, no, so that you may not fall under judgment. (James 5:12)

Do not allow your mouth to get ahead of your brain.

…let him know that he who turns a sinner from the error of his way will save his soul from death and cover a multitude of sins. (James 5:20)

Do not forget the power that is provided to one who saves another from sin.

Therefore, since Christ has suffered in the flesh, arm yourselves with the same purpose, because he who has suffered in the flesh has ceased from sin, so to live the rest of time in the flesh but no longer for the lusts of men, but for the will of God. (1 Peter 4:1–2)

Follow God's will and sin will fall away from you.

…The Lord knows how to rescue the godly from temptation and to keep the unrighteous under punishment for the day of judgment and especially those who indulge the flesh in its corrupt desires, and despise authority. Daring, self-willed, they do not tremble while they revile angelic majesties. (2 Peter 2:9–10)

This is especially true when false teachers speak rashly in disbelief of the power and authority of the majesties of God.

... If after they have escaped the defilements of the world by the knowledge of the Lord and Savior Jesus Christ, they are again entangled in them and are overcome, the last state has become worse for them than the first. For it would have been better for them if they had known the way of righteousness, than having known it, to turn away from the holy commandment delivered to them. It has happened to them according to the true proverb, "A dog returns to its own vomit." "A sow, after washing, returns to wallowing in the mire." (2 Peter 2:20–22)

This presents a graphic example of a man returning to sin after experiencing Christ and regressing even more deeply into sin than before.

I read something recently about resisting sin in an *In Touch* booklet that I would like to share. "Wishing and hoping can't help you overcome sin and live victoriously. You must decide to fill your mind with God's truths. Then, as you absorb them into your life, they'll guide your decisions, protect you from deception, and shape your relationships." Hopefully, this will help you with how you think and behave when you are faced with evil. I offer a word of caution, however. Be very careful of any elements of sin hiding in your heart.

Let this verse in Romans 12:21 guide you: "Do not be overcome by evil, but overcome evil with good; be helpful in your endeavor."

If we say we have no sin, we are deceiving ourselves, and the truth is not in us. If we confess our sins, He is faithful and righteous to forgive us our sins, and to cleanse us from all unrighteousness. (1 John 1:8–9)

This means for us to walk in obedience to God's ways.

…He Himself is the propitiation for our sins and not for ours only, but also for those of the whole world. (1 John 2:2)

Christ is the only offering that satisfied God concerning everyone's sin.

SORROW

This is often experienced over the loss of a loved one, either by accident or by the harm inflicted on them by someone else. An individual may also experience sorrow through failures in their career or in business. Lastly, sorrow may be experienced in the decline and loss of principles of one's native land.

Be gracious to me, O Lord, for I am in distress. My eye is wasted away because of grief, my soul and my body also. For my life is spent with sorrow, and my years with sighing; my strength has failed because of my iniquity, and my body has wasted away. (Psalms 31: 9–10)

In this psalm, David, while praying to God, bewails his poor health and the dangers he faces. He pleads for help in his distress.

Many are the sorrows of the wicked, but for he who trusts in the Lord, lovingkindness shall surround him. (Psalms 32:10)

Narrow is the gate that leads to eternal life. Always trust in God alone. As *Streams in Desert* shares it: "The sorrows of life cause us to rise to God for comfort and understanding. Our burdens become our wings."

…The days of our lives they contain seventy years, or if due to strength eighty years, yet their pride is but labor and sorrow for soon it is gone and we fly away. (Psalms 90:10)

Days pass slowly for the young, but they really accelerate as you grow older. The self-reliant, who try to illumine the darkness by their own light, will only know sorrow. Instead, trust in the Lord and Him alone.

For the sorrow that is according to the will of God produces a repentance without regret leading to salvation; but the sorrow of the world produces death. For behold what earnestness this very thing, this godly sorrow, has produced in you what vindication of yourselves, what vindication, what fear, what longing, what zeal, what avenging of wrong! In everything you demonstrated yourselves to be innocent in this matter. (2 Corinthians 7:10–11)

In the circumstances of this verse, sorrow has worked the right kind of repentance.

SPIRIT

This element lies within each of us and it is up to us how we live and move and have our being. Be cautious and do not let your spirit lead you into evil.

...For Thou art my strength. into Thou hand I commit my spirit... (Psalms 31:4–5)

Committing one's life to God is the epitome of faith.

The Lord is near to the brokenhearted, and saves those who are crushed in spirit. (Psalms 34:18)

Never fail to ask God for comfort and peace. He is forever present.

The sacrifices of God are a broken spirit. A broken and a contrite heart O God, Thou will not despise. (Psalms 51:17)

We must openly acknowledge our dependence upon God and not ourselves.

Nothing so hinders the working of hidden spiritual forces as a spirit of anxiety and unrest. Are you happy with your spiritual life? Have you asked God for help and guidance? I suggest you open your heart to Him. Remember He is always available.

Like a city that is broken into and without walls is a man that has no control over his spirit. (Proverbs 25:28)

If a man is to be truly content, self-control must be exerted.

...The dust will return to the earth, as it was and the spirit will return to God who gave it. (Ecclesiastes 12:7)

Man's spirit returns to God for judgment.

Now may the God of peace Himself sanctify you entirely; and may your spirit and soul and body be preserved complete, without blame at the coming of our Lord Jesus Christ. (1 Thessalonians 5:23–24)

A two-verse prayer that closes with instruction and exhortation.

...The Spirit explicitly says that in later times some will fall away from the faith, paying attention to deceitful spirits and doctrines of demons, by means of the hypocrisy of liars seared in their own conscience as with a branding iron, men who forbid marriage and advocate abstaining from foods, which God has created to be gratefully shared by those who believe and know the truth. (1 Timothy 4:1–3)

Does this sound familiar to you? I'm sorry to have to say this but this sounds like the present to me.

We are from God; he who knows God listens to us; he who is not from God does not listen to us. By this we know the spirit of truth and the spirit of error. (1 John 4:6)

Chew on this one. Think about it. Where do you fit?

TEACHING

This word means much more than teaching in school or college. Let me explain. As believers, we have a purpose to not just keep what we have learned to ourselves but to share our faith in God and our Lord Jesus Christ with friends and associates, and, particularly, with our family.

Listen O my people, to my instruction. Incline your ears to the words of my mouth. (Psalms 78:1)

These words of God from many centuries ago are relevant for us to consider today.

Teaching our children is exceptionally important. It does not mean just taking them to Sunday School and church. It also means explaining your personal relationship with the Lord to them, answering their questions and explaining the need for them to establish a meaningful prayer life. In school, your kids have report cards to determine their progress. I encourage you to have thoughtful reviews with your children to determine where they are in their relationship with God and help guide them in their faith. I feel that I failed in doing this and it grieves me greatly. Unfortunately, when time is past there is no turning back the clock. Please, please do not repeat my error. Family prayer is important as well and implants in each mind that a family that prays together, stays together.

For I give you sound teaching; do not abandon my instruction. When I was a son to my father, tender and the only son in the sight of my mother, then he taught me and said to me, "Let your heart hold fast my words; keep my commandments and live." (Proverbs 4:2–4)

I want to ask you a serious question. Do you take the time to review with each of your children the importance of having Jesus Christ in their hearts? And do they know that this is the key not only to their immediate future but, more importantly, for the salvation of their souls?

The teaching of the wise is a fountain of life, to turn aside from the snares of death. (Proverbs 13:14)

The term "the fountain of life" is a symbol of spiritual vitality. Do you have it?

There are very few things we do in our lives that are more important than consistently teaching our family the need for a Christian lifestyle.

THANKFUL

It is most important that we express our thanks and gratitude for all of the benefits that we receive. Unfortunately, too many of us fail to comprehend that all that we receive is truly due to the hands of our Heavenly Father and not through their own efforts. I ask that you express your thankfulness to the proper source. Likewise, show your thankfulness to others who do good and pleasant things for you.

I will give thanks to the Lord with all my heart… (Psalms 9:1)

Make a concerted effort to do this on a daily basis.

Oh give thanks to the Lord; Call upon His name. Make known His deeds among the people. (Psalms 105:1)

Do not be shy but gladly witness to others about all the Lord has done for you in your life.

Before leaving this topic, it is important to understand that the Bible teaches us to be thankful for all things and not just for what we consider to be good for us. Even when we face unforeseen trials and problems, we need to be thankful for them as well because the Lord is helping us to learn and understand His purpose for us. This may not be easy for you to accept at first but I encourage you to allow God's perfect timing to become reality in your life.

And let the peace of Christ rule in your hearts, to which indeed you were called in one body; and be thankful. Let the word of Christ richly dwell within you, with wisdom, teaching, and admonishing one another with psalms and hymns and spiritual songs, singing with thankfulness in your hearts to God. (Colossians 3:15-16)

Paul's appeal is to experience what you already are by God's grace.

In everything give thanks for this is God's will for you in Christ Jesus. (1 Thessalonians 5:18)

Make every effort to follow this advice.

Lastly, let us be ever thankful for our redemption and salvation through our Lord Jesus Christ.

THANKSGIVING

I encourage every person who reads this to open their hearts and express their personal thanksgiving to God who has so richly blessed us and our families. We do this each year in November on a national holiday, but we should not overlook the obligation to do this on a daily basis.

Let us come before His presence with thanksgiving; let us shout joyfully to Him with psalms. (Psalms 95:2)

This is a call to worship God as He is our creator.

Enter His gates with thanksgiving and His courts with praise. Give thanks to His name, bless His name. (Psalms 100:4)

Praise the Lord for the many blessings we receive.

Be anxious for nothing, but in prayer and thanksgiving let your requests be made known to God. (Philippians 4:6)

Sound advice. Pay heed to it.

Devote yourselves to prayer, keeping alert in it with an attitude of thanksgiving. (Colossians 4:2)

God is always available to each of us but we must talk to Him.

Each November, our country celebrates Thanksgiving which we observe with family and friends and a joyful meal and fellowship. We are a very fortunate to be able to celebrate abundance and I trust each of you will take the time to thank our God and Father who makes everything possible.

TRUST

This attribute is one of the most important elements of a person's character. When anyone gives another their word, it is critical that this can be depended on as accurate and completely truthful. Your word must be your bond; if not, trust does not exist. How do you feel on this subject? Are you to be trusted? I pray that you are. If not, do a turnaround in your life. It is never too late.

O My God in Thee I trust. (Psalms 25:2)

You can always trust God in any and all things.

The Lord is my strength and my shield; My heart trusts in Him and I am helped. (Psalms 28:7)

This is pertinent today and in all ages.

Commit your way to the Lord; Trust also in Him and He will do it. (Psalms 37:5)

Trust in the Lord always, no matter what you face. Carrying out God's will requires a heart and soul that not only trusts Him but is willing to accept, without question, the results, whatever they may be.

How blessed is the man who has made the Lord his trust... (Psalms 40:4)

Truer words were never spoken.

Another of my near-death experiences occurred in 2011. My Internist told me that if I did not have a small section of my colon removed, it would very likely become malignant. I proceeded with the surgery and the anticipated time in the hospital was to be ten to fourteen days.

The surgery went fine and there was no malignancy, but I then developed, in succession, pneumonia, a-fib, and, finally, a gall bladder problem. I was confined for twenty-five days. Toward the end of this time, I was asked by one of the doctors if I had any instructions should it appear, I would not survive. I assure you that got my attention. Fortunately, I did survive but I did have to spend another two weeks in rehab.

Some weeks later, after I had recovered, and while attending a party, a doctor friend told me he was very glad to see me as I almost did not make it. Fortunately for me, I had placed my trust in God and I survived.

Think on this for a moment: "Nothing that is not of God's will come into the life of one who trusts and obeys God." What a comfort to know. (from *Streams in the Desert*)

God is our refuge and our strength, a very present help in trouble. (Psalms 46:1)

When you are facing trial or trouble, where do you place your trust for protection and guidance?

We are never without a pilot as God is always close by.

When I am afraid, I will put my trust in Thee. In God whose word I praise in God I have put my trust; I shall not be afraid. (Psalms 56:3–4)

I have a question for you. When you are faced with a difficult situation, in whom do you place your trust? Is it family or friend? Do you trust God? Consider that God is in control of all things. Does it not make sense to place your trust in Him and to follow His guidance? Please utilize His presence always. Do this and be at peace.

Take a moment to think over this note from the booklet *Our Daily Bread:* "To trust God in the light is nothing, but to trust in Him in the dark – that is faith."

In God I have put my trust; I shall not be afraid, what can man do to me? (Psalms 56:11)

There is no better place to put your trust than in God.

….For I trust in Thy word. And do not take the word of truth utterly out of my mouth, for I shall wait for Thy ordinances. (Psalms 119:42–43)

Do not allow the threats of others sway you from having trust in God.

Trust in the Lord with all your heart, and do not lean on your own understanding. In all your ways acknowledge Him and He will make your paths straight. Do not be wise in your own eyes; fear the Lord and turn away from evil. (Proverbs 3:5–7)

Overly confident individuals often lose their way but the wise trust God. I read these verses daily. I hope you will give this a try, too.

"Quiet tension is not trust but compressed anxiety." Take the time, be still and listen patiently for what God has to say to you to help you solve your problems. This is from *Streams in the Desert*.

He who trusts in his riches will fail… (Proverbs 11:28)

Money will never buy true peace of mind. God's way is *the* answer.

Only the foolish put their trust in mankind rather than God. Can you think of any better place to place your trust than with God? It is fact. There is no better place now and there will never be.

TRUTH

Make sincere effort to be honest when talking to others regarding any subject. Do not parse words. Aim for complete truthfulness and not just partial truthfulness.

Consider the New Testament quotation of our Lord Jesus Christ when He said "I am the way, and the truth and the life; no one comes to the Father, but through Me."

We must never forget the power and meaningfulness in this statement of truth.

Only fear the Lord and serve in truth with all your heart for consider the great things He has done for you. (1 Samuel 12:24)

Practice this philosophy, from yesterday, today and forevermore.

Lead me in Thy truth and teach me, for Thou are the God of my salvation. For Thee I will wait all the day. (Psalms 25:5)

I often refer to this very meaningful verse.

All the paths of the Lord are lovingkindness and truth to those who keep His covenant and His testimonies. (Psalms 25:10)

Do things God's way and not our way.

The sum of Thy word is truth. And every one of Thy righteous ordinances is everlasting. (Psalms 119:160)

This is an absolute fact.

The Lord is near to all who call upon Him. To all who call upon Him in truth. (Psalm 145:18)

Pay close attention to the wording here. Unless you call upon the Lord in truth, and not half-truth, do not expect to be heard.

Do not let kindness and truth leave you; Bind them around your neck, write them on the tablet of your heart. So you will find favor and good repute in the sight of God and man. (Proverbs 3:3–4)

Be truthful in all you do and say.

…Grace and truth were realized through Jesus Christ. (John 1:17)

Thanks be to God for this gift.

"But he who practices the truth comes to the light, that his deeds may be manifested as having been wrought in God." (John 3:21)

Pay attention to these words of Jesus. Be sure that when you speak everything is both true and right.

…you shall know the truth and the truth shall make you free. (John 8:32)

This is a revelation; that your soul shall gain freedom when you follow this course.

Laying aside falsehood, speak truth, each one of you, with his neighbor, for we are members of one another. (Ephesians 4:25)

Lying will bite you; it will only be a matter of time. Ouch!

For if we go on sinning willfully after receiving the knowledge of the truth, there no longer remains a sacrifice for sins. (Hebrews 10:26)

I encourage you not to waste the opportunity for salvation.

JOHN H. (JAN) DOLCATER, JR.

If we say we have fellowship with Him and yet walk in the darkness, we lie and do not practice the truth. (1 John 1:6)

You can never deceive the Lord. Only yourself.

UNDERSTANDING

Humankind is fortunate to have been granted, by God, the gift of understanding, especially concerning the Word of God. Be thoughtful as you explore this blessing with all your heart, mind and soul. I firmly believe that if the utilization of the Word of God is ignored, or only casually used, your life will be both hollow and futile.

"But where can wisdom be found? And where is the place of understanding?..." (Job 28:12)

In the Word of God.

"And to man, He said, "behold the fear of the Lord, that is wisdom, and to depart from evil is understanding." (Job 28:28)

True wisdom is showing holy respect and reverence for God while shunning evil.

Do not be as the horse or the mule which have no understanding... (Psalms 32:9)

Get with it. Take the time and follow Jesus Christ, our Savior.

...the meditation of my heart will be understanding. (Psalms 49:3)

Be still, take time, relax and allow the Lord to speak to you and you will gain understanding.

Man in his pomp yet without understanding is like the beasts that perish. (Psalms 49:20)

We should praise God, and not ourselves, for any good fortune and accomplishments that we have and also for our adversities by which we learn lessons of humility.

The fear of the Lord is the beginning of wisdom. A good understanding have all those who do His commandments. (Psalms 111:10)

This is a valuable lesson. Do not forget it.

Give me understanding that I may observe Thy law, and keep it with all my heart. Make me walk in the path of Thy commandments. (Psalms 119:34–35)

A very strong recommendation for you to follow.

From Thy precepts I gain understanding; therefore I hate every evil way. Thy word is a lamp to my feet, and a light to my path. (Psalms 119:104–105)

Once again, this is a pearl for you to know, understand, and, perhaps, to memorize. It works for me as I read this daily.

The unfolding of Thy words gives light; it gives understanding to the simple. (Psalm 119:130)

Allow the words of the Lord to open your heart and soul to greater understanding.

...Give me understanding that I may live. (Psalms 119:144)

When you are faced with a difficult situation, turn to God in prayer and ask humbly for guidance.

...His understanding is infinite. (Psalms 147:5)

Think long and hard on this powerful thought.

For the Lord gives wisdom; from His mouth come knowledge and understanding. (Proverbs 2:6)

There is no better resource of wisdom and understanding than our Almighty God.

Trust in the Lord with all your heart, and do not lean on your own understanding. In all your ways acknowledge Him and He will make your paths straight. Do not be wise in your own eyes; fear the Lord and turn away from evil. (Proverbs 3:5–7)

I read these verses daily and find them very helpful. Try it.

How blessed is the man who finds wisdom and the man that gains understanding. (Proverbs 3:13)

Take a little time and let this sink in. Huge benefits are available to you if you will. I also read this passage often.

Long life is in her right hand, in the left hand are riches and understanding. (Proverbs 3:16)

This verse, and the one preceding it, are powerful and meaningful. I also read this verse on a daily basis.

The Lord by wisdom founded the earth. By understanding He established the heavens. (Proverbs 3:19)

Wisdom often has a dynamic effect on human life. The guiding hand of God created all things and has given us so many opportunities to gain understanding.

Does not wisdom call and understanding lift up her voice? (Proverbs 8:1)

These two attributes are linked. One leads to the other if sought with care.

The fear of the Lord is the beginning of wisdom and the knowledge of the Holy One is understanding. (Proverbs 9:10)

I consider this verse to be an important life lesson. I hope you will agree.

He who despises his neighbor lacks sense, but a man of understanding keeps silent. (Proverbs 11:12)

Silence is often golden.

He who is slow to anger has great understanding… (Proverbs 14:29)

Hold your tongue regardless of the pressure you are experiencing.

Wisdom rests in the heart of one who has understanding… (Proverbs 14:33)

The wise do not parade their knowledge but the fool boasts of the little he has.

He who rejects discipline despises himself, but he who listens to reproof acquires understanding. The fear of the Lord is the instruction for wisdom and before honor comes humility. (Proverbs 15:32–33)

Please read and reread the above verse several times and allow it to soak into your heart and soul. It is a solid foundation for anyone's life.

A fool does not delight in understanding, but only in revealing his own mind. (Proverbs 18:2)

Have you ever met this individual before? Unfortunately, I have met him far too often.

A man who wanders from the way of understanding will rest in the assembly of the dead. (Proverbs 21:16)

Do not end up on this dead-end street.

Harlotry, wine and new wine take away the understanding. (Hosea 4:11)

Always avoid harlotry and be prudent and cautious with wine. If you do not, it will overwhelm you and take you away from your best interests.

...making the most of your time, because the days are evil. So then do not be foolish, but understand what the will of the Lord is. (Ephesians 5:16–17)

Life is fleeting. With this in mind, try to understand the purpose that God has for your life.

That their hearts may be encouraged having been knit together in love, and attaining all the wealth that come from the full assurance and understanding resulting in a true knowledge of God's mystery, that is Christ Himself. (Colossians 2:2)

Please search for this understanding of Jesus Christ.

JOHN H. (JAN) DOLCATER, JR.

Who among you is wise and understanding let him show by his good behavior his deeds in gentleness and wisdom. (James 3:13)

The answer to the question posed here is "the person who remembers and practices his moral responsibilities."

VANITY

This characteristic occurs in an individual when he becomes very self-important due to financial or professional success, the recognition and praise of others, or the self-indulgent approval of his own personal appearance or attributes. When this type of behavior surfaces, it does not provide a positive attribute for the person who indulges in it.

Let not the foot of pride come upon me... (Psalms 36:11)

Very pertinent advice.

Man in his pomp will not endure; he is like the beasts that perish. (Psalms 49:12)

Vanity is but a thin veil.

They speak from on high. They have set their mouth against the heavens, and their tongue parades through the earth. (Psalms 73:8–9)

All seems to be well with the wicked but what fate awaits them? Vanity and self-indulgence are self-defeating realities.

There is a kind – oh how lofty are his eyes! His eyelids are raised in arrogance. (Proverbs 30:13)

Pompousness and self-important vanity are on display here.

...Vanity of vanities! All is vanity. (Ecclesiastes 1:2)

Far too many things people consider valuable are, in reality, utterly worthless. Be careful what you pursue.

...I considered all my activities my hands had done, and the labor I had exerted and behold all was vanity and striving after wind and there was no profit under the sun. (Ecclesiastes 2:11)

Where do you fit? Are you self-satisfied? If so, please change this destructive attitude.

He who loves money will not be satisfied with money, nor he who loves abundance with its income. This too is vanity. (Ecclesiastes 5:10)

Very true and meaningful advice.

...He who boasts, let him boast in the Lord. For not he who commends himself is approved, but whom the Lord commends. (2 Corinthians 10:17–18)

The boastful individual deludes himself and only obtains a feeling of pride and vanity.

Do nothing from selfishness or empty conceit, but with humility of mind let each of you regard one another as more important than himself; do not merely look out for your own personal interests, but also for the interests of others. (Philippians 2:3)

If you will follow this advice your future will be fruitful, indeed.

VISION

The ability to successfully perceive a different future state when analyzing opportunities and plans. This characteristic offers the person who has vision many advantages over others that lack this ability. Visions may be either for the good or bad of man, but, hopefully, good will be exercised when your opportunities appear.

Where there is no vision the people are unrestrained...(Proverbs 29:18)

In this type of situation, trouble is usually close by.

I want to mention another type of vision that I experienced many years ago. Earlier, I talked about my traffic accident involving a tractor-trailer and how I came very close to not surviving it.

One morning at about 4 AM, after being in intensive care for just shy of two weeks, and just as I was rousing a bit, I had a vision of Jesus and was told that I would survive. I had never experienced anything like this before and nor have I since. It was quite startling and overwhelming, to say the least. However, the following day, I responded to tests in a fully-cognizant manner for the first time during that two-week period and was discharged and home within several days. This vision I shall always treasure and remember.

Some individuals have another kind of vision; and that is regarding the location of evil spirits and how to deal with them. Read more on this in *The Odds Are Too Great* by the Rev. Scott Davis of Fairhope, Alabama.

And a vision appeared to Paul in the night; a certain man of Macedonia was standing and appealing to him and saying to him, "Come over to Macedonia and help us." And when he had seen this vision, immediately we sought to go into Macedonia; concluding that God had called us to preach the gospel to them. (Acts 16:9–10)

This journey by Paul into Macedonia was his first into Europe. He was later joined there by Luke, the physician.

And when I saw Him, I fell at His feet as a dead man. And He laid His right hand upon me saying, "Do not be afraid I am the first and the last." (Revelation 1:17)

Jesus is plainly stating in this vision that He is the Alpha and the Omega and will endure in this manner now and forever.

WISDOM

Some people are fortunate to have this inbred in them. However, wisdom may also be obtained by patience, persistence, and placing trust and commitment in our Almighty God and Father. Keep in mind, wisdom should never be confused with intelligence nor can wisdom ever be purchased at any price.

...A bribe blinds the eyes of the wise and perverts the words of the righteous. (Deuteronomy 16:19)

Being on the take is a dead-end street. If you ever run into this type of situation, get away from it as quickly as possible. I have experienced this several times when calling on buyers of large companies. When approached like this, I left as soon as possible.

"But where may wisdom be found? And where is the place of understanding?..." (Job 28:12)

Where do you think wisdom may be found? Have you ever searched for it? Why not try God?

...The testimony of the Lord is sure making wise the simple. (Psalms 19:7)

The testimony of the Lord is available to all to understand and appreciate; it is not just for the elite.

My mouth will speak wisdom; and the mediation of my heart will be understanding. (Psalms 49:3)

Again, wisdom and understanding are joined.

...Teach us to number our days; that we present to Thee a heart of wisdom. (Psalms 90:12)

A wise man will do this; a fool pays no heed.

The fear of the Lord is the beginning of wisdom. A good understanding have all those who do His commandments. (Psalms 111:10)

Commit this verse to memory, as it needs to be indelibly etched in your mind.

To know wisdom and instruction...to receive instruction is wise behavior, righteousness, justice and equity. (Proverbs 1:2-3)

Make effort to use wisdom in a practical and successful manner. Utilize instruction to achieve wise dealing which will lead you to success.

A wise man will hear and increase learning and a man of understanding will acquire wise counsel. (Proverbs 1:5)

A prudent individual learns from and listens quietly to those who have wisdom.

The fear of the Lord is the beginning of knowledge. Fools despise wisdom and instruction. (Proverbs 1:7)

Fear of the Lord is the starting point and the essence of wisdom. Fools will never submit to His will.

For the Lord gives wisdom... (Proverbs 2:6)

Are you open to acquiring this through the Lord?

...Acquire wisdom and with all your acquiring get understanding. (Proverbs 4:7)

The first step in acquiring wisdom is to make up your mind that you want it. Then, strive to obtain it and, by doing so, you will gain understanding.

Wisdom is better than jewels and all desirable things cannot compare with her. (Proverbs 8:11)

No jewel has ever been found that can compare with wisdom.

Do not reprove a scoffer lest he hate you. Reprove a wise man and he will love you. (Proverbs 9:8)

Simply do not waste your time and effort with the undisciplined as their understanding is non-existent.

When pride comes then comes dishonor, but with the humble is wisdom. (Proverbs 11:2)

Pride comes before a fall. Be careful where you land.

The wisdom of the prudent is to understand his way, but the folly of fools is deceit. (Proverbs 14:8)

The wise individual carefully considers his conduct and his habits but the foolish sidestep the truth with their frivolous lifestyle.

Wisdom rests in the heart of one who has understanding... (Proverbs 14:33)

When an individual has both of these attributes, his life will be productive.

He who neglects discipline despises himself, but he who listens to reproof acquires understanding. The fear of the Lord is the instruction for wisdom and before honor comes humility. (Proverbs15:32–33)

Always attempt to understand your errors and acknowledge them with humility.

Wine is a mocker; strong drink a brawler, and whoever is intoxicated by it is not wise. (Proverbs 20:1)

Have you done this? How did it work out? Well, or poorly?

By wisdom a house is built and by understanding it is established... (Proverbs 24:3)

Remember this when undertaking any significant project or effort.

Know that wisdom is thus for your soul, if you find it then, there will be a future and your hope will not be cut off. (Proverbs 24:14)

If you are blessed to have wisdom, your future should be bright.

Do you see a man wise in his own eyes? There is more hope for a fool than for him. (Proverbs 26:12)

Do you know someone like this? I hope that someone is not you.

The sluggard is more wise in his own eyes, than seven men who give a discreet answer. (Proverbs 26:16)

Pathetic but very true.

...He who trusts in the Lord will prosper. He who trusts in his own heart is a fool. He who walks wisely will be delivered. He who gives to the poor will never want. (Proverbs 28:25-27)

This verse contains several valuable lessons. Learn from it.

A fool always loses his temper, but a wise man will hold it back. (Proverbs 29:11)

It would be prudent for you to review many of these passages from the Book of Proverbs on a regular basis.

I listened to a sermon recently by Dr. Charles Stanley regarding utilizing wisdom in establishing friendships. Let me enumerate them for you.

1. "Be willing to meet the needs of others.
2. Be willing to risk rejection.
3. Be open to loving spiritually.
4. Be open to committing to the spiritual growth of the other person.
5. Allow the principles of Scripture to be shown to others."

Also, as you determine whom to befriend, avoid the following types of individuals: gossips, the hot-tempered, the disloyal, the indulgent, the gluttonous, and those of poor morals. Any mixture of these elements in the nature of an individual will certainly not lead to anything of a positive nature.

...I saw that wisdom exceeds folly, as light exceeds darkness. (Ecclesiastes 2:13)

Sound discernment. I offer this from *Our Daily Bread*; "Wise is the person who would rather give honor than receive it."

...Wisdom is protection just as money is protection. But the advantage of knowledge is that wisdom preserves the lives of the possessors. (Ecclesiastes 7:12)

Well said and nothing new here. This was understood centuries ago.

Ecclesiastes, like the Book of Proverbs, is an excellent source of both wisdom and understanding. Do not neglect these valuable resources.

For the word of the cross is to those who are perishing foolishness, but to us that are being saved it is the power of God.... Because the foolishness of God is wiser than men, and the weakness of God is stronger than men. (1 Corinthians 1:18 & 25)

Strive to gain the wisdom of God through Jesus Christ. This is simplicity and yet it is perfection. The worldly wisdom highly prized by the Corinthians is the very antithesis of the wisdom of God.

Therefore be careful how you walk, not as unwise men, but as wise making the most of your time, because the days are evil. So do not be foolish, but understand what the will of the Lord is. (Ephesians 5:15–17)

As true today as it was in the first century.

Divine wisdom has two sides to it: one as man sees it and another known only to God.

Conduct yourselves with wisdom toward outsiders making the most of the opportunity. Let your speech always be with grace, seasoned, as it were with salt, so that you may know how to respond to each person. (Colossians 4:5–6)

Far too often, people rush to respond without enough forethought. Take a little time and avoid awkward situations.

Who among you is wise and understanding? Let him show his good behavior by deeds in the gentleness of wisdom. (James 3:13)

The answer to the question posed above is "the person who remembers and practices moral responsibilities." Be wise and make decisions according to God's principles and not your own personal preferences as they may lead you to foolish and sinful choices.

But the wisdom from above is first pure, then peaceable, gentle, reasonable, full of mercy and good fruits, unwavering without hypocrisy. And the seed whose fruit is righteousness is sown in peace by those who make peace. (James 3:17–18)

These verses are back again. I truly value this advice and I hope you do as well.

In closing this topic, please consider the following advice from the booklet *Our Daily Bread*, "Monitor your heart daily to avoid wandering from God's wisdom."

WITNESS

True witness must be done by the power of the Spirit of God. All earthly things are limited, but the word of the Lord our God is infinite. Never be shy or hesitant to share your witness of God with others. He will guide you and strengthen you as you proceed.

He came for a witness, that he might bear witness of the light, that all might believe through him. He was not the light, but came that he might bear witness of the light. (John 1:7–8)

John the Baptist was the witness to the light of Jesus Christ.

"But the witness which I have is greater than John; for the works the Father has given Me to accomplish, the very works that I do bear witness of Me, that the Father has sent Me." (John 5:36)

Here Jesus bears witness to His mission on earth.

Jesus answered and said to them, "Even if I bear witness of Myself, My witness is true, for I know where I came from and where I am going; but you do not know where I came from or where I am going." (John 8:14)

Jesus is stressing that His testimony is to be trusted and believed.

"I am He who bears witness of Myself and the Father who sent Me bears witness of Me." (John 8:18)

In this Scripture, Jesus testifies of His own witness and that is the Father's will.

"You shall receive power when the Holy Spirit has come upon you; and you shall be My witnesses in Jerusalem and in all of Judea and Samaria, and even to the remotest parts of the earth." (Acts 1:8)

Jesus is stating, quite plainly, that the gospel must be preached and witnessed throughout the entire world.

"This Jesus, God raised up again, to which we are all witnesses..." (Acts 2:32)

The apostle Peter explains to those assembled that he and the other disciples witnessed the resurrection of Jesus.

Of Him all the prophets bear witness that through His name everyone who believes in Him receives forgiveness of sins. (Acts 10:43)

All who believe in Jesus receive forgiveness of their sins.

Therefore, since we have so great a cloud of witnesses surrounding us, let us also lay aside every encumbrance and the sin which so easily entangles us, and let us run with endurance the race that is set before us, fixing our eyes on Jesus, the author and perfecter of faith, who for the joy set before Him endured the cross, despising the shame, and has sat down at the right hand of the throne of God. (Hebrews 12:1–2)

Never forget the sacrifice made by the Lord Jesus Christ for each of us.

I recommended back at the beginning of this topic not to be shy about bearing witness to your faith. I do not recall what year it was (it was within the past twenty years) when our priest asked several of the parishioners if they would be willing to witness their faith during a Sunday service.

I accepted this request and during a Sunday service I told of my trials during by business Chapter 11 bankruptcy which was not something I really liked to discuss. My trials had existed in Florida and no one present was aware of them but I felt it was important to let others know how Almighty God helped me through seven devastating and exhausting years. And, that there was no way I could have gotten through it without my faith and commitment to Him.

This was not easy, but I recommend that whenever the opportunity arises to witness for Christ do not let that opportunity be missed. Ask for His help in prayer and all will be OK.

WORSHIP

This is our opportunity to express, either privately or publicly, belief and commitment to our Lord and Savior, Jesus Christ, and to God the Father. Although many believers do this only on Sundays, I urge you to do this each and every day in quietness and truth. When you make this a part of your everyday life, I believe with all my heart, not only will you establish a personal relationship with Him, but, in addition, your life will blossom, and you will experience growth beyond your perception. Please do not waste this opportunity.

…beware lest you lift your eyes to heaven and see the sun and the moon and the stars all the host of heaven and be drawn away and worship them…. (Deuteronomy 4:19)

Avoid temporal things of all kinds that may tempt you. Instead, focus on God for your guidance and understanding.

Worship the Lord with reverence, and rejoice with trembling. (Psalms 2:11)

Be humble in thanksgiving with joy in your heart and soul.

Come let us worship and bow down; Let us kneel before the Lord our Maker. For He is our God and we are the people of His pasture and the sheep of His hand. Today, if you would hear His voice. (Psalms 95:6–7)

Do not let this opportunity escape you.

Their land has been filled with idols. They worship the work of their hands. (Isaiah 2:8)

Do we, in our country today, worship our possessions and other temporal things or do we truly worship the Lord our God, as we should? Examine your own heart regarding this. If you feel changes are necessary, get involved.

"God is spirit, and those who worship Him must worship in spirit and truth." (John 4:24)

We should worship God's worth in spirit, in contrast to material things. And in truth, in contrast to falsehood.

A few years ago, our priest told several of us about a Christian renewal program called *Emotionally Free*. I agreed to go to Washington state to take the course as a test. After returning, I recommended that our parish take on the project. I was asked to give a sermon to our parish, as well as to two other churches in our community, to explain the program. In an effort to reach as many as possible in our area, I also made calls on quite a few pastors and preachers of other dominations.

We were successful in bringing in participants from a wide area. Our mission of bringing spiritual awareness to many individuals was accomplished. I mention this so that if you are ever offered this type of project to elevate worship in your community do not be shy but do all you can to make it a successful event.

I urge you therefore, brethren, by the mercies of God, to present your bodies a living and holy sacrifice, acceptable to God, which is your spiritual service of worship. (Romans 12:1)

Do this each day and do not be just a "Sunday Christian."

This quotation from *Our Daily Bread* places the proper focus on worship. "Worship takes the focus off of us and places it where it belongs – on God."

YEARNING

Spiritually, this emotion is a longing for a closer relationship with Jesus Christ and God the Father. Often, a person may experience a feeling of emptiness which can only be filled with the fellowship and understanding of our Creator. However, when this is accomplished, you gain both a joy and peace of mind that cannot be matched in any other way. Although you may not recognize the trigger that sparked your feelings in pursuit of this relationship, it actually is fact that this is your response to the Lord's call to you.

O God, Thou art my God; I shall seek Thee earnestly. My soul thirsts for Thee, my flesh yearns for Thee…. (Psalms 63:1)

My soul longed and even yearned for the courts of the Lord; My heart and my flesh sing for joy to the living God. (Psalms 84:2)

I stretch out my hands to Thee. My soul longs for Thee… (Psalms 143:6)

Each of the above verses exemplify the meaning of the emotion of yearning.

My soul is crushed with longing after Thine ordinances at all times. (Psalms 119:20)

JOHN H. (JAN) DOLCATER, JR.

The psalmist yearns for the word of God in order to be near to Him.

At night my soul longs for Thee, indeed, my spirit within me seeks Thee diligently. For when the earth experiences your judgments the inhabitants of the world learn righteousness. (Isaiah 26:9)

As you proceed on your spiritual journey, persevere in this quest.

For indeed in this house we groan longing to be clothed with our dwelling from heaven. (2 Corinthians 5:2)

The believer here is imagining his resurrection and how he will be clothed in it.

My prayer for all who read this book is that you open your heart to our Lord and Savior, Jesus Christ. Do so at all times regardless of your situation and whether it is good or perilous. Never let your yearning for His presence in your life to drift or falter.

ZEAL

From a religious perspective, zeal is an enthusiastic and passionate pursuit of a purposeful and holy lifestyle. Exert your efforts to make this a definitive element of your active search to establish your fervent relationship with God.

For zeal for Thy house has consumed me and the reproaches of those who reproach Thee have fallen upon me. When I wept in my soul with fasting it became my reproach. When I made sackcloth my clothing, I became a byword for them. (Psalm 69:9–11)

David suffered unjustified persecution for his maintaining faith in God.

The Lord will go forth like a warrior, He will arouse His zeal like a man of war. He will utter a shout, yes He will raise a war cry. He will prevail against His enemies. (Isaiah 42:13)

The complete fulfillment of this verse will be at Armageddon.

For I bear them witness that they have a zeal for God, but not in accordance with knowledge. (Romans 10:2)

Intelligent reasoning is the basis for witness.

Never be lacking in zeal, but keep your spiritual fervor, serving the Lord. (Romans 12:11)

This verse emphasizes the enthusiasm needed in serving the Lord.

But God that comforts the depressed, comforted us by the coming of Titus; and not only by his coming, but also by the comfort by which he was comforted in you as he reported to us your longing, your mourning, your zeal for me; so that I rejoiced even more. (2 Corinthians 7:6-7)

Paul describes his relief because of the good news Titus brought of the reaction of the Corinthians to Paul's most recent letter.

…A Hebrew of Hebrews; as to the Law, a Pharisee; as to zeal, a persecutor of the church; as to the righteousness which is in the Law, found blameless. But whatever things were gain to me, these things I have counted as loss for the sake of Christ. (Philippians 3:5-7)

Paul commits to Jesus and becomes the apostle most responsible for taking the gospel to a large portion of both Asia Minor and the Mediterranean area.

ZEALOUS

An eager and ardent search for our Almighty God describes this word. It is always good to pursue good things, and nothing is better to pursue than God. I ask you to consider whether you are zealous for God or perhaps other things instead? All too often what we do for God is half-hearted and lacks full commitment. Be passionate in your desire to achieve purpose with our Lord and you will find a solid relationship.

And after he had greeted them, he began to relate one by one the things which God had done among the Gentiles through his ministry. And when they heard it they began glorifying God and they said to him, "You see brother, how many thousands there are among the Jews of those who have believed, and they are zealous for the Law..." (Acts 21:19-20)

Paul helped to bring together both Gentiles and Jews in the acceptance of Jesus Christ. However, some of the Jewish sect would not conform to this unity in spite of the strength of his ministry of Christ.

So also you, since you are zealous of spiritual gifts, seek to abound for edification of the church. (1 Corinthians 14:12)

Utilize your zealousness to edify your church.

For the grace of God has appeared bringing salvation to all men, instructing us to deny ungodliness and worldly desires, and to live sensibly, godly in this present age, looking for the blessed hope and the appearing of the glory of our great God and Savior, Jesus Christ; who gave Himself for us that He might redeem us from every lawless deed and purify for Himself a people of His own possession, zealous for good deeds. (Titus 2:11-14)

Be forever thankful for what Jesus did for you and for all of mankind.

"Those whom I love I reprove and discipline; be zealous and repent. Behold, I stand at the door and knock; if anyone hears my voice and opens the door, I will come in to him and will dine with him and he with Me." (Revelation 3:19-20)

Never reject the love of Christ because of discipline that you have received but remember that all deeds done in sin have consequences.

MY CLOSING THOUGHTS

It is important to observe a quiet time each day when you can open your heart to the Lord and express your thanksgiving in prayer for His forgiveness, guidance and understanding. Although you may have a pressurized job and feel as if you are always in a tight time constraint, make the time happen. In my opinion, the best possible time to do this is first thing in the morning when it is quiet. Identify a room or a place for this and simply get in the habit. If this procedure is followed, I am confident this will be effective for you. Without a doubt, your day will be more successful.

As you move forward in your pathway of faith in Christ, you will be tempted in various ways. Do not be discouraged by this as there is no way any of us can avoid the elements of temptation that swirl around us in this secular atmosphere. When you come face to face with a situation for illicit financial gain, or an opportunity for an immoral practice, utilize your defense by depending on the Word of God as your source of strength in order to resist it. Keep this powerful verse close to you:

No temptation has overtaken you but such as is common to man; and God is faithful, who will not allow you to be tempted beyond what you are able, but with the temptation will provide you the way of escape also, that you may be able to endure it. (1 Corinthians 10:13)

Always maintain this advice within your spirit.

Lastly, I cannot stress too strongly to always maintain your faith and commitment in your relationship with Jesus Christ, our Lord and Savior. If you will follow this advice, it will transform your life.

Peace within – I fear no evil, for Thou art with me.

ABOUT THE AUTHOR

John Dolcater (known as Jan) spent most of his life in Florida in the building materials business before moving briefly to Florence, Alabama to take a manufacturing job as VP of Sales & Marketing. He finally settled on the coast of Maine where he continued his sales career until retirement.

Wherever he has lived, Jan has participated in and committed to various levels of church work. In Florida, he served as a Vestry member several times and also as a lay reader and lay assistant. He also taught ninth grade Sunday school and coached the church basketball team. Jan was a leader in organizing renewal events and both he and his wife, June, participated in Cursillo.

Throughout the three years living in Alabama, he also served as both lay reader and lay assistant.

After moving to Maine in 1994, Jan served multiple times on the Vestry at St. Thomas Episcopal Church in Camden, Maine, as well as serving as lay reader and lay assistant and teaching Sunday school. He helped to initiate the renewal program, *Emotionally Free*, which drew participants from a number of other local communities across the midcoast of Maine.

Both in Maine and in Alabama, the clergy asked him to give sermons to their churches and others in the community.

Jan has served for eight years as his church representative to the local Food Pantry and for six years led the effort to raise funds for local low-income individuals and families who had lost a large percentage of heating assistance funds. This effort raised over $150,000, without incurring any fundraising expenses.

Three years ago, he began working on *Peace Within Through God's Way* to provide guidance for individuals of all ages who are believers in God and also non-believers who are having difficulty dealing with anxiety and lack of peace of mind.

BIBLIOGRAPHY

Cowman, Mrs. Charles, *Streams in the Desert*. Grand Rapids, MI: Zonderman Publishing House, 1984.

Ryrie, Charles Caldwell, ThD, PhD, *The Ryrie Study Bible* - New American Standard Translation, Chicago, IL: Moody Press, 1986, 1994.

Bible Gateway – a division of the Zonderman Corporation, Grand Rapids, MI, 49546

In Touch Ministries – Dr. Charles Stanley, Atlanta, GA, 30357

Our Daily Bread Ministries, Grand Rapids, Michigan, 49546

Made in the USA
Middletown, DE
17 October 2024

62303625R10199